MOVING INTO SPACE

Geoff Chandler

MOVING INTO SPACE

The Myths and Realities of Extraterrestrial Space

edited by
Larry Geis and Fabrice Florin

with
Peter Beren and Aidan Kelly

PERENNIAL LIBRARY
Harper & Row, Publishers
New York, Cambridge, Hagerstown, Philadelphia, San Francisco
London, Mexico City, São Paulo, Sydney

Illustrations on page 93 and page 145 reprinted with permission of The Portable Stanford; from *The Galactic Club: Intelligent Life in Outer Space* by Ronald Bracewell (Stanford, CA: Stanford Alumni Association, 1974; New York: W.W. Norton, 1978).

Photographs on pages 2, 32, 52, 163, 275 courtesy of The New Dimensions Foundation.

Drawings on pages ii, xviii, 30, 132, 174, 244 by Geoff Chandler

This work was originally published under the title *Worlds Beyond: The Everlasting Frontier* by And/Or Press, P.O. Box 2246, Berkeley, CA 94702. It is here reprinted by arrangement.

First PERENNIAL LIBRARY edition published 1980.

ISBN: 0-06-080499-8

80 81 82 83 84 10 9 8 7 6 5 4 3 2 1

Dedication

"Spaceship Earth" is a term we owe to Buckminster Fuller, who coined it before we ever saw the magnificent photographs of our blue-green planet hanging in space. Although most of us know him as the inventor of the geodesic dome, few of us realize that his work in mathematics and geometry is even more revolutionary; that the principles he has discovered point to the fundamental patterns by which all matter and energy are organized in the universe.

During the more than eight decades of his life, he has witnessed and participated in the incredible transformations brought about by advances in science and technology. Yet even today, this octogenarian retains a childlike wonder and youthful enthusiasm, as he continues to probe the awesome complexity of our universe.

For his vision, for his insight, for his willingness to share, and for the gift of his life to the service of humanity, we lovingly dedicate this book to him.

Foreword
JACQUES VALLEE

In the small French town of Pontoise, where I was born, some elderly booksellers may show you a naively colored print that has amused generation after generation of local amateurs. It shows a classroom in a village schoolhouse, the kind that existed in the time of the Emperor Napoleon. A dozen little boys are sitting on rough benches, and the male teacher wears a long black coat. An extraordinary incident has just occurred: as she was reaching for a book on a very high shelf, the young (and pretty) servant has lost her balance and is hanging precariously, her skirt caught in some highly ornamented piece of furniture, offering her graceful behind to the view of all present.

Standing between the embarrassed girl and the group of startled schoolboys, the teacher is thundering: "Close your eyes, or you shall lose your sight!" Indeed, most of the terrified boys have already buried their heads into their arms crossed on the table, while others turn away from the girl in utter dread. Even the cat is running.

There is a single exception to this scene of disciplined terror: one daring little character has deliberately raised his head toward the forbidden wonders so exceptionally revealed. True, he has squarely covered the left half of his face with his hand, but he is avidly staring with his right eye, as he tells the teacher: "I shall risk one!"

I feel a certain degree of sympathy, even kinship, with this naughty little person. When a self-proclaimed higher authority—be it scientific, religious, or bureaucratic—forbids me expressly to question a theory or to consider a certain subject, I at once wonder what ulterior motives, what human pettiness, this authority hides; I even suspect that it may be attempting to prevent my gaining a more perfect knowledge of its own weakness. And the stronger the commandment, the more tantalizing my urge to behold the soft and tender mysteries whose exposure inspires such dread, such terror, such an abject flight all around me.

This volume affords just such a rare opportunity to probe the hidden structures that support what we experience as space, time, and the events of our lives. It gives us permission to question the statements of Authority on the laws of physics and the rules of the world. Here we have a whole classroom of naughty kids who have decided to steal a good look up the dress of Lady Nature, and the result of their collective exercise is the kind of uproar that could shake science and technology from their rotten cultural moorings, Hallelujah! sending them downstream into a future nobody's ready for.

Yet it would be a grave mistake to read this simply as a book about the Future. The Future, as everyone knows, belongs to Herman Kahn and the Rand Corporation. It is characterized by linearity and mythlessness. It has no contradictions. The Future, Ladies and Gentlemen, MAKES SENSE.

Not so here.

This book is full of contradictions nobody has tried to hide. There's going to be trouble, and we know it. The vision we have is nonlinear; it is mythological; and it doesn't apologize for either of these characteristics.

Perhaps because the authors have ceased to apologize for the mythology and the nonlinearity, this book also represents something new. We have agreed that we were dealing with *discontinuity*, and we have collected essays to cover, roughly speaking, three types of events: the endogenous (which comes from within human society), the exogenous (which comes from outside), and the utterly unpredictable.

Under this classification, the book talks first about those sudden changes that our own institutions are capable of engineering: space colonies, for example. The economic exploitation of outer space is a conscious decision, even if the impulse is atavistic, archetypal, and dark. To the rocket engineers, the discontinuity of launching an artificial planet for thousands of humans to admire, hate, praise, or sabotage is common sense. Such technologists and their theoretical gurus, such as the governor of California, who would "summon up" all that energy and human talent to launch it toward the stars, are represented in Phase 1 and Phase 2 of this book.

Contradictions, I said.

Consider this bizarre image: proponents of space industry and chip manufacturers from Silicon Valley in bed with what's left of the counter-culture of the last decade; the most naive in both camps, locked in amorous embrace. In this strange perspective, it is the naive who survive. They would get thousands of factories turning day and night, creating millions of new jobs in California and elsewhere, using untold amounts of metals and fuels to manufacture the ultimate "appropriate technology": a spinning cylinder, a few miles long, at the Lagrangian point; and inside it, Stewart Brand's vegetable garden, where at last he can grow the cheapest carrots this side of Andromeda and change his climate at will from New England mist to Hawaiian sunshine.

That was only the beginning.

The second kind of discontinuity is not coming from within. It simply arrives from the night out there, asking no permissions. If there are intelligences in space already, they may have some preconceived notions about its utilization and, yes, its "exploitation." Perhaps the Galactic Federation has long ago decreed that the solar wind shall only sweep the flowerbeds of some space-dwelling entity which despises vegetables. Perhaps Stewart Brand's carrots will be frowned upon, Gerry O'Neill deported to some remote cluster, and the governor of California severely chastised by the morose pundits of Arcturus.

How would we ever know that we had tiptoed through the wrong tulips? NASA has some ideas about that; scientists come into these pages to propose vast arrays of radiotelescopes they would tune in to the likely frequency of the "Galactic Club."

One can hope they would pick out more than reruns of space soap-operas from romantic Centaurians and advertisements for obsolete Lagrangian condominiums. Retire on Ganymede, says the cosmic DJ. Watch the comets go by.

Yet even if we got from deep space only the same kind of cultural junk we have been broadcasting, the notion that it might be *somebody else's junk* would be exciting enough to justify every megabuck spent on radiotelescopes. Such projects as Cyclops and SETI, described in Phase 3, thus appear to be quite sensible. They are not free from contradictions, however. Why would extraterrestrials be restricted to the use of radio? Could Humankind be on the threshold of a totally different communication era, which might make obsolete the way in which we are using the electromagnetic spectrum? How seriously should we take the premise that no signal can travel faster than light? When we are talking about such immense investments into irreversible changes for Earth's cultures, can we afford to refrain from speculation? We cannot, in fact, even if we want to, as Phases 4 and 5 of this book make quite clear.

The third way in which something discontinuous can happen to each and every one of us is through myth. We are not concerned with the polite, dressed-up mythology of Sunday school and fairy tales. The myths to come will not be catalogued by orderly librarians. We are expecting a new explosive, creative, *operational* mythology, so alive it can even embrace the mythology of science itself, the fairy tale of the rational acquisition of knowledge which we are patiently telling to the sleepy children in our universities. Enter Timothy Leary, one of the most impatient of the people who have gone through the official conditioning and rejected it as garbage. He now believes in the mythology of migrations to the point of making his home on "the west coast of California," as he says in a magnificent slip of the tongue. The old mapmakers, too, drew California as an island.

And speaking of islands, Leary would leave the Turks and the Greeks on Cyprus, and the Protestants and Catholics in Ireland, struggling for their ancient bitterness. We don't have a hell of a lot to learn, he argues, from the outcome of their pitiful fights. Our genetic future is westward. When you stand on the seashore in Los Angeles, all you can see is the Milky Way. So that's the next frontier where we expect the new mythology to come from.

The flying saucers are part of it; they have complied with our expectations. They have been coming increasingly into our consciousness, with Hollywood as their port of entry from their multidimensional world to the two-dimensional screen. They have been zipping around the sky, causing no physical harm to our structures, as the Air Force was quick to point out. If the nation can be regarded as secure as long as the buildings keep standing up and the flag keeps flying high, then the UFOs are as harmless to national security as an enemy's neutron bomb. If, on the other hand, the UFOs turn out to be APDs — Airborne Psychotronic Devices — programmed to unzip our collective unconscious, no amount of military intelligence is going to sanitize the mythological fallout. Those who argue, like Stanton Friedman, that the UFOs are somebody else's spacecraft (in other words, part of *our own* mythology) clash with those who argue, like John Billingham, that they are nobody's business. They are trying to drop into a scientific square hole the round peg of a religious issue. The prophets of the space age care little about the tenets of technology. It is there to be used.

The notion that the history of man is the slow but irresistible emergence of the rational mind out of irrational darkness is one of the most curiously persistent falsehoods of intellectual life. It is denied by careful examination of the development of science, as Lynn Thorndike observed in his masterly work on the *History of Magic and Experimental Science* (Columbia University Press). Every age uses the latest in available technology and applies it equally to the rational and the irrational. Accordingly we should expect to see very soon entire computing centers devoted to compiling horoscopes, and laser devices attempting to communicate with sylphs and mermaids. The only reason such things have not yet taken place is that the equipment has been too expensive.

Here again a discontinuity is upon us. Next year or the year after, Silicon Valley will turn out lasers for ten bucks and disposable computers labeled not IBM or Control Data, but, more prosaically, "No deposit, no return." When such technology becomes readily available at the corner drugstore, a big market is bound to exist for astrological subroutines and remote mediumship by computer.

Although in June 1976 I and a few friends organized the first Solstice celebration by collective networking—an event that linked us coast to coast through portable terminals in our homes—I am willing to recognize that this mythological explosion, if it goes on unchecked, will lead our rationalists to despair and technology to the edge of absurdity. Yet no one is challenging the myth, except in the tired words of reactionary minds who will believe nothing new. I make an appeal to skeptics. They could do much to raise the standards of research in all the areas we have reviewed. With UFOs, for instance, the most serious obstacle to the progress of research is not lack of government funding for some Flying Saucer Institute, but simply the absence of informed, interested, and intelligent skeptics. Such an intervention by critical minds is an outcome the reader could promote. This intervention is essential if we are to survive tomorrow's mythological immersion, and go on to the glorious synthesis this book promises.

At the end of our story, the fair maiden is not left hanging with her skirt in the air. She jumps, strips, and runs away. And the reader, if he dares, can be the one-eyed boy she runs away with.

Preface

During the late 1950s, there was a heated discussion about the political and social significance of "Sputnik" in my high-school social-studies class. At that time the United States had not launched a tennis ball into space, much less a satellite or an orbiting weather station. No one could foresee the impact space exploration would have.

Today, Buck Rogers is alive and well, living at NASA Headquarters. Twenty years ago, what has since become reality was only fantasy or science fiction.

Who can forget those first pictures of Earth beamed back to us by human beings in space? Whatever our national origins, political persuasion, or cultural heritage, those pictures brought to everyone an experience of the planet Earth we had never had before.

Global awareness is upon us. This book is a reflection of our emergent understanding of the connection between us and the rest of us. No longer can we deny the relationship. And we have photographs to prove it. Exploring the farther reaches of space has brought you and me closer together. This, perhaps, represents the single most striking result of the space program.

As we explore outward, the inward search becomes deeper. The farther out, the further in, is the name of this new game. Looking at new possibilities, new choices, new solutions as they emerge, is part of the play. This book is one of the results of our playing with many people through the medium of radio. Most of the material in this book has been transcribed and edited from conversations we've broadcast on public radio stations. Because of the exciting nature of the information, it seemed appropriate to make it available in book form. Frankly, at the beginning, we weren't sure the aliveness and vibrancy of the material would translate into print. But it does, I'm happy to say. So we're able to expand the game to include you, the reader. Welcome to the sandbox with no sides.

A preface could not be complete without acknowledging all those dedicated persons who contributed to bringing this book into being. There are so many, I cannot list everyone. A special thanks to: Sebastian Orfali and Peter Beren of And/Or Press, who demonstrated faith from the beginning; Fabrice Florin and Larry Geis, who tirelessly listened to countless hours of tapes, and meticulously edited reams of material; Justine Toms for supporting the vision; Will Noffke, Byron Hayes, Re Couture, Abigail Johnston, and Lou Judson for performing a myriad of tasks that were needed to support the project; and to all the others I have not named, but who contributed all the same.

Michael A. Toms
Founding Director
New Dimensions Foundation

Contents

Phase One
Reaching Outward
The Adventure of Space

Buckminster Fuller

Prolog

An Exercise in Perspective
BUCKMINSTER FULLER

R. Buckminster Fuller has been called "the planet's friendly genius" and "the Leonardo da Vinci of our time." His inventions have been patented in 49 countries. Over 200,000 geodesic domes have been built around the globe. His major published works include No More Second-hand God, Operating Manual for Spaceship Earth, *and* Synergetics: Explorations in the Geometry of Thinking.

To you and me the ocean looks very deep. We are amazed when we can see the bottom at a depth of twenty feet in extraordinarily clear tropical waters. If we can swim very well, and it gets any deeper, we start to be fearful. But we now know that in some places in our oceans the depth reaches five miles. And the average depth of all the waters on our Earth is about one mile. That seems to us incredibly deep.

However, our Earth is a sphere 8,000 miles in diameter. And we can visualize this ratio of 8,000 to 1 by imagining a steel ball 12 inches in diameter. Also imagine that this ball is highly polished, like a mirror. Now, if you breathe on it, the film of condensation from your moist breath would be *deeper* than our ocean.

Reaching Outward — *A fortunate few of the human race have seen with their own eyes the awesome spectacle of our planet, alone in the dark void of space. These explorer-adventurers join the roster of others who have captured the imagination of history, as they collectively focus the questing spirit of mankind. Will these individuals be remembered by name, as we recall Alexander the Great, Genghis Khan, Columbus, Napoleon, Byrd, or Lindbergh? How many of us recall the name of the first man to escape gravity and orbit the Earth? Who was the first human to set foot on the Moon?*

Nowadays, in the minds of most of us, these individual personalities become easily submerged in Big Government personas: The Russians (not Yuri Gagarin) were first into space; the Americans (not Neil Armstrong) won the race to the Moon. Perhaps that is as it should be, since those undertakings were more miracles of computer-assisted organization, administration, and applied technology than they were exercises in personal tenacity and bravery.

The veteran astronauts and cosmonauts would probably be the first to agree with this view. Yet we, as a collective part of that endeavor, can only fantasize about what it is like to contemplate our planet, our world, our Earth, suspended against the stars.

The first phase of our multidimensional journey into the unknowns of space will explore the feelings and emotions, the insights and effects, of going beyond the limits of gravity and atmosphere. As the first man-in-space decade ends, we may find startling new attitudes about what is now possible in the future.

L.G.

Sequence 1

An Everlasting Frontier

EDMUND G. BROWN, JR.

The beckoning adventure of space is changing our attitudes about life on Earth. Our embryonic spaceflights brought home a harvest of photos and images that showed our globe to be wondrous and fragile. Unexpectedly, our first steps outward boosted our ecological consciousness. Nowhere is this seeming paradox of perspective more apparent than in Governor Jerry Brown's endorsement of a renewed effort in space. The California Governor organized the first "Space Day" in July 1977 to bring industry and space program administrators together with environmentalists. He has recently proposed a $5.8-million project to buy communications channels aboard the Syncom IV satellite, scheduled for launch from NASA's space shuttle in 1980.

The remarks here were made extemporaneously at a symposium held in July 1977, sponsored by the Governor's office and entitled "California in the Space Age: An Era of Possibilities." One can easily see the influences of Russell Schweickart (see "One Man's Approach to Space") and Stewart Brand (see "The Origin of Space Colonies"), special advisors to the Governor, who contend that "ecology and technology can find a unity in space."

As we look at the whole Earth, and see the thin film of soil and atmosphere that makes life possible, we are struck by the fact that we're in a closed system, and there are very definite finite limits to what is possible. Several years ago, some academics wrote a book about *The Limits to Growth*, trying to calculate what was possible, given geometric expansion, in the various economies of the world. Although some of their assumptions have

5

Governor Jerry Brown at Space Day, a conference that brought business leaders, scientists, and others together to explore the effects of space research on California's future.

been discredited, the basic question still remains, as we deplete our air and water and resources, that stresses are imposed on our society, on our ecology and, ultimately, on our future survival.

I'm struck by the limits that press in against us, both materially and economically, psychologically and politically. Those limits must be respected, in some cases must be reverenced, when they deal with the natural environment.

An Alternative to Closed Systems

But as I look out into space, and as I look at the possibilities that an expanding universe (and an expanding exploration of that universe) makes possible, I sense in my own mind not only immediate benefits in a practical economic sense, but—in a far more profound way—benefits for the people of this Earth. The Earth map is drenched with the blood from a million conflicts, over recorded history. We're divided along arbitrary geographical lines, separated into ethnic categories, and divided into various linguistic groups. Yet when we look at the Earth and the human species from a few hundred miles up, we can't help but sense the oneness of the human race, this species that has been part of the universe for such a limited period of time.

This also brings to mind the closing of the frontier, the closing of the West, and what that does to the psychology of a people. As long as there is the safety valve of unexplored frontiers, the aggressive and exploitive urges of human beings can be channeled into long-term possibilities and benefits. But as those frontiers close down, and people begin to turn in upon themselves, that jeopardizes the democratic fabric itself. I don't happen to think that the frontier *is* closed. It's just opening up in space. That frontier that is opening up, that exploration, is first and foremost a discovery of the unknown, a breaking-out of the egocentric, man-dominated perceptions that still tie us down here below.

Infinite Possibilities

As we break out of that narrow conception and see the possibilities, endless as they are, throughout the entire universe, we can concentrate the creative energies of the best and most talented of those among us and their by-products here on Earth, whether they are monitoring the oceans or the land, protecting the environment, knitting together the human family through transportation and communication and other scientific breakthroughs, or just exciting the imagination. In space, we summon up more energy, and more concentrated human talent, than in almost any other human endeavor.

The mind of man will develop, will expand technologies. Some of these technologies are destructive; some of them kill millions of people; and some of them open up untold new horizons. You can't limit the mind of science and technology.

You can't limit human beings, as they put things together, as they synthesize, as they combine thoughts and information in ways that have never existed before. Here in California, where we've witnessed the creation of new industries, where we witnessed the Gold Rush, the creation of the airplane industry, the movie industry, and the record industry, we also discover that we're on the cutting edge of the aerospace industry: space development and exploration.

Practical Applications

As I look at the communications network around this globe, I think of the tremendous practical applications of space exploration. For example, with communications satellites, instructional television, we can take the work in the Mediterranean, at Harvard, in Berkeley, and by two-way communication we can take it right into the ghettoes and the low-income high schools. We can let the young people of this state sense what is possible, if we can just inspire them and summon up the talent that they have. That's what I'd like to do. There are a lot of bummers in this world, and a lot of bad vibes, but there's a lot of positive potential. And that positive potential is in our industries, in our skilled work force, in our universities, and in our dreams and ideas. It's just a matter of political will: it's a matter of making the right choices, making them at the right time, and being willing to take the risks. We don't know if all these ideas that have been spun out about the future will work. Some of them may be failures. But there's no doubt that we're going to look up, as we look within.

Space and the Imagination

It is a work of human imagination to break down the parochialisms which, seen from space, seem so arbitrary. We divide up people into Californians and Mexicans, Arabs and Israelis, Chinese and Americans; yet, as we circle the globe, we see what it is that we are: *one very rare species*, existing for a moment in universal time. In that moment, however long it lasts, we ought to make the most of it.

The space shuttle Enterprise *is* truly like laying the last spike on the Transcontinental Railroad, only much more so. Those of us who see it will also see, in the next ten or twenty years, a base on the moon manufacturing from moon material or from asteroids. It's *going* to happen. The only question is: how will it happen?

Will it be the Japanese, or the Germans, or the Russians—or will it be *all* of the world? Working through the leadership of the developed countries, we can bring along all the other countries to try to promote a better quality of life, to reverence the Spaceship Earth, to realize that the oceans flow through all of us and through all of our land.

We're going into space as a species. We'll be there whether we're labeled Americans or Russians or Chinese or Brazilians.

Courtesy of NASA

A modified Boeing 747 takes the space shuttle aloft for its fourth test.

The human race is going out and throughout, wherever space will permit us to go. It's only a question of when, and who, and what kind of leadership will take us there. And I, for one, don't think we ought to be looking just down here below.

When the day of manufacturing in space occurs and extraterrestrial material is added into the economic equation, then the old economic rules will no longer apply. It's a moment and a time that many of us are going to witness; it's just a question of the political will, the leadership and the imagination; and the ability of the private sector, the Federal and the State governments, the universities, all working together, *sensing* the potential: not looking back to ten years ago or a hundred years ago, but looking to the future with confidence, and with the collective power to realize the common purpose of this whole species, as delicate as it is.

Our Evolutionary Potential

I sense that the potentials are unlimited, if we just put our minds to working at it, giving full vent to our human imaginations. It's all there, waiting for *you*, and the rest of the people who stand behind you throughout this world, waiting to get into space, to go into the oceans, to understand ourselves, and to create the quality of life that will really achieve our evolutionary potential.

We've got to keep on going; we have to keep on pushing, because that *is* the human impulse. Instead of fighting it or ignoring it, we ought to develop it and respect it, encourage it and celebrate it. That's why we're here: because the potential of this state and of this country and of this species has just begun to be tapped. It's just a matter of courage; it's a matter of investment, of work, of collective effort, of common purpose. That's been the destiny of California, of America, and it's going to be the destiny of this world as those of us on this planet work together to push back the new frontier which is the everlasting frontier: space, the universe itself.

Sequence 2

One Man's Approach to Space

RUSSELL SCHWEICKART

Astronaut Russell Schweickart, the first human to walk in space without an umbilical, was Lunar Module Pilot for the Apollo 9 Earth-orbital flight. He is now Assistant for Science and Technology to the Governor of California, Jerry Brown, and is involved in a $5.8-million space program for the State of California, concentrating on the use of communication satellites as a public service.

In this sequence he candidly discusses his experiences before and during spaceflight, and extrapolates on their possible significance for our future understanding of ourselves.

There were very special times for me in building up to the Apollo 9 flight, especially at that time, back in early 1969 and late '68, as the mission got closer. Bill Anders, who is a very close friend of mine, and who flew on Apollo 8 with Frank Borman and Jim Lovell, had flown around the Moon in December of 1968. As Bill went off on that mission, I was very sensitive to the kind of experience that he was going through, being the first crew to leave the gravitational influence of the Earth and go out around the Moon. Apollo 8 did not land, but circled the Moon and then returned to Earth. I think Bill's experience and my sensitivity to it, because of our friendship, brought me closer to the reality of what I would be doing several months later.

The last four or five months before the flight, my wife would go off on Sunday evenings to sing in the local choral group, and the kids were in bed, and Sunday nights became my sort of private time. Not for studying the manuals or the handbooks or the procedures, but to turn out most of the lights in the house, and put on some good classical music, and surround myself with expressions of human experience: books, poetry, occasionally letters from friends, other expressions of what life is all about and what is meaningful in it. Some of these were from "way back" and others very recent. And in those Sunday nights I gradually selected a number of these expressions, phrases, occasionally individual sentences, and put them together in a kind of assemblage of the experience of life. I had them printed on parchment in gold leaf and took them up in flight with me. That was my way of bringing the total human experience on the surface of the Earth up there to this new frontier of the human experience.

Those Sunday evenings became very precious times to me.

Courtesy of NASA

Apollo 9 Lunar Module Pilot Russell L. Schweickart during preparations for a launch.

A Unique Cargo

As we moved toward flight, there had been much trouble on the previous flights of adequately documenting what was going on. So many things happened so fast that it was really difficult to take notes, and if one didn't take notes, then by the end of the day you were so filled with information that you began to lose track. So on our flight—Apollo 9—we decided to take along a little Sony tape recorder that we could use to record, by voice, information about major maneuvers, tests and results of main engine burns, and things of that kind.

It turned out that the batteries we carried were adequate for about 1.8 cassette's worth of tape. Just to insure that we didn't lose any data, the policy was that we'd change the batteries for each cassette. But now we still had a set of batteries that were good for another .8 cassette's worth. We took up with us, on agreement, cassettes with music on them—or whatever we wanted, for that matter—and we could use the .8 batteries for our own entertainment.

I took up two of the pieces of classical music that I used to play on those Sunday evenings. Unfortunately, one of my good friends up there—who will go nameless, but it wasn't Jim McDivitt—didn't particularly care for my brand of music. So, strangely, my cassette of music disappeared until about the ninth day of the flight. But I finally found it. At lunch on that day, rather than just eating with the headset on and monitoring the radio as we normally did, I decided to take the earphones off and put them aside, eat lunch, and put the cassette player on the shelf next to me and play the music. I did it almost casually; it was no big deal.

Suddenly, I was transported in a most physical and deeply emotional way back to those quiet Sunday evenings when I was preparing for these flights by going back through human experience. And there I *was*. It brought the reality of being up there back to those periods of preparation and integrated the two. It was one of the most powerful emotional experiences I've ever had. It almost jerked me bodily out of that spacecraft. I wasn't in any way prepared for the experience. It was really a surprising thing. I realized through that experience how much I was into the activity of the space flight, how much I was really involved in what I was doing there. *That* experience brought me back to the Earth. And to home. And to music, and to life back there.

The Effect of Space

I really can't speak for anyone else, but at least in my own experience, in reflecting back on it, there's certainly no question that I am today—as a result of my experience of space flight— quite a different person from what I was before I flew. But in trying to analyze what stimulated that change, or what the process of change was, it was not just the flight. In some ways the flight itself was probably less of a factor than the preparation for the flight. The flight was central, of course, being the actual culmination of all the training, as well as the experience of being there. But then after the flight, the reflection of what it was that I had been through, and what I had seen and observed, and the integration of that total process—the preflight, the flight, and then the after-flight reflection—were all part of it. It's not something that comes in and commands your attention.

For the most part, during a flight like that, you're quite busy. If there are no interruptions and you press on with the flight plan, throw the switches, make the readings, do the maneuvers, and use all the skills that you've developed in the training, you can totally occupy yourself with these activities. In fact, during the flight, I found that I thought about the nature of the experience I was undergoing only when I caused it to happen. That is, when I took the time. I interrupted what was happening, and took the time to think about it, what the experience of space was in and of itself. I brought it consciously into mind, and actually it was almost an accident.

On the fourth day of the flight, I was to go outside the lunar module for a test of the backpack which we were to use later on the surface of the Moon, in order to explore the Moon. This was to be the first flight of that backpack. I was, on that day, going outside the lunar module and, in fact, went out for 47 minutes. During that time, Dave Scott—who was over in the command module—also depressurized the command module; and although he was not on a backpack but had to stay hooked to the umbilicals, nevertheless, he partially exited from the hatch in order to recover some thermal samples. Part of the program at that point was to photograph the exterior surfaces of the lunar module and the command module for discoloration due to pyrotechnic events and things of that kind, which might change the thermal characteristics. So Dave and I were photographing the vehicles.

I was to progress up a set of handrails up to the top of the lunar module and across to the command module. That was to verify, in case we couldn't go through the tunnel between the two vehicles because of some problem with the docking, that we could transfer from one to the other externally—if worse came to worse. Dave was to photograph that, for engineering purposes, to see how well I could control my bodily position and whether I would bang into the radar antennae . . . things of that kind. While Dave was preparing for that, it turned out that the camera jammed.

Dave called a halt to everything and said, "Give me five minutes to try and fix the camera." Which is no simple task in a pressurized spacesuit, you know, outside in a vacuum. So while Dave was messing around with the camera, I had about five minutes where, in fact, I had nothing to do. Except to take that time to think about what I was doing . . . and look down at the Earth. And of course this is an absolutely spectacular sight; at that time, we were coming up over the west coast of the United States.

I'd gotten out at dawn just after we'd crossed the equator over the Pacific. By this time, I was coming up over the western part of the United States. I was looking down, going over the southern part at 17,000 miles per hour. When there is no communication coming in, as you use that portable life-support system, the radios are completely dead. There's absolutely no sound at all. Now, when you're going along at 17,000 miles an hour with this incredible, spectacular panorama below you—and absolute, total silence—you can't imagine how beautiful it is.

Mysticism is something that I am interested in, in a way. In another way I react against the idea that the space experience is, in and of itself, a mystical thing. I think that has been implied by many people in looking at the kind of changes that have occurred

The docked Apollo 9 command/service module and Lunar module "Spider," with Astronaut David R. Scott standing in the open hatch of the command module "Gumdrop," photographed by Russell Schweickart from the porch of the "Spider."

in some of the astronauts: Jim Irwin, after his flight on Apollo 15, started the High Flight organization and became an evangelical preacher; Ed Mitchell, going into ESP; Al Woden writing poetry. Somehow the experience of space does something to people. I react against that concept when it takes on the guise of something imposed almost from the outside, something controlled by the experience. It's not that. Certainly this was not the case for me. I don't believe that it was for anyone that I know, including those I've mentioned. I think it's something that one permits. I think space is a very profound experience. There are many analogous experiences here on Earth, or under the sea, or in many areas of life.

In many cases, unique human experiences come about only after one gets the attention of the person—as the story goes, hitting the mule between the eyes with a two-by-four to get his attention if you want him to do something. Space travel, at least in the early days of it, where things were pretty exciting, was a fairly big two-by-four. In terms of getting one's attention and causing one to think why one is undergoing that experience— a "How did I get here?" kind of thing—space travel has that aspect to it. Then the experience itself is, in terms of the perspective, the enlarged physical perspective of the Earth. This is the identity which develops as you circle the Earth every hour and a half. At least this is the case in Earth-orbital missions. As you go around, you develop an expanding identity, one which starts by recognizing the familiar features: home, the places you spent your time. However, this enlarged perspective is something that stays with just about everyone who has flown in space. The consequent and subsequent expression of that experience, in terms of a changed lifestyle or what one does afterward, assumes different forms for different people. For some people, it's personal and internalized. They consider this to be a private matter. For others, it's something which demands a different type of commitment.

In my case, I have always felt quite strongly that by becoming

an astronaut I accepted a kind of responsibility for that experience as a representative of humanity in this new environment,
and not as something which was my private property. So, to me,
sharing that experience and bringing that back in some way to
other people has been a part of what I consider to be my responsibility. But I think it varies a great deal from one individual to
another.

The space experience itself is unique. A person does not do
this on a routine basis. Any space flight that you're assigned to
may be the only one you fly, or if it's a second one, it may be your
last space flight. They don't come that frequently, and so there
is, certainly, a sense of wanting to capture the experience because
it is something which doesn't happen frequently. In some form,
though perhaps less purposeful than the one I just described for
myself, I think that probably everyone prepared for the missions. But I suspect there was a great deal of variation in the
consciousness or the specifics of how different people went
about it.

Simply going into space is not going to produce change in
consciousness. When you get up there, you are still you. And if
you are open, then the experience takes on a different meaning
for you and has a different significance than if you were an
"eyes-straight-ahead" or "on-with-the-job" type of person. But
that's also true of those same two people if they go out into the
woods, or if they go scuba diving at night, or any other experience of that kind. The one type of person will experience something quite different from another who is less open to the broader
perspectives.

It's not the environment that forces the experience, though the
environment certainly provides a rather pregnant setting. I've
often thought that there are people who need (if you will) an idea
that "if only I were there I would have this experience." There
are people who need many things and in some sense they create
them out of that need. Whether they're there or not, perhaps, is
not as important as the opportunity for them to create something
they need.

Prospects of Living in Space

We're already living in space. It's not as if we have been isolated from space. In an ironic way, we lived in space more in the past than we do today. Before we had city lights and electricity and houses with solid roofs and other things, nighttime was a very cosmic time. Today, however, nighttime is a very electronic time. We sit in front of a tube, and we're entertained by other people under bright lights. So we've lost, I think, a little bit of the sense of the cosmos that mankind had earlier in its development.

In the future, in some ways, as we move out into the cosmos, I think there will be a much greater awareness of our position in the cosmos. Again, as with individuals who have gone out into space and come back, I think there will be a sense of a changed perspective. The view of the Earth which was brought back from Apollo, both subjectively and in the form of photographs, I think altered irrevocably the sense of what the Earth was and what its place is in the cosmos; and what our responsibility for the Earth is.

As more people move out into space operations in the future, as they become more commonplace, and less exceptional, and at the same time much more personal, more people will experience that new perspective and will express it in their own way— I would hope in a much greater variety of ways than we've been able to express it so far.

I think that we will develop a longer-range view of the evolution of intelligence. There has been an assumption, although not an explicit one, that the evolution of life is limited to the planet, that we are in a closed system. The whole assumption behind the limits-to-growth concept is that we are in a closed system: that the Earth is it. I think that as we move out into space, that perception will change; that erroneous assumption will in fact gradually disappear. That's not to say that there is any disregard for Earth, or for our responsibility to Earth. In fact, I'd say it's the other way around. Certainly, from the astronauts who have flown, looking back on the Earth makes the Earth that much more precious in a subjective way. It doesn't create a disregard for it, because you're much more aware of the universe around the Earth. It makes it even more precious.

Transcending the Limits to Growth

As the idea of a closed environment is gradually modified, moving out into the universe will form the assumptions on which our children operate. In fact, my children operate that way now. They are the kids of the space age.

The reality of migration away from the Earth, of a gradually increasing sphere of consciousness and awareness of different life forms, is something which we're seeing in its embryonic stages. To some, that's a shock; to others, it's dismaying, because they see it as *either* space *or* Earth. I think that's totally invalid. In fact, in some ways, it seems to me that the environment of Earth will be enhanced as we move out into space, because we open up a much larger environment for utilization and for interaction; whereas, without doing that, we are limited to using the resources here on the planet only.

This whole issue of the limits to growth, which provides a psychological, as well as a physical, cap on potential expansion of activity and awareness, has had a very depressing effect on many people. It is now beginning to be reexamined in a critical way through a lot of the activities brought about by O'Neill's concept of space colonization and other developments. I don't for a moment think that there's any concept which anyone's working with now which will be followed as a straightforward scenario. But the idea embodied in concepts such as space colonization or space industrialization, or availability of nonterrestrial resources, is fundamental, and it will change the way in which people look at the future.

I know that my kids, and I don't think they're in any way atypical, assume that this is part of the future. They will provide the imagination and the creativity which will bring about this kind of an evolution.

Sequence 3

Space: A Totally New Perspective
EDGAR D. MITCHELL

Captain Edgar D. Mitchell was the sixth human being to walk on the Moon; his moonwalks totaled nine hours. He also conducted a successful telepathic experiment between space and Earth. After leaving government service, he devoted himself to studies of how latent human potential might influence alternative social futures, founding the Institute of Noetic Sciences (now located in San Francisco). He serves as Chairman of the Board of the Institute. He is also currently a director, consultant, and senior stockholder in Information Science Incorporated, an international firm in human resource management.

In this sequence, Captain Mitchell discusses the ways in which spaceflight can alter our perceptions of ourselves.

What is the best way to describe the experience of space flight? Perhaps the best way to describe it quickly is to say that it produces a changed perspective. We have the saying, "You're so deep in the trees you can't see the forest." Getting away from Earth, and looking at Earth from deep space, allows us to see the forest as well. This provides a totally new perspective on what we're all about, a deep emotional perspective. I had what the psychologists call a "peak experience," or what the mystics would call a "mystical experience," in which it was as though my awareness was greatly expanded, and I had brief flashes of insight that were very personal and profound, sufficiently so to make me change my life and go find out what all of this meant. I have spent the past several years investigating mental phenomena, exceptional human mental capabilities, what "peak" and "mystical" experiences really mean in terms of fundamental science and, more importantly, what they mean in terms of human ability to choose and implement acceptable behavioral and social futures.

Edgar D. Mitchell

Not A Unique Experience?

Certainly the type of experience I had in space has been recorded by people standing on a mountaintop and looking at vast reaches of the Earth. For example, from the top of Mount Everest, or in the case of pilots flying high-altitude airplanes, or mystics in meditation—all of these people have had similar experiences. So the likelihood is that my experience resulted from the fact that I was ready for it in my life and from the changed perspective of seeing Earth from 240,000 miles away. Both are very provocative ideas: that a person becomes ready for an experience, and that a *metanoia** can take place.

It was the type of experience that has been well-reported in the mystical literature, and is now starting to be reported more in the psychological literature, much in the same way as a "peak experience" or a euphoric experience whereby new and deep insights become available to the mind.

There are pseudo-ways to produce such insights and such experiences. We know that the psychedelic drugs have produced highs, and changed perspectives, but they also have had some horrendously bad side effects. Such mind-altering substances have also produced psychosis, in that the yearning for this psychological experience became so great that people kept trying to reproduce it with more drugs; then the side effects took over, and their lives were destroyed instead of enhanced. It is possible, perhaps, that as a clinical tool the psychedelic drugs have some significant utilitarian value. But for public use to produce insights and "enlightenment," these drugs have no value whatsoever. As a matter of fact, they take you in the wrong direction.

Causes of Peak Experiences

We have begun to understand the psychology of the mystical experience and of the peak experience, but so far only a little of

* *Metanoia* is a Greek term used in the New Testament. It means literally "change of mind" (or heart), and is usually translated as "repentance." Ed.

the physiology. This is where science has really been derelict. We have tended to say that these types of mental functioning are aberrations, that they are hallucinations — which is not the case at all. They can be produced, and they can be controlled. A study of Eastern philosophy, traditions, and techniques of producing mental phenomena shows that it can be done consistently, under controlled conditions; and many individuals of the Eastern tradition spend their lives studying and learning these techniques. Therefore, it is not aberrant or hallucinatory at all. It is a trainable technique which apparently has a great deal of utilitarian value in helping an individual to learn to calm his body, to cope with stress, to cope with chaos, to learn more satisfying thought and behavior patterns. This is achieved by learning to maintain an inner calm, an inner peace, and an inner feeling of fulfillment and good will, regardless of what's going on around the individual.

In that sense, this experience can be utilitarian for our society. That the broad social implications are so great for a distressed society is one reason why it's of such interest to those of us who have been studying this area of human functioning.

Is Space Migration Part of Our Evolutionary Destiny?

I think there are several things to be considered before we really take space migration seriously. Space stations, habitation in space in near-Earth orbit: by all means, that will be done. However, when we start thinking of the vast distances required to go to other habitable-type planets, it becomes an exceedingly difficult problem, given even the wildest extrapolations of our current technology. Furthermore, many of the problems here on Earth are solvable problems, and I would not like to see us export our own brand of insanity to the rest of the universe. Let's learn to cope with our problems here first, rather than saying, "Let's launch off to space to colonize other planets." We need to become far more wise about what we're doing here on Earth, for example, how to cope with our own emotions, with our own relationships with other people, other societies, other nations, *first*. I don't really think we are evolved enough here on Earth even to think about exporting ourselves elsewhere in the universe at this time.

The Space Environment

Space is a hostile environment, in which you must be protected because there is no atmosphere. The extremes of temperature are enormous; if your body is not pressurized, it will obviously die very quickly. However, under the proper conditions of protection, like a spacecraft or a spacesuit, space is euphoric. Psychologically it could be a very nice place to live. But it is exceedingly hostile, and everything has to be manufactured and taken there: your oxygen and water supplies, your food, and so on. Now, a sophisticated space station could become ecologically self-sustaining. However, that's going to require a bit more technology, and the question is, "Why do it?" Well, if it enhances our ability to solve problems on Earth, which we think it will, then it is obviously worth doing. But to do it just because we're overpopulated, or we have too many problems to solve and we want to get away from them, is to do it for the wrong reason. Only if space exploration helps us solve our problems *here*, by providing greater understanding of Earth systems and humanity, only then will it have true utilitarian value.

The Importance of Apollo

The Apollo mission was important not only in my life but, I think, in the whole social structure of the Earth. Aside from the enormous technological and scientific benefits that came out of the program, there are economic benefits: that program returned about seven dollars into the economy for every dollar invested.

Courtesy of NASA

President Nixon with his hands on his side in dismay, after dropping the NASA Distinguished Service Medal to be presented to Apollo 14 Lunar Module Pilot, Edgar D. Mitchell.

No other government program in the history of the world has been that successful. But perhaps the most important benefits that have come out of the space program are the new management techniques that had to be devised to run a program of that size successfully, on schedule, on cost, and safely. That's a first in man's history. And perhaps another of the most important benefits, and one that was never predicted, was this new perspective on Earth and of ourselves. We gained this perspective by going into space and looking back, and seeing ourselves in a new reality, as we really are: as a finite, tiny, harassed, ridiculous little planet with many puffed-up egos and a lot of inhumanity to each other, when it doesn't have to be that way at all. Seeing ourselves in this new light may be the single most important element to bring about a turning point in the history of Earth. This new perspective may have more effect on the history of the planet than any other single thing that came out of the Apollo program.

Sequence 4
Preparing to Go into Space
PATRICIA COWINGS

---

*Patricia Cowings, Ph.D., is Director of the Psychophysiological Depart-
ment at the NASA Ames Research Facility at Moffett Field, California.
She specializes in research on control of involuntary states. She has
applied for a position as Mission Specialist on the upcoming series of
space-shuttle flights.*

*The domain of space beyond our atmosphere has traditionally been the
exclusive province of males. There are changes here also, as women move
into positions of responsibility in the further exploration and development of space.*

*The space-shuttle program involves a vehicle that can make many
trips into Earth orbit and return. Six of the astronauts in this program
will be women.*

*In this sequence Dr. Cowings discusses her reasons, both as an
individual and as a scientist, for wanting to go into space.*

There was a reason why very few women were involved with the
space program in the past. It had to do with the old school of
astronauts. They were the superhuman beings of this planet.
I know some of them, and they are really amazing individuals.
But I think the biggest drawback for women in the space program up to this point was the requirement for so many thousands of hours of flight time in jets. There's no way you can get it
if you're a woman, not in the military until just recently, or
unless you own your own jet. But women are equally qualified as
scientist-astronauts.

27

I'm from the Star Trek generation. The idea of riding on the USS Enterprise was one of my major fantasies. That's the main reason I work at NASA. I try to get the most mileage out of my fantasies that I can. I get a lot of personal satisfaction out of the fact that I really feel my work is going to be worthwhile for the space program.

I want to go into space, but I'm both afraid and excited about the prospect. Going into a totally alien environment, where life is threatened on all sides, produces a certain amount of anxiety. If I went on an exploration in a sealab, there would be a certain amount of anxiety about that. Scuba diving is anxiety-producing, too: you can die if you don't check your tanks and your decompression computer. But at the same time, I go because it's exhilarating, just trying to stay on top of it. Your heart beats faster, but it's from excitement. I think I would be terrified, but I would go anyway; especially when I look at the films of the crew after they've adapted to zero-G and it's home away from home. In a zero-G [weightless] environment, you can *fly!* You don't walk from place to place; you sort of ice-skate or push yourself along—that must be terribly exhilarating.

As far as your world outlook changing, let me put it this way. Suppose you were standing on the Moon and looking at the Earth, would you at that time think of yourself as a citizen of Palo Alto, a Californian, an American, or somebody from that planet? All the little things we tend to classify ourselves in sort of go away. You're all from that planet. I know some of the astronauts have become terribly concerned with ecology. You go outside the planet, and you *see* parts of it that are spoiling, and that it's just a little ball, and there's all this big open space around it, and it could be hurt irreparably. Then they become terribly concerned about ecology, because they see the big picture.

Technology is advancing at lightning speed. I am not a member of the school of thought that believes that machines will take over humanity. My field is essentially a glorification of biofeedback. I've discovered that, with the help of my machines, a subject can now become aware of how much blood is in the little finger of his left hand, something he could not have been aware of before. Eventually he doesn't even need the machine; he can be aware of it on his own. This is an example of how machines can be used to increase human ability.

I study the relationship between mind and body in human subjects. We are developing in our laboratory a method, based on biofeedback and partly on self-hypnosis and attention training, for training human subjects to control several of their own physiological responses simultaneously. This therapy would allow people to adapt to the condition of zero gravity much more rapidly than they normally would, without the use of drugs. Drugs often have side effects that would be dangerous in a life-threatening situation like that of space, where you really have to be on top of what's happening.

We have found that the more often a person practices his learned control, the more likely it is that he won't have to think about it much. It becomes automatic. The body will make the optimal change it needs to make. It's like exercising muscles for a long period of time; after a while, they become strong.

The therapy we use in combination with biofeedback is called autogenic therapy; it's somewhat modified from the standard routine. It consists of a series of self-suggestion exercises. For instance, a person focuses attention on his right hand, hopefully to the extent that he's aware of nothing else, and gives the suggestion that his hand is beginning to feel heavy. That's highly correlated with a reduction of muscle activity, because the mind is directly controlling it. Then he would suggest that his hand feel warm *and* heavy, and that is correlated with an increase in blood flow to his hand. By constructing these exercises in such a way that you can produce a known pattern of physiological responses, you can prevent arousal reactions to stress, and you can produce a more relaxed profile in the individual.

It should be noted that the techniques involved in biofeedback and autogenic therapy are suitable for any type of stressful situation encountered in human experience, not just trips into space. Many individuals have found this training helpful in alleviating everyday job-oriented anxieties.

Geoff Chandler

Phase Two
Space Industries
A Design for the Future

Buckminster Fuller

Prolog

The Universe Is Technology

BUCKMINSTER FULLER

The universe is technology; all biology is technology. Anything that operates under cosmic laws—reciprocity, interconvolutarity—is technology. The universe is *nothing but* technology. We, as individuals, represent a most complex technology: the total ecology of the interplay of all the biological elements, the Sun's radiation, the cross-pollination and so forth, the chemistries we develop on this planet are all part of an incredible preexisting technology.

If we want to examine space-age technology, we should keep in mind that we are in space and have never been anywhere else. The space-age technology of getting this planet populated is the most extraordinary space-age technology that has ever occurred. What we've been doing is absolutely childish compared with what nature's already done. Space-age technology is something that's always been going on; it's a mark of great ignorance to speak of it as if it weren't.

Such attitudes are similar to the geocentric idea, which is still around. There are cultures that still think the universe is going around us; there are *scientists* who are still seeing the *Sun set*. The level of self-misinformation is very high.

We are already a space colony. If we can't make it in this beautifully equipped colony, we're not going to make it anywhere else, either. And we're not going to carry on any of our space colonies, except by virtue of being colonies from the mother ship. If the mother ship can't be made to work, the colonies aren't going to work.

There is no independence in the universe. Everything in the universe is interdependent. The kind of phenomenon *we* represent—60 percent water, to give us hydraulic compression, distribution of loads, noncompressibility, the whole shape—this is an extraordinary piece of structuring. We don't know any other planet with water, just this tiny bit of water on the surface of our globe, which looks deep to you and me, but is almost negligible on a planetary scale. If I take a six-foot steel ball, polished, and breathe on it, the condensation of my breath will be deeper on it than the oceans are on Earth. So that water could be vaporized and lost very rapidly, if it weren't for the beautiful set of spheres around it: the Van Allen Belt, the troposphere, all beautifully interacting to hold what we have down here, while we continually take on energy and give off energy. So that surface has to be kept in balance.

It's important, then, to keep in mind that the Earth is already in space, rather than to think of us as going out into space from it. All the things that are going on are simply a discovery by humanity of how the universe operates. We're gradually getting in, a little bit, on our own control system. We're not introducing new technology; we can't invent anything. All we can do is discover what *is*, and employ it.

Many new tools are evolving with us, as independent entities. However, in the world of the machine, I don't talk about "cybernetic intelligence" (as some do). I talk about the technology of cybernetics, of steering-system *feedback*, for example, but I don't refer to feedback as intelligence. To discover an error in an angular course and correct it is not intelligence. We have a cultural propensity for talking about things in a way that's really stupid. Newspapers, magazines, need headlines that will sell; so they apply the word "intelligence" to a machine. No machines will ever be intelligent. They never have been and never will be.

There is a physical universe, and a metaphysical universe. The universe, as we began to find out at the beginning of this century, in Einsteinian terms, is all energy. Energy can neither be created nor be destroyed. The physical universe is all energy;

radiation is energy. A needle on an instrument will be moved either gravitationally or electromagnetically. Anything that is metaphysical will not move needles. The sound I make when I talk to you is physical, but the meaning within the sounds is completely metaphysical. Your whole intellect is utterly metaphysical, whereas the cybernetic deals very much with the physical—like the arrow, or the needle, which shows that your course is wrong. That's why "cybernetic intelligence" is a contradiction in terms.

It's similar with the so-called world of the machine. I've said that the universe is nothing but technology. People have been so careless as to think of us as some kind of china doll with nothing underneath the surface. Now we're beginning to learn about what's in that brain; and it's incredible!

What is really going on is that *mind is discovering the principles of brain to be only a special case*, coordinating the input of all the senses—olfactory, auditory, optical, tactile—and, to some extent, the esthetics and the intuitions. All that's happening is that we're discovering the principles that have always been there, and learning to employ some of those principles, and discovering more about how they operate.

The ocean's been working the same way all the time, the waves have moved that way all the time, those bubbles in the surf have been the same all the time. It's just that we know a little more about them. We have been able to participate a little bit in nature's own carryings-on. We're not introducing anything new in the universe.

Evolution is continually working, continually transforming, intercomplementarily transforming by laws which operate in such a way that we have an eternally regenerative universe. Coevolution is, then, the increase of our knowledge about what's going on, that's all.

Human beings have developed words so that we can communicate our experiences: that's what education is. Although we became able to write, and to compound all the experiences and information of all the people before us, gradually discovering the principles operating in that information, we were misinterpreting the special case of ourselves, and missing completely what its significance was. That makes the present cultural change a fascinating one: each child born, successively, is given less misinformation; the old misinformation becomes simply irrelevant. Moreover, each successive child is being born in the presence of more reliable information. It doesn't make much difference how they use their senses, how they get it.

When I was young, people wanted to get what they considered a desirable job, to look fancy. I learned it didn't make a difference what the job was. If it was just sweeping, I could learn an incredible amount by sweeping. I learned what makes a floor. I learned about microbes. I learned the principles of sweeping! I've never had a job that wasn't just full of the most beautiful information.

This is why I say I'm not worried about the way new information gets to children, whether they're sitting in front of a TV set, looking at the newspapers, or just looking at the cartoons. The kids are going to latch onto whatever it may be.

The fact is that latching onto the TV is really a most wonderful thing. An apparent problem is that we're using it as a means to make money—to sell toothpaste, and so on. The kids, however, aren't really so much interested in that information, but just in the way the thing is working. They love the technique; they're studying the technique all the time. They take in the use of language much more than they do the message. Parents think their kids go for the story; but a child has stories in which he can play "Shoot Grandma," and it doesn't mean a thing. You can shoot Grandma twenty times, and it doesn't really mean shooting Grandma, but they'll play it over and over. Similarly, as far as they're concerned, what's going on on TV is another game. What really counts is the things that are behind this: that you're really feeling Grandma's love, that she really did get you some cookies. Something else is going on all the time.

My hope would be that we take advantage of the fact that the kids are glued to the set, and give them some of the synergetics, the mathematics, that will really fascinate them. Then the 99 percent of humanity that doesn't understand that the universe is nothing but technology, who think that technology is something new and undesirable, who can be fooled into using phrases like "cybernetic intelligence," will be able to catch on to nature's way of producing. They can learn about the way things grow, what a structure is, how you employ the principles in the most economical way so you can harness all the wonderful energies that are available in your own little home. All these things can come about if the world will realize that we really have the option to make it.

We must no longer be engaged in "It's you or me—I have to make a living." We're really here to solve local problems in the universe. Each one is to find out what it is he or she has a proclivity for, and begin to solve those problems.

Our young world is in love with truth. You used to be able to say to kids, "I want you to be loyal to our family, loyal to our team, our school . . . and everyone else is a foreigner, dangerous and obnoxious." Kids won't do that any more. They're beginning to see human beings as human beings. Their values are figured in terms of judging what is true themselves. They just can't stand hypocrisy; they can't stand pretension; they can't stand fake glory. Our values are getting purer, richer, and more reliable.

Space Industries — *Today's deep-space probes and manned launchings inspire much less wonder and awe than the achievements of the 1960s. The glamour wears thin; appropriations diminish; media coverage is nil. Is space becoming commonplace?*

An unlikely new group of visionaries doesn't think so. For them, the excitement is just beginning. They speak seriously about building cities in orbit within the next 30 years. More importantly, they are also making plans to go up there and live.

These individuals are not wild-eyed, star-blinded dreamers. They have long, distinguished pedigrees. They hold responsible positions of authority. They teach physics at prestigious universities, do advanced engineering research for NASA, head large corporate concerns, write complex technical articles, and publish magazines and newsletters.

Phase two of our exploration of potential worlds beyond is the province of these technocratically trained humanists who, faced with a bleak apocalyptic future, have said "No!" to Doomsday. They are comfortable with enormous economies of scale. And here they explain exactly how and why they foresee up to a million people living and working in space by early in the next century.

L.G.

Sequence 5

The Origin of
Space Colonies

STEWART BRAND

Occupying the front position in each edition of Stewart Brand's Whole
Earth Catalog *is a category called "Whole Systems." Most of the
information listed refers to books and materials by Buckminster Fuller.
Indeed, the first line states, "The insights of Buckminster Fuller initiated this catalog."*

*Stewart Brand has always been fascinated by information, especially
about how personal creativity and ingenuity can apply scientific technology in practice to meet basic human needs. His efforts have helped all
of us "conduct our own education, find our own inspiration, shape our
own environment, share our adventures with each other." In 1975,
Stewart shared the "potential" adventure of building self-sustaining
colonies in the virtually unlimited space that exists beyond our atmosphere.*

*After creating and supervising the editing of a succession of quarterly
"Whole Earth Catalogs," Stewart combined the cream of the informa-
tion into* The Last Whole Earth Catalog. *It turned out not to be "the
last" word from Stewart, since demand for a sequel called forth* The
Whole Earth Epilog *and a current successor,* The CoEvolution
Quarterly *(Box 428, Sausalito, CA 94965). As Special Consultant
to the Governor of California, he introduced Jerry Brown to Russell
Schweickart and to Gerard O'Neill.*

*In this sequence Stewart shares his personal insights into the work of
Gerard O'Neill and into the importance of human expansion into space.*

Gerard O'Neill spoke at a World's Future Conference that I
attended in Washington. Several thousand people collected to

talk about the future, if any. Most of them decided to be interested in the idea that there wasn't one. It was a beautiful example of what Ken Kesey calls "looking through the problem box trying to find a solution." Well, there's nothing in the problem box but problems. If you want a solution, you go to the solution box.

The World's Future Conference was almost entirely a problem box this time, except for this one guy, this character O'Neill, who was talking on the subject of "the High Frontier": colonies in space. I think his talk was attended by a grand total of maybe thirty people. It was embarrassing. There were just a few chairs filled by people, while all the other meetings, about how the

Stewart Brand rowing to work.

economy was going to pieces, and how the Third World was going to pieces, and how lifestyles were going to pieces, were jammed to the doors.

No one was at O'Neill's. But they are coming now. There's been a major change, and the change is this.

Making Physics Relevant

In 1969, pressured by all of us who said that science and engineering, the military, and so on, were irrelevant, O'Neill was teaching basic physics at Princeton University. Like a good elitist, he was also really deeply involved with the course. He was leading one of the sections, and was pretty much involved in the problems the students were having with their roommates who said, "Ah, engineering. That's not about anything real. Get into communes, man. Try some dope. Get into politics." So he started to try to see if there was a way to make physics relevant and basic physical design relevant.

Looking in the Solution Box

He held a seminar of his best students, ten or twelve first-rate individuals. They met once a week with him. I guess about the second week, he put the question to them this way: "Is the surface of a planet the best place for an expanding technological civilization?"

So they started to see if it was, and, even more interestingly, if it were *not*, then where *would* be the best place for an expanding technological civilization? They quickly ruled out not only the Earth's surface, which is famously bad for this, but also other planetary surfaces, including the Moon, because you're at the bottom of a gravity well, which means it's hard to move things around. You're in an atmosphere in some cases, which means that when anything goes wrong, it goes wrong for everybody. In addition, it's often hard to do industrial processes with an atmosphere where you don't want it. They came to realize, also, that energy—plain old solar energy—that reaches the surface of planets is so dilute that you have a major problem there, too.

So then Dr. O'Neill started looking at free orbits: free spaces, they came to call it. There, you've got solar energy coming in twenty times better than any place on the Earth's surface. Furthermore, there's no night and day: you can just stay pointed at the Sun as long as you want, and collect energy, richly. Working without gravity, you could have three-dimensional structures instead of flat. For instance, he once asked someone at Chrysler what size their many square miles of plants would come to if they could work in three dimensions, and they came up with a cube a couple of hundred yards on each edge. And again, a whole lot of industrial processes want to go on in a vacuum if they can.

Now suppose that's the case, and you now want to make a place where people who prefer to live there, rather than on the planet's surface, can do it. What he came up with was something that looks like a tin can; some of the later models are maybe five kilometers in diameter and thirty kilometers long. This is a very large item. It's got six stripes from one end to the other, and these six stripes are alternating window and land. Above each window is a mirror which reflects the sun onto the land opposite, so this is a three-fold symmetry on a cylinder. The cylinder is pointed at the sun, and stays pointed at the Sun. You can raise and lower these thirty-kilometer mirrors to give night and day if you want to do that.

The Birth of Practical Space Colonies

Then the students started seeing things about the real practicalities of this. One of the things they discovered is that you can make it quite desirable, because, in an atmosphere that size, you have weather, and a blue sky, and each of these three strips of land—which they came to call valleys—could be made anything you wanted. If you wanted it to be like the area around Carmel, that's how you could make it. Would you rather be in New England, with a changing climate? Fine, you can do that. Hawaii? Fine.

To be sure they weren't going off the very deep end, they started checking out the economics of this, and found that it was readily possible to get 95 percent of the material from the Moon. In fact, it doesn't take very much Moon to make one of these. I think they said that the strip-mine operation for the first model, which would be a planet for 10,000 people, would be 70 yards by 70 yards by twenty yards; that's the size of the hole left in the Moon to accomplish all of this. The students found that by moving the lunar material to handy gravity points called Lagrangian points, which are sort of Sargasso Seas in space, in front of and after the Moon in its Earth orbit, you could send up lunar material cheaply, using magnetic mass-drivers, as they call them. It reaches zero velocity just at the Lagrangian point. You just reach out with any kind of local robot and push it over to where you're going to process it. They know from the Apollo flights that the lunar material has everything you need—30 percent aluminum oxide and things like that—not as fantastic as the asteroids, but that comes later.

The time to get these going: the first one, for 10,000 people, could be done, speaking conservatively, fifteen years after time zero, the start of the project. These become economically profitable, because, if you've made a planet like this, you can now easily do two other things: first, make more planets like it, or more tin cans; and second, make solar collectors much more efficiently there than anywhere else, to be put in synchronous orbit around the Earth and beam down endless amounts of clean microwave transmission of solar energy. Then these planets start making more of themselves. They would get into, I think, a doubling time of about every six months.

The Space Colonies Expand

They would be designing themselves to be extremely attractive to colonists, which they've got the full range of abilities to do. For

Pair of cylindrical space colonies.

example, you could have mountains in the end caps—at the end of the cylinder—which would have the peculiar property that as you go up the mountain you get lighter, until at the top you can put on some nice feathers and fly. At the base of the mountains, you might have a river which goes clear around the cylinder, so you could get into a canoe and visit all three valleys and be back home in a couple of hours, riding downcurrent all the way.

The engineering on this has been subjected to good, detailed critiques, which have been met by detailed better solutions. They've started to put the effort into it. The feasibility is there, the economic feasibility and the engineering feasibility. This is with on-the-shelf technology. It's there now, just using Skylab materials, Apollo, the space shuttle, and so on. The cost of doing the first one is about equivalent to the Apollo program.

Five years after it's up, it starts to pay for itself. The people on board become fabulously rich and proceed, presumably, to make more of these things. If the procedure started now—again, this is O'Neill's conservative estimate—by the year 2018 the population on this planet's surface would commence to decrease, as more people would spend the $3,000 it would take to join a colony.

The colonies, of course, can be anything they want to. Each one is its own culture, if it wants to be that. Diversity could be encouraged or discouraged, as you wished. If you wanted to do a different kind of economy, you'd be free to try. This is the place to do it.

It's a little scary because Gerard O'Neill has taken away the energy crisis, the population crisis, and—because these things are terrific food producers—the food crisis as well. So much for the Apocalypse we've known and loved for so long.

Our Universe Will Expand

Part of my commitment to the colonies is that, as their possibilities are realized, you may get some of the intellectual and spiritual ferment going on that was going on in Europe when North America opened up, which fed back and forth as the pioneers over here were roughing it and the intellectuals over there were talking up the new ideas and possibilities. These possibilities filtered across the Atlantic, and the pioneers came up with some pretty interesting governmental ideas. I think that kind of process would take off again. Also, if you want the spiritual end of it, for example, the American Transcendentalists were an interesting crew. Would Walt Whitman have happened in Europe? I doubt it. It's an extension, I think, of the period of time when we started seeing photographs of the Earth from outside; the kind of self-consciousness that this brought may be really beneficial in promoting the idea of *other possibilities*.

What's even nicer is the fact that these possibilities can get extremely far out, and it's all right; because even if the space colonists blow it, if they destroy themselves, that only happens within that particular tin can; it doesn't take everyone else down with them.

That's the problem that makes us feel constricted—even claustrophobic—on the Earth now. You can't get too far out, or you blow it for everybody. Dr. O'Neill sees a time when these space colonies would be all over in Earth orbit; there would be a lot of them off to the asteroids; a few of them might set off for distant stars—which is all still in the realm of physical engineering practicality. And the Earth may be pretty much preserved and reverenced as a kind of park.

Seduced by the Design Elegance

My first question to Dr. O'Neill was, "Okay, you've got a new ecological niche opening up. That means there's going to be some limiting factors: space, atmosphere, or something like that. What's the limiting factor here? What will people find an excuse to make war over, for example?"

He said, "Well, it's not material. There's material for a population some 50,000 times the size of our present population, just in the Moon and handy asteroids.

"I was seduced—willingly—by the design elegance of the original notion. I liked especially the idea that mistakes could be made in space and wouldn't really hurt anyone else." In space, there is genuine isolation of most problems, even using hydrogen explosions to move asteroids around. On the planet, they're evil; in space, they're negligible. The solar wind will carry away any products, and the products themselves have nothing to impinge upon that's dangerous. As the whole exotic nature of the space environment—getting some personal sense of what it's like there—is perceived more clearly, the Earth and the care of the Earth will be better perceived as well.

The Main Inconvenience of Space Colonies

Inconveniences are always something different from what you expect. You imagine the inconvenience of an ocean voyage will be the endless ocean, and it turns out the real inconvenience is the other people in the crew. So anticipating overmuch, I think, is to some extent a meaningless exercise. As a design exercise, of course, it's important, but it happens incrementally anyway. We already have the experience of Skylab in this country—and that was a space colony—to help us figure out what's right for the next level and the level after that. Space industrialization is getting to be the buzzword for what's coming next: a much wider involvement in space by various nations and various corporations. With the arrival of the space shuttle, NASA becomes more and more just the busdriver.

Life in Space

People say, "Do you want to go into space?" That doesn't really occur to me. Space colonies make people either angry or religiously enthused, and therefore they fight with each other. Why bother with something that's got its own course of development? Massive human participation in space has its own momentum. There's a point at which you say "Here's an interesting subject, people," and then when enough people get interested, you don't have to say that any more. So I start looking around for what else might be going on. That's why I don't have a lot to say about space colonies by now. They may be good or bad for you, I'm not sure which. They will probably occur.

Those who want to go into orbit are basically saying, "Pocket calculators and telephones are where it's at, and I'm going to go where they lead." Technology is not following the aspirations of humankind; we are trying to catch up with technology. That gives you either despair or elation, sometimes depending on the time of day.

It's a religious question. People who feel that some type of technology is all right have a dedication to it which you'd have to call religious. They feel that people who despise that are somehow anti-Christ, somehow wicked. And the people who despise it think the technologists are wicked, and there's a lot of finger-pointing going on. This keeps editors like me busy.

As for myself, I like wooden boats. I use power saws to make them work. Just enough technology to get by and keep yourself interested. I'm too old-fashioned to really dive into computer science or, probably, space colonies. But I admire the ones who are willing to go out that far and cut off quite a bit behind them. That's pretty serious bridge-burning. In computer science, to join in an incredibly symbiotic relationship with equipment, this is already here and is increasing. There are people who live with computers all the time; they live out of the Coke machine next to the computer and sleep on a cot. They're young and they have the power. If they go out, it's to see *Star Wars*. In some fundamental way, *Star Wars'* reality is their reality, because they have this projective reality that's as fluid as the special effects in *Star Wars* or *Close Encounters of the Third Kind*.

Communications Satellites

My own suspicion is that what will be coming out of the communications satellites will be much more revolutionary for human behavior than most of the things we're talking about in space applications. And in that line, I have one alarming scenario, which goes something like this. As we get larger and larger antennae in geosynchronous orbit, they can deal with much smaller receivers and senders on the ground, down to the level of wrist-radio-type communications. For instance, individual amateur sailors would be able to use these satellites to pinpoint their location down to practically a few feet. What I worry about is the combination of these two abilities, so that anyone using communications of any sort could be trackable to a few square feet at all times.

On some fundamental level, the illusion of being able to get away with things is sort of necessary. Buckminster Fuller puts forward the idea that the outlaw area is where real invention goes on. What worries me is that recent forms of surveillance might be used by recent governments, and possible governments to come, to pay more attention to people who disagree with them than us potential outlaws might want them to.

Space Mutants

I talked at the California Maritime Academy. One question was, "How do you think people will physically evolve in the future in space?" I said, "Either they will remain exactly the same, because we have enough control over the environment that we can make it suit us, or, because the complexity of computer capabilities is fast approaching biological capabilities, you'll have two heads: yours and the computer's." Alan Kay of Xerox Research Center says the juice that it takes to run your brain is about what it takes to keep a 25-watt bulb lit. With the increasing sophistication and cheapening of the components of computer technology, it'll get down to your head and *its* head, which will be the same size and equally talented.

The terms—I love them! There's "hardware," which is the equipment, in computer science; "software," which is the programming; and "jellyware," which is us. And they're merging. For a long time we thought we'd have to adapt to the machines; but we've adapted the machines so far to us that you can no longer distinguish. So I said that either people will be the same 50,000 years from now, or they'll be so unrecognizable that they have nothing in common with us, except for being alive.

Russell Schweickart said—and here comes the natural history instead of speculation—"In space, at least in zero-G, you find the most useless thing you have on your body is legs. They're big, they fly around and get in the way, they make you crowded, they have no function. Oh, they do have a function: you have feet on the ends of them, which you can hook into things and make a leash to move around at the end of." He figures that if astronauts of the future keep working in zero-G, it will be like those guys on skateboards whose hips end in wheels, and they'll have enormous forearms and hands. He says working in a pressure suit outside in space, the first thing that gets tired is your forearms. So your theoretical mutant might have no legs and huge arms.

Whatever Happened to "Small is Beautiful"?

We did a space-colonies book and several issues on the illusion that either small is beautiful or big is beautiful, and either you're low-tech or you're high-tech, and that's it. I've come to think those distinctions are so stupid and illusory as to be negligible.

It may be because at an early point I promoted the idea of getting a picture of the whole Earth, which is a high-tech project. Lots of Indians, hippies, musicians, and so on, have claimed to have traveled out and seen the empyrean realms and seen the whole Earth before their eyes—but they didn't bring back photographs. The crewcut Bible-thumpers of Dallas did. It changed ecology, it changed Indians, it changed all the good things that we love. I say if an advance here helps an advance there, how can you have an either/or proposition? They are somehow the *same* proposition, and "small is beautiful" is a luxury that you can afford when you have some other way to grow that doesn't threaten the wild places. I think Governor Brown feels there is a synthesis there which is not contradictory. "Small is beautiful" on Earth; big may be beautiful in space; we don't know yet.

Ivan Illich talks about convivial tools like the bicycle. And in the same breath he says the telephone is a very convivial tool. Pocket calculators in most of their uses seem convivial tools. The making of pocket calculators is not a cottage industry. It *makes possible* a lot of cottage industry. You've got wonderful symbiosis, so far anyway, between large and complex enterprises and quite small and complex enterprises. Centralization/decentralization. It's like the economy: we aren't socialist or capitalist; we're a mongrel. But mongrels are the smartest dogs.

Sequence 6

Breakout into Space

GERARD K. O'NEILL

Gerard K. O'Neill, Ph.D., is Professor of Physics at Princeton University. In his research specialty, high-energy particle physics, he invented the colliding-beam storage ring, which has been adopted for use in nuclear accelerators worldwide. Professor O'Neill is a Fellow of the American Physical Society, and a member of the American Institute of Aeronautics and Astronautics, Phi Beta Kappa, Sigma Xi, the Soaring Society of America, and the Experimental Aircraft Association. His book The High Frontier: Human Colonies in Space *was published by Bantam Books in 1977. He also edited* Space-Based Manufacturing from Nonterrestrial Materials, *which is Volume 57 in the series* Progress in Astronautics and Aeronautics, *published by the American Institute of Aeronautics and Astronautics, New York, 1977.*

In this sequence, Professor O'Neill recounts the origins of his proposals for space colonization, and discloses their relationships to the changes in social values that took place during the 1960s.

The year 1969, in the United States, was about the peak of the disenchantment with the sciences. I found myself teaching a big freshman physics course at Princeton. It was perhaps the worst possible choice of years. In order to answer some of my own questions about the values of science and technology, and in order to try to explore for the students whether it was, in fact, useful and productive and "right" to be going into technical fields, I took a few of them aside, those who were interested, and said, "Look, let's address the question, Are there some large-

51

Photo by David Roberts

Gerard K. O'Neill

scale engineering programs which could be carried out completely within the technology which either is right here, now, or will very shortly be with us, that could involve you in a way *that you could feel is benefiting, in some profound fashion, the mass of humanity?"*

As the outcome of that question, I asked, "Look around: we see all the limits-of-growth problems. We see energy usage going up very rapidly, desperate need for more energy, particularly in the developing nations. We see the connection of wealth and low population-growth rate. We see every reason to try to bootstrap up a large fraction, hopefully all, of the population of the world to a better standard of living. Is there a way—where the industrial revolution has brought us so many of the things people regard as necessary—*is there a way in which technological growth can go on, but not in a harmful fashion?"*

As I began to explore those questions with the students—the fundamentals of energy, how to get it, and how to get rid of it after you've used it and it's become waste heat, how to recycle materials in such a way that you don't get pollutants—as we addressed those questions, it became more and more obvious that a logical long-term solution was to establish human habitation not on a planetary surface, but in space itself, where free energy is available all the time and can be turned either on or off very easily.

Why Have Human Colonies in Space?

By using the material and energy resources that are out there in space, resources which can be used without any damage to our environment and without stealing anything from anyone, we can probably have a greater positive benefit on our own planet — on our own spaceship here — than it seems we are likely to have by any other comparable effort. To be specific, we're concerned about the question of energy for the long term. The Alaska pipeline will supply us with energy for a short time, but if we were to run even our electric generators in the United States on that alone, it would run out completely within a very few years. So we need a long-term source of energy: it ought to be clean, something we can use without damaging our environment.

We've become aware that there *is* a source of energy kindly provided for us, a nice thermonuclear reactor that's a hundred million miles away and has all of its own shielding: the Sun. Solar energy is mostly wasted, and we could be using some of it, sending it down to the surface of the Earth in the form of low-density microwaves, and using it to supply all the energy we would ever need for millions of years to come. The question is: why don't we use it?

One reason is that the lift-costs of bringing up big power stations, big generators, is just too great. However, there are sources of material for such things available, for example, the Moon, from which you can bring materials off into space at about one-twentieth of the cost in energy that it would require to take them from Earth. There are even some special asteroids that may be easier to reach, easier to bring materials from into space, than if we were to start here from the Earth.

So I think when you ask, "Why human colonies in space?" the likely first reason is that people out in space, working in a useful and productive way, can be doing more good for us here — and more good for the Earth's biosphere — than we're apt to have from the same number of people working in any other way.

Why is Space Industry Important?

As we come to understand the possibilities of living and working in space, in the long run we're going to find two things. One is that the energy problem is with us right now: it's urgent on a time scale of one or two decades. Therefore, we feel that going after this energy is extremely practical. However, on a time scale of a century or so, we're going to have a very different problem, even more fundamental, and that is the heat balance at the surface of the Earth. If we continue to grow in energy usage, even only at a slow pace in the developed nations, and the underdeveloped nations go through their industrial revolutions — which they're desperate to do — we're going to find in about 80 to 130 years that we are upsetting the heat balance of the Earth and changing the climate. On the time scale of a decade or so, I think we should solve our energy problems by means of space. In a century or so, we will need habitats in space, and industry in space, for the even more fundamental reason that this is the only way of having industrial growth without spoiling the climate of the Earth.

In satellite solar power, you spend very little waste energy in the Earth environment; you use almost everything that comes in.

Solar Power on Earth

The average solar intensity on Earth is only about a sixth as much, even in favorable places, as it is in space; and it gets turned off every night. It is unreliable because of weather. The cost of energy made in that way goes up enormously. When we decrease our use of fossil fuels, and go more into an electrical economy, we will depend more and more on what we call "base-load power," energy that you know is going to be there all the time. Here's the baby in the crib in Boston in January, and it's very cold: that's not the time for the solar-energy collector to turn off.

The national power grids are very complicated, and things like mountain barriers are very important for those grids. But reliability is more important. The power that space can provide us with is energy that we know is there all the time, whereas solar energy on the Earth is wonderful for running air conditioners in Phoenix, because the power is there exactly when it's needed. But that's not good enough for base-load power. The utilities people say, "There might be a really cloudy January, when clouds are going to be over the solar cells for two weeks; we're going to have to build standby plants, fossil-fuel backup plants, to take care of those two weeks. Otherwise people are going to die." Learning to store power very cheaply would really be a new scientific breakthrough.

An International Interest

At the beginning, when this work began to get public interest, I got letters from other countries which expressed, almost always in the first paragraph, a fear that the U.S. would do it by itself. Those people who wrote to me felt that this was an important development for all of humanity, and it was very important that their own nation be part of it. COMSAT is an excellent example of a multinational effort. My friends in that organization point out that it's the only international organization where there are 80 member nations, and every member nation pays its dues promptly at the beginning of every month; there's no argument at all. It's perceived as a genuine need which is being satisfied, and they're willing to pay their bills.

I've talked about these things in Buenos Aires and Saudi Arabia, and there was strong interest there. In Buenos Aires, very bright young Argentinians came up to me and said, "Now that this is a possibility, we're determined to be part of it. We don't know how. We want cooperation; tell us how we can get involved." I get this very strongly from people all over the world.

Our Timid Approach to Space

We are now in a tremendously useful and productive period of space exploration, but one which I think we must honestly describe as timid, not because of the timidity of people within NASA, but because of the timidity of the people who give them the money. Since the great days of Apollo, when for a while NASA was a number-one employer, it's now down to number 52 in the United States, just behind Borden's Milk.

These days, we send robots into space instead of going ourselves. Much as we all love R2D2, I think it's about time we stopped letting him have all the fun. I also feel that if we don't do it, somebody else will. Not necessarily the Russians; maybe the Japanese, or the West Germans, who are technologically fully capable of it. The Japanese have already said they're going to have a shuttle of their own within the next twenty years. How are they going to be helped to do it? They're going to be helped by the American aerospace engineers, who can't find jobs in a shrinking American aerospace industry. So a by-product of a vigorous thrust into space, I believe, should be a very direct human involvement, again.

We're planning to work with a bootstrap method, which requires lifting only a relatively small quantity of equipment from the surface of the Earth, and building habitats for a work force and solar-power stations, in space, from the lunar materials. We made a big investment in Apollo, and as a result we know that the lunar surface is about 30 per cent metals, 20 per cent silicon, and 40 per cent oxygen, by weight. The energy cost to take those

Courtesy of NASA

Space-shuttle crew puts finishing touches on a solar-power station in geosynchronous orbit. Thé station will beam a continuous stream of microwave energy to Earth.

lunar materials into space is only about a twentieth as much as it is to take equivalent materials from the surface of the Earth. Therefore, the shuttle is the most important development leading to the possibility of manufacturing in space, and eventually space settlement. It has a tremendous importance. We want to really put the shuttle to work, adding maybe 50 or 60 flights per year to the program of the shuttle in the later 1980s.

Problems and Solutions

Satellite solar power is a problem looking for a solution. The solution has to be a way of doing it cheaply, without developing a launch-vehicle fleet, which would mean enormous vehicles going through the atmosphere almost every hour and depositing tremendous quantities of at least water, if not anything else, in the upper atmosphere.

Space manufacturing is, on the other hand, a solution looking for a problem. It's very general, and it could produce objects needed in high orbit very cheaply. But you have to have an economic reason to justify that initial investment. It looks as if satellite power and space manufacturing are excellently matched to each other for that purpose. The electric utilities are going to have to spend 800 billion dollars in the next 25 years on new generator capacity, 25 to 50 billion dollars a year.

Where will that money come from? It will be borrowed from the life-insurance companies, who have a cash flow of one billion dollars per week. It comes in all the time, and it must be invested or it piles up. Obviously, we're talking to both the electric companies and the insurance companies at the present time.

Total investment to light the fire of space manufacturing looks like something comparable to Apollo, about 50 billion of today's dollars. However, the calculated productivity of space looks like it will easily return that much every year.

Sequence 7
Industries in Orbit
J. PETER VAJK

J. Peter Vajk received his Ph.D. in theoretical physics from Princeton University in 1968 with a thesis in general relativity. He spent nearly eight years in research at the University of California's Lawrence Livermore Laboratory, where he became deeply involved in the implications of space colonization. While still at Livermore, Dr. Vajk researched and wrote the landmark report, "The Impact of Space Colonization on World Dynamics." He is now a staff scientist at Science Applications, Inc., where he is a major contributor to a long-range planning study being conducted for NASA on space industrialization, space settlements, and solar-power generating satellites. Dr. Vajk describes an attractive future scenario in his first book Doomsday Has Been Cancelled.

In this sequence Dr. Vajk sets forth his forecast of the most plausible ways in which large space settlements, of up to a million people, may become possible in the relatively near future.

In discussing space colonies, it is helpful to consider an evolutionary viewpoint. If we think back about 3 and a half billion years, the first living things on this planet were tiny one-celled creatures, primitive organisms that were not at all like the modern complicated cell. If you looked at one of these simple creatures through a microscope, it would look like a tiny sphere or rod with no internal structure to speak of. Almost all of these creatures lived by eating large organic molecules in the ocean. Where did these large, complicated molecules come from? They came from simple molecules such as methane, ammonia, carbon dioxide, and water, which were synthesized into more complicated molecules by inorganic processes, including lightning and the tides at the edge of the ocean. The primitive organisms ate those complicated molecules, broke them down, and released the energy that had been tied up in them; that's how they lived and grew.

J. Peter Vajk

Of course, the rate at which these inorganic processes could produce food for these organisms was very limited. But everything changed about two billion years ago, when some of these little creatures invented photosynthesis, and the blue-green algae suddenly appeared on the face of this planet. They stepped outside of the existing system and found a way to tap into an outside energy source, namely, the energy coming in from the Sun. They used that energy directly, in a biological process, to synthesize complicated molecules out of the simple molecules in the environment. These new biological sources of food were more efficient and far faster than the inorganic processes. There was a sudden explosion of life on the planet, and it became feasible for life, which had been confined to a narrow band along the edge of the ocean, to spread out into the middle of the ocean and, eventually, out onto the land.

The End of Limits

In a sense, modern civilization is in a similar position today. We're feeling the effects of limits. If we look more closely, there aren't as many limits on energy sources as we had previously thought, but we are feeling some strains. Maybe the time has come for us to reach outside the existing system and tap into new sources of material and energy. That's what space colonization is, in essence: a way to reach out and tap the solar energy that's streaming out past the planet day and night, all year round, at prodigious rates, and to use some of the abundance of materials in space for the purpose of propagating life beyond the planet Earth.

Space colonization has been talked about publicly for four years, since Professor Gerard O'Neill at Princeton first brought these issues into public discussion with the astonishing claim that space colonization might come to pass within the current generation, with existing or soon-to-be-had technology. I've been actively involved in this for about three years. This is perhaps the most exciting thing I've done in my life, because it's a reaching out for something new. This is a response to a deep drive to explore, to know, and to reach out into what's new.

Projections for the Future

How is this going to be done? My own hunch is that by 1995, give or take a couple of years, we will have several thousand people living and working in space. For the last year and a half, I've been involved in a study contract with Science Applications, Inc. We have a contract with NASA to draw a preliminary road map of "space industrialization." We already have a handle on what will be technically feasible; now we're trying to see what's likely to be economically profitable and socially desirable during the next 30 years. "Space industrialization" is a phrase that very few people have heard yet, but it is something that already exists. Communications satellites have been profitable as well as serving useful social functions for almost ten years now. This is one area that is going to grow like crazy in the 1980s, as the space shuttle comes on-line and we can reduce the cost of launching large satellites into orbit.

With large satellites assembled in orbit from multiple space-shuttle payloads, we would be able to deploy very large satellites out in geosynchronous orbit 22,800 miles above the Earth's equator. At that distance from the Earth, the satellite goes once around the Earth in exactly one day; so it appears to hang fixed in the sky. Most of our communications satellites today are in geosynchronous orbit. A communications satellite placed out there, large enough to require the use of the space shuttle, multiple payloads, and assembly in orbit, reduces the ground station you need to communicate with that satellite to a very small size, small enough to fit into a wristwatch-size device — in other words, a wristwatch telephone — which allows you mobile personal communication with anyone else on Earth who has one. It will be no more expensive to call a friend who happens to be hiking in the Himalayas than to call your next-door neighbor.

Is this socially desirable? I think communication is an essential feature of any socially desirable program. Certainly, our modern way of life is impossible without communications. Our friendships are based on a much wider community than just the people next door. We all know relatives who live at a long distance, school friends living on the other side of the country, and associates in far-flung interest groups. Maintaining daily communication with all those friends by telephone or its equivalent would be a socially desirable thing in terms of fulfilling personal interests. Economically, the benefits are rather clear, if you're trying to run a large corporation with offices scattered across the world.

How about the company that invests in this kind of system? About 15 years after a system like this is first deployed (that is, by about the turn of the century), assuming reasonable rates of market penetration, similar to what we've seen in other industries, we expect this company could have annual revenues between ten and twenty billion dollars. Large satellites like this are a sure bet to go.

Profits in Space

Other things in space are more uncertain, but the chances are excellent that there will be large profits to be made. With the space shuttle, the cost of transportation into Earth orbit and then back down will be about $350 per pound. Now, that sounds like a lot, but a substantial portion of the U.S. economy involves products in that price range, particularly electronic components, pharmaceutical products, specialized optical equipment, and jewelry.

Can you do anything in space for any of these products? The answer is yes. Many industrial processes could be done much better in a zero-gravity environment. You can do them better and cheaper, and you can do new things. Suppose you try, here on the Earth, to form an alloy of aluminum and antimony. These two metals have very different densities. If you melt both of them, then, as soon as they start freezing, the aluminum floats on top. So you can't form that alloy here on Earth in commercial quantities. Such an alloy could provide a new material for manufacturing solar cells that would be about 35 per cent more efficient than the best solar cells we know how to build today.

Hundreds of products like this have been examined and are technically feasible, but it's impossible to say which of them will be commercially viable in the 1980s, because we don't know what the competing technologies are going to be down here on the ground for doing the same function by other means. Certain materials-processing applications, the communications satellites, and information-processing satellites, such as Earth-resource prospecting satellites, are likely to involve significant numbers of people working in space in the mid-to-late 1980s.

Manufacturing in Space

Large communications satellites might not require much in the way of construction facilities, but would require a few dozen people for maintenance. It's not likely that these construction and maintenance facilities would be at the same place as the manufacturing facilities. Manufacturing facilities, I suspect, will be located in one or more "industrial parks" in Earth orbit. It will probably be the most economical for some commercial enterprise to provide a basic habitation facility, basic power and communications utilities, and a basic structure onto which other companies could mount their small manufacturing modules or their small experimental facilities. Depending on how successful these manufacturing processes work out to be, and how fast they penetrate the market, a few dozen to a few hundred people might be living and working in orbit by the end of the 1980s.

Going into the '90s, we would expect the next-generation launch vehicle, which would be significantly cheaper than the space shuttle, to become operational. There's reason to believe that the cost of transporting payloads into orbit could be ten to twenty dollars a pound. At that point, an interesting thing happens. The cost of carrying a person into space and returning him or her to Earth becomes just a few thousand dollars. This is comparable to the money people now spend in going for three-week ocean cruises in the Pacific. Thus space tourism suddenly becomes a genuine possibility in the early 1990s. People could go up into space just for the pure joy of having the experience, looking back at the Earth, experiencing zero gravity, doing some of the fun things you can do in zero gravity that you can't do down here.

Space Resorts?

Rather than a single-purpose resort, it's more likely that the habitation facilities of an industrial park would expand to serve as a hotel. If we're thinking about several hundred people working in space, we know they're going to be having fun and playing games when they're off duty. Doubtless, they'll develop new sports and new recreational activities that take advantage of zero gravity. If the tourists are paying their rent, I'm sure they, too, will participate in the fun and games.

Practical Solar Energy

The biggest single enterprise that has been talked about, which would require the biggest investment, is building large solar-power satellites in space to collect solar energy. Freely available 24 hours a day in suitable orbits, solar energy would be converted into short-wavelength radio beams that are sent down to Earth for conversion back into electricity. The economic projections strongly suggest that such satellites could be very competitive in the early 1990s, assuming we make a large-enough investment in the 1980s, with any of the alternative sources of electricity that we're presently considering for the 1990s. If this happens, then we are contemplating several *thousand* people working in space by the end of the 1980s. But we can't say today that some cheaper new energy technology won't become available here on the ground before that time.

The Long-Range View

If we look at a long-term construction program that would convert the entire energy consumption of Earth over to solar-power satellites, it would probably take about 30 years to fulfill the Earth's energy demands, even if the space-manufacturing facilities double in capacity every two years.

For a program that large in scale, the total weight of the material that has to be placed in space for these enormous satellites is too huge to consider launching from the Earth. We are thus talking about obtaining the materials for building these things from other sources in space, from the Moon, for example. We know there are abundant metals there, abundant oxygen, and most of the other materials we need. Silicon, for example, which can be used to make solar cells, is abundantly available on the Moon.

We're also looking at the Earth-crossing asteroids, a new family of asteroids that have been discovered in the last few years. These asteroids have orbits that bring them very close to the Earth at fairly regular intervals. It would be possible, with the technology that is foreseen for the 1980s, to retrieve one of these asteroids (say, about 100 meters in diameter), bring it into an orbit around the Earth, and begin manufacturing things in space from the material in that asteroid.

By the turn of the century, we might be able to import nickel from such asteroids to the Earth at prices significantly lower than what we're paying for nickel today. If any of these things happen, we are talking of populations possibly approaching a million people in space by the end of the century. Most of them would be in orbit doing the manufacturing and construction. A relatively small number would be involved directly in the mining operation, which would be highly automated; large machines would do most of the work, just as in mining operations here on the ground.

A Million People in Space?

If we're talking about a million people living and working in space by the end of the century, this will obviously have major ramifications. Now, obviously, we would have to provide large facilities; so we're talking about building space cities, space colonies, space settlements, whatever phrase you like to use. These could be large structures providing a fairly Earthlike environment, in the sense that you would have normal weight in the residential areas. There would also be a more or less normal atmosphere. This might not be quite sea-level pressure, but with half sea-level pressure or higher, and certainly with sufficient oxygen, you wouldn't feel any different in terms of your ability to do work. In the early stages, most food would still be imported from the Earth. Not too far down the line, though, the cost of supplying food to people living up there becomes a little too high, and it becomes more advantageous for the spaceworkers to grow their own food supply in space. The space environment probably is going to be a pretty good place for doing that very efficiently. If you look at some kinds of closed-environment agriculture in use here on Earth, such as greenhouses with artificial light to prolong the length of the day, and with increased carbon-dioxide concentration inside the greenhouse, the productivity per acre of such a system is amazingly higher than the best we can do in the Kansas cornfields. Under such optimized conditions, we can probably support several thousand people from a single acre, in contrast to the one or two per acre which is the worldwide average down here today. Learning to do that well will obviously have some implications for how we do agriculture down here. When we develop a new technology for one use, it can proliferate very rapidly to other uses *if it's better*.

Space Designs

We've been talking about structures perhaps five miles in diameter. In fact, some of the more grandiose designs that are postulated for the second or third decade of the next century would be communities in the form of cylinders, perhaps as long as the San Francisco peninsula. With *five acres per person*, we could fit a million or two million people into it, and still have lots of room left for open space, planting trees and forests, and other landscaping. However, we will have to be very careful about how we manage the environment.

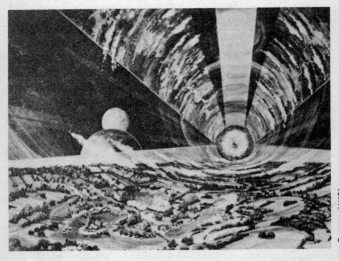

Interior view of Earth-habitat space colony, supporting anywhere from 200,000 to 2,000,000 people.

Research Spinoffs

Even in researching such possibilities, we will be learning a lot about what makes earthly ecosystems tick, how our environment really works, how dozens of species of plants and animals interact, and how they manage their own waste products.

One of the spinoffs I see from this program is learning better ways for industrial processing with more recycling. In refining metals down here, we frequently use all sorts of lyes and acids to get the desired end products. It turns out the easiest, cheapest thing to do is not to clean up the acid for reuse; it's cheaper just to dump it. But in the space habitat, where raw materials will be coming from literally astronomical distances, it gets to be a real drag to have to keep reimporting the processing materials, and the system is very strongly driven to recycle the processing materials. Therefore, we will learn better ways to do recycling for closed-cycle manufacturing: better and cheaper, and that will have spinoffs on how we do manufacturing here on Earth.

The same thing applies to ordinary living. A space community has lots of room for people, but there is only so much room, and there's no place to dump a lot of junk. We can't just throw it out the window because we'd have to resupply equivalent material, again from astronomical distances, and that gets to be a drag. Yet we don't want to have to recycle everything we own once a year, because *that* gets to be a drag in just running a recycling facility. What I think we get pushed toward is an ethic in which we minimize our wastes, and maximize durability of our goods; and if all our furniture is meant to last 30 years, then we're not going to want it to be plastic junk, and we're not going to want it to be identical to what the guy next door has, who's also going to have his for 30 years. What will probably happen is a resurgence of individual craftsmanship, of quality, durable goods. Now, things won't necessarily turn out this way, but the system does push us in that direction.

The Immediate Motivations for Space

The feasibility of power satellites is the only motivation in the next few decades that would push us toward large-scale colonization fast. If, for some reason, the power satellites turn out to be the wrong direction because we've found a better way, then I think we will still see space cities, but they may be much smaller, a few hundred people, maybe a dozen or more communities. Many of these considerations will still apply. In any case, a significant point is that it won't be just one Spaceship Earth flying around the Sun; it will be a formation flight of several independent biospheres. The biosphere which has been here for two billion years has finally matured enough to spawn daughters of its own.

A Personal Vision

When I first heard of Gerry O'Neill's ideas three years ago (and in 1974 we'd just come through the OPEC embargo, with long gasoline lines), I was almost convinced that, in fact, the limits-to-growth era was here and that, from here on, civilization was going downhill. But I didn't want a narrowly restricted, progressively more regimented future for myself, let alone for my children. So I thought going into space in a big way, and soon, was vitally important. I thought, "Let's get this show on the road so I can emigrate to a better place." Ten years ago, a lot of people concerned about the Vietnam War were very actively thinking about emigrating to Australia. It's a somewhat similar feeling.

Now, though, it has become much clearer that these "limits-to-growth" concepts are simply illusions. In fact, if we have the will, we can solve any of the material or energy problems foreseen by doomsday prophets. I'm not sure I want to emigrate to the space colonies any more. Once they exist, I certainly would want to go for an extended visit, but I don't know if I will want to settle there. I'll have to wait and cross that bridge when I get there. What is important to me is that the extension of human civilization into space be done in some fashion or other. I think it's an important and valuable thing for the human species to undertake.

Rusty Schweickart, one of the astronauts on Apollo 9, which was a flight to check out the Apollo system in Earth orbit, has eloquently described his experience of going around the Earth every hour and a half, and seeing it again and again. The astronauts' work schedule was such that they woke up in the morning just as they were crossing the Mediterranean and the Near East, and so every morning there's this breakfast scene of looking down and knowing that there in the Middle East are these people fighting over an imaginary boundary, a national boundary that you can't even *see*. It's not real! It's purely an imaginary thing. It's something we've created in our minds.

Suppose we have 20,000 Americans — that is, about one out of every 10,000 Americans — living in space at the turn of the century. In every town of 10,000, there would be a very good chance that, even if you don't know the space colonist in person, you would know his or her family, and the colonist will come back occasionally for a vacation and visit the old home town. We've put a couple of dozen astronauts in space; yet how many of us know an astronaut personally? But when it's somebody who lives in your own town, who writes back regularly, who comes and visits, and you find out what it's like, you may realize that national boundaries don't really matter. It's no longer a global village; we've transcended the global village. It's not just a global system we're living in, but a *transglobal* system. National boundaries become much less relevant. From a political point of view, I think maybe that's the biggest change in perspective to anticipate.

I strongly believe space industrialization is going to be happening in the next 20 to 30 years on a fairly large scale, by U.S. corporations, by multinationals, by Japanese corporations, by West German corporations; it's going to be done by a lot of different people.

Space and the Third World

When considering the Third World, we have to go back to the question, "What are we going to be doing *economically* in space?" Solar-power satellites seem to be one of the big options, and if this option is chosen, that is going to have a major impact on the Third World, not because the Third World needs electricity, but because they desperately need energy. Electricity from a solar-power satellite can be converted on the ground into synthetic liquid fuels, liquid fuels any peasant in India or Bangladesh knows how to use.

Right now, in much of the Third World, the people who don't live in the cities (and that's still the bulk of the population, on the average, around the world) use an average of one ton of firewood per person, per year, just for cooking. The environmental damage from that in the Third World far exceeds the worst that has happened in North America, from a superindustrialized economy. The deforestation of the foothills of the Himalayas has increased erosion of the soil in the foothills, and has increased flooding downstream in the prime agricultural lands of India, Bangladesh, and Pakistan, aggravating a situation that's already bad.

It has been estimated that in India, in 1975, they were burning off 80 million tons of dried cow dung every year for cooking purposes, instead of using it for fertilizer. Why? Because kerosene, which is a petroleum derivative, has become too expensive. Firewood is scarce and becoming too expensive. Cow dung is very expensive in India now; it has become a prime commodity. Since the cow dung is not going back into the land, the land is getting depleted. The nutrients in that 80 million tons amount to one-third of India's fertilizer needs; and importing that fertilizer has a major impact on India's balance of payments.

Solar-power satellites will not generate electricity for India's 600,000 villages. However, they may supply synthetic fuels derived from electricity.

Environmental Impact of Synthetic Fuels

The environmental impact of burning things like methanol (wood alcohol) is minimal. These materials can be synthesized from air and water, if you've got a primary source of energy like the electricity from solar-power satellites. When you burn these synthetic fuels, they just go back into air and water, with no environmental impact. Since you're substituting these fuels for cutting down all the trees again, that's a positive environmental benefit, as well as an economic benefit.

In central Africa, the average manual worker spends 25 to 30 per cent of his annual income on buying firewood. In many of these countries, since the OPEC price increases of 1973–1974, the price of firewood has tripled. Something has to be done about that, because that kind of deforestation is a major contributing factor in the spreading of the Sahara southward, which has been part of the cause of the famines we saw in the early '70s.

Effect of Space Systems on the Economy

Sweden, at the end of the Second World War, was almost entirely agricultural. Sweden is now a major industrial nation, because the Swedish government fostered the movement of available capital into new industries and new technologies, which have consistently provided the largest economic return. In the United States, that's not really the case. The many signs of economic stagflation result, at least in part, from the fact that our tax laws are set up in a way that encourages reinvestment of capital in the same old companies and technologies.

Investments in research and development for space hardware have been the most productive, economically, of any R&D spending in the U.S. for the last 20 or 30 years. In terms of new products that have disseminated very rapidly into the economy and the tax revenues that those have produced, we have probably already paid off the whole Apollo program. The payoff on investments of a few billion dollars a year in the 1980s in space industries will be even faster and greater.

Sequence 8
Building the First Colonies
GERARD K. O'NEILL

In this sequence, Professor O'Neill explains each step in the chain of events that he foresees as the most practical way in which space colonization can begin.

The basic approach to getting into space is not very complicated or profound. It's simply a way to reach a substantial level of space manufacturing and production payback within the limitations of the space-shuttle system, very much with the help of a kind of mass-driver reaction engine and a mass-driver lunar transporter.

The Mass-Driver Machines

We like to think of a mass-driver as a special type of rocket for space, and also as a lunar-materials transport machine.

There are about 20 coils in the mass-driver model; they're about six inches in diameter, wound of square copper wire. Those coils are assembled on pieces of plumbing pipe, which the bucket that carries the material rides on. The 20 coils make up an eight-foot acceleration section. It's done in a very simple-minded way: the bucket has just one big driven coil. It rides on its automobile starter brushes, and as it goes past each drive coil, it triggers a microswitch which fires a capacitor through a silicon control rectifier, and that coil gives the bucket another push, so

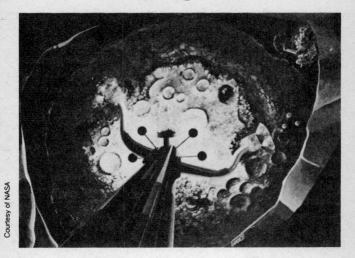

Courtesy of NASA

Mass drivers in operation, transporting lunar materials.

that there is a sequence of 20 such pushes that does the complete acceleration process. Then the bucket gets friction-braked to slow it down, but the contents keep on going.

We had a mass-driver model at Princeton. It was run on only one test, with liquid nitrogen cooling the bucket coil. It was designed to be operated that way, but we did only one test because we didn't have any adequate way of stopping it. We cooled it down so its resistance would be low — the bucket is fed by current from a set of automobile storage batteries — and the device for stopping the bucket when it flies off the end consists of a lead brick. We were able to recover the bucket, even though it did penetrate about a quarter of an inch into the lead brick. (We're not planning to operate the mass-driver any more, a good reason being that, every time we run it, it breaks a microswitch or two.) The second model will be built with optical triggering, and will, I hope, be considerably less crude.

The performance of the mass-driver in that test was that it accelerated the bucket from zero to 80 miles per hour in a tenth of a second, within a space of eight feet: that's 35 Gs of acceleration. The second model is designed for much more. As far as we can tell, the theoretical limits for these machines are far above a thousand Gs. In a production version of the lunar machine, we expect to be running in the 100- to 200-gravity acceleration range. For the mass-drivers to be used as rocket engines, using powdered external tanks from the shuttle as reaction mass, we expect something more like a thousand Gs of acceleration.

A Sample Mission for a
Mass-Driver Reaction Engine

Once the shuttle gets working, people will want to go up into low orbit and begin learning how to do practical tasks. A contractor working for the Johnson Space Center has developed a concept for a low-orbital workshop in space. It would involve taking up beam sections, which would be extended from the shuttle. Then a beam-builder would extend them still further. A little zero-gravity equivalent of a crane house moves along, placing things along a type of strong-back device. Something like that is going to be a first step, no matter where we go from that point.

A typical mass-driver reaction engine would be several kilometers long, with a total mass of two or three hundred tons. The total power is about three megawatts. It should run at about 75 per cent efficiency, and would be able to put out roughly a fifteenth of a kilogram of material per second. We would get the material by powdering the external tanks from the shuttle, which is the reaction mass that we can get* most easily and cheaply in low orbit for these tasks. The idea would be to operate by collecting six months or so of shuttle payloads in low orbit, and then taking those payloads—some 700 tons or so—out to the distance of the Moon, roughly a 150-day trip. The 700 tons of payload would be deposited in lunar orbit.

The mass-driver would return in a rather short time, because it would now be unloaded, using the remainder of the reaction mass. It would end up back at the shuttle again after about 200 days. During that same 200 days, another 700 tons or so would have accumulated from shuttle flights, assuming something on the order of 50 or 60 shuttle flights per year. After two or three years, it would be possible to emplace up to two thousand tons of material in the right place.

The key items, adding up all the bits and pieces really needed on the lunar surface, would total about a thousand tons, of which the mass-driver is less than a quarter. With that material a mass-driver could be put into operation on the Moon. It would be able, in terms of the capacitors, the aluminum coils, and all the rest of the components it contains, to put out about 600,000 tons per year of the lunar materials. However, the power supplies that would be emplaced on the lunar surface would be adequate for only one-twentieth of that throughput, because the power supplies, being photovoltaic, turn out to be far more massive than the mass-driver itself. That's an illustration of a key element in this sort of bootstrap approach, making a minimum investment at each stage, and getting a maximum return.

We assume that the regular crew on the lunar surface would not have to be more than ten people, requiring only about 40 tons per year of resupply from Earth. That's ten kilograms per person per day, a pretty husky resupply allotment.

For the 1,000 or 1,100 tons needed on the lunar surface, an equivalent mass of ordinary chemical propellants, such as liquid hydrogen and liquid oxygen, is also needed. These propellants must be brought up from the low orbit, where the space shuttle brought them, and that's all added into the budget.

There are a lot of other small bits and pieces needed from the Earth's surface, pushing the total up to 3,000 tons—something on the order of 100 shuttle flights. At a traffic model of 50 flights per year exclusively devoted to this kind of program, at $20,000,000 per flight, the total expenditure is one billion dollars per year, certainly not an excessive travel budget.

Completion of that project would create the basic ability to bring 30,000 tons of material off the surface of the Moon and receive it at a particular point in space each year. Therefore, an ante of 3,000 tons at shuttle altitude nets roughly ten times that amount per year of lunar material coming out. However, getting to this point will be no small task.

Building the First Colony

Processing all that material is the next phase. We have concluded that a total personnel force of 150 people would be required in space, working in the processing facility. That would be sufficient, according to our 1976 study, to process those 30,000 tons per year of lunar materials, resulting in approximately nine kilotons per year of fabricated silicon and metals.

Chemical process plants, mass-drivers, and all other fancy aerospace hardware are the sorts of things properly manufactured on the surface of the Earth, and brought up in pieces in the shuttle. Manufacturing in space, in the early days at least, is limited to very simple and repetitive objects. The thing needed more than anything else turns out to be just habitats, "costing" ten tons per person.

There was a study carried out in the summer of 1970 by our Group 2, headed by John Shettler, of what sort of initial habitats would be used. His conclusion was that the most natural thing was to convert the shuttle external tanks into 21 separate apartments for as many different people. One would connect cables to these tanks, and spin them for whatever gravity is required, since the tanks are already designed to take considerably more than one G. It seems to be, at first blush, a reasonable way of arranging the initial habitats. Eventually, of course, most of the people would be living in habitats which had been manufactured in space, presumably very simple and repetitive ones; a kind of Levittown, I think. We could hope to go to something a bit more couth a little bit later.

Input 8.1
The "Space Shack"
RICHARD D. JOHNSON

Richard D. Johnson currently is the Chief of the Biosystems Division at the NASA/Ames Research Center at Moffett Field (near San Francisco), California. The group's work is primarily focused on the conduct of life-sciences experiments in space, and, as such, is responsible for development of hardware systems for such experiments. For example, the current emphasis is on preparing experiments for flight on the space shuttle, starting in 1980. The experiments will study biomedical questions and use laboratory animals in flight.

Dr. Johnson is a physical-organic chemist by training, having received his B.A. at Oberlin College in 1956, and his M.S. and Ph.D. from Carnegie Tech in 1960 and 1961. He did postdoctoral study at UCLA, and then worked at JPL before coming to Ames in 1963. Dr. Johnson was a principal investigator for the Apollo 11 lunar sample, and worked on the study of space colonization in 1975. He has authored more than 30 articles in the scientific literature, lectures in aeronautics and astronautics at Stanford, and is an amateur winemaker on the side. He resides with his wife, Caye, and son, Eric, in Los Altos Hills, California.

I think when we have the first space colony, we probably won't even know we have it, in the sense that we won't call it by that name. As much as we hate it, and contrary to what all the more social-minded people would like, the first colony will be fairly crude.

Input 8.1 (Cont.)

My analogy is that it will be like living down in the bowels of an aircraft carrier in the middle of the ocean. You will hardly even know what's outside. Machinery will be rumbling, and everything will be painted gray. I have a hard time believing that the practical issues—technology, economics—won't overwhelm everything, so that the more fantastic ideas we talk about now will disappear one by one. Eventually the idyllic ideas will start coming back, and they'll decide to build a new version with more amenities.

At some point you'll say, "Hey, we've got a space colony," but initially we talk about building construction shacks. I think the people used the word "shack" with meaning and intention, because they're really saying, "The first ones are probably going to be a little bit on the gross side, because our purpose is to get the job done, not to make something fancy." So the fanciness inevitably comes later.

A lot of people have their ideas built around something Earthlike: cows, and in some cases streams and rivers. I see much of this as fantasy. More practically, I think a spirit of teamwork, dedication, and orientation to the job will be overriding, making these fantasy lands less important. The progress that people are capable of making will be significantly greater than what people are used to. The group dynamics as a whole will be fairly dedicated to seeing the purpose accomplished very well, very fast, and expeditiously.

In this more social sense, I think you'll see the kind of things that go with really smooth-working teams. If you had a thousand or five thousand people who really knew, "This is what's supposed to happen," and every energy was devoted to seeing that it happened, this would influence the whole resulting lifestyle. It's sort of like a kibbutz in Israel, in places where there's a lot of purposefulness in

---

Input 8.1 (Cont.)

what the people are doing: people working hard, still enjoying themselves, but they know why they're there and what they're doing. They'll be working for their future and for that of their children, rather than requiring all the comforts of Earth. But the sense of aliveness will be great, and the comforts not missed.

The next most massive thing required is photovoltaic power supplies, not only to operate the process plant, but also to upgrade the lunar mass-driver, eventually, to its full capability of more than half a million tons of material per year. After consulting with professional extractive metallurgists, and redesigning the chemical processes to be used in space, we were able to reduce the peak temperature occurring anywhere in the process cycle from 2,300 degrees, which is mighty hot, down to about 1,100 degrees, right in the normal range for typical chemical processes used here on the Earth. That took us a big step closer to a practical operating system. I think the next obvious step is to set up something with bits of aluminum and glass tubing and retorts and Bunsen burners on a bench top, and have something where you can pour in, perhaps, a child's sand shovel of artificial lunar soil at one end, and get out silicon and aluminum and liquid oxygen at the other end. That's not by any means out of the question, but it's clearly going to require some money to do that.

The Bootstrap Point

Just to sum up where our balance sheet is at this point, we've had to put in about two years' worth of shuttle flights to get to the point where we could bring out the lunar materials in reasonable quantity. Then another year of shuttle flights, on this model, would bring us to the point where we could process that 30,000 tons per year of materials. So already we're at a bootstrap point; that is to say, we're producing on the order of nine or ten thousand tons per year of finished products in space, plus a lot of oxygen, from a total investment, up to this point, of only three or four thousand tons that we put in over a period of several years. So we already have a big leverage multiplier in our favor.

I'd like to give you a sort of over-all growth pattern for the manufacturing capability in space, during a hypothetical seven-year period. We assume, as I said, about 50 flights per year for the first three years, then 60 per year for four more. After three

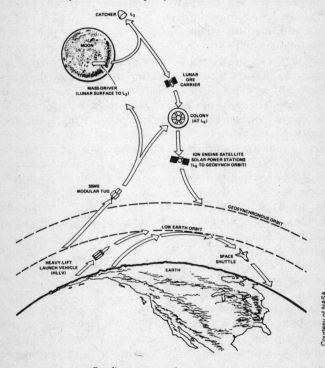

Baseline transportation system.

years, the process throughput capability in space goes up to the initial 30,000 tons. Then, during the next four years, it builds up, at about 150,000 tons per year per year—like the units of an acceleration. The 3,000 people needed in space at the end of those seven years, assuming that we still haven't developed agriculture in space or built any big space habitats, are still living in converted shuttle tanks, and must be resupplied from the Earth. At that point, the fabricated output rate in tons per year would be almost a hundred times the resupply rate that would be required for those people. So it seems there is some very useful leverage.

The Big Question of Economics

The next big question is that of economics. We shouldn't throw money down the drain unless we're going to get it back. Investment analyses indicate that if we were to sell stock in this (we're not at that point yet), even at high interest rates it would probably return a substantial profit and give us a large benefit-to-cost ratio.

It is essential, for economic payback, that our program experience an exponential growth. A simple linear growth (putting in X dollars of input, say, launch capacity, in order to get Y dollars of throughput of your space manufacturing, with the same multiplier between the X and the Y) will never pay back your initial investment. You must have exponential growth of the productive capability if you're going to come out with a benefit-to-cost ratio that is higher than 1.

This leads us to the economics of our hypothetical seven-year program. The first year of such a program—presumably after an already substantial amount of lower-level research and development—will require a billion dollars. That's very consistent with the scale of the shuttle, which in its peak year, I think, just passed with something like 1.5 billion. The next year will cost two or three billion—these are Apollo-like numbers in this region—finally building up to our peaks, which get into the range of five to eight billion dollars in our particular model. The numbers go up mostly because we assume that we will be paying 10 per cent interest in constant dollars all during the time we're constructing our manufacturing capability.

For the first several years, all production in space goes into increasing productive capacity—the buildup from near-zero to 600,000 tons per year. The question is, how do you value the products which you build? The typical model that everyone tends to use is satellite solar power, whether or not that will turn out to be the prime target for space manufacturing. It's a convenient model, because it's been studied fairly thoroughly. Studies show, for example, that a satellite power station for 10,000 megawatts is going to end up weighing something like 100,000 tons. If we then assign it a value of $500 per kilowatt of installed generator capacity, that figure being taken from the electric-utility industry, we can make some valuation of the products of this space manufactory. And the valuation which has been assumed, in this particular scenario, is on the basis of about $500 per kilowatt on the surface of the Earth. That transforms back to earnings at the rate of about $18 per kilogram of throughput in the space manufactory.

It should be noted that we've biased things in a fairly cautious manner by assuming, first of all, research and development costs to get to this stage which are taken straight out of the shuttle experience, and that means thirty to sixty million dollars per ton of hardware that has to be developed. We're referring to noticeably different hardware; we're not talking about repetitive things.

The interesting point is that, although the hardware we have to lift into space is assumed to cost us something on the order of $1,100 per kilogram to make, then another $200 to $700 to put up to low orbit, and we are producing things that are worth only $18 per kilogram, even then we make a profit. The reason, of course, is that we are getting an enormous amount of leverage from the bootstrapping which goes on.

We can see how that leverage occurs if we assume the construction in space of a number of 10,000-megawatt satellite power stations. If we build enough satellites to produce enough power to supply all of California, for example, or all of the United Kingdom, there's quite a value associated with such scale. Naturally, the earnings picture turns around as well. We have profits rather than losses, even though we're still paying interest on all the previous investment. When that particular scenario takes off, the profits really go out of sight.

A detailed view of this same approach, done by Shettler, Vajk, and Engel, indicates that we will need to invest something on the order of an Apollo project, between thirty and sixty billion dollars, in today's dollars, to reach the point where we begin earning money. However, when you begin earning money, it's quite a lot. It gets up into five, ten, and more billions of dollars per year. The market, as far as we can see, if satellite power were to work out, is very big indeed. It's somewhere between 100 and 400 billion dollars per year, worldwide.

So, even though the investments involved are comparable to the Apollo project (for scale, that's about one twentieth as much as we're going to have to be spending on electric generators of one kind or another over the next 25 years anyway), the question really is, Shouldn't we be spending a few per cent of this money on a limitless source of energy which will remain just as good a thousand or a million years from now as it is right now?

We're looking at something which is a very exciting possibility. It is only a possibility; there's an enormous road of research and effort ahead of us. If, however, a time-scale is followed which was traced with great detail, it might see the first lift-off supporting this effort as early as 1985, and the first power station coming on-line by about 1991, with most of the Earth's energy supply being picked up by satellite power plants constructed in space by the late years of this century or the early years of the next.

But very clearly, to realize the vision of the High Frontier, it's going to take people—all of us—and we need all the help we can get, so that we can see, hopefully within our lifetimes, the humanization of space.

Sequence 9

Some Questions About Space Colonies

answered by

GERARD O'NEILL

What kind of training will be required? As much as for the astronauts?

It will be much more like the education of Peace Corps people than that of the astronauts, because the numbers are much more similar. There are, after all, only 50 or 75 astronauts, who are necessarily tremendously highly trained; the Peace Corps people number ten or twenty thousand. They are also dedicated, but the degree of training, and the rigidity of programming, is far, far less. The astronauts are each being asked to do the work of ten or twenty men during the time they're in space; we certainly don't expect that of colonists who are going out simply to do a job.

What chance is there for the average person?

What other kind of people are there? That's the kind that will be going to even the early habitats, I believe. The sort of people who'll go into the first space habitats will probably be the sort you'd see cooking in restaurants and running laundries and doing every sort of human activity that is necessary and productive. When you have ten thousand people, you have a community; you need everybody.

Can one apply to be a member of an early space colony?

That's the most frequent question of all. I think we're deliberately not taking any sign-up lists yet. People may make them up informally, but it's just too soon for that. Students often ask, "What field should I go into?" The only honest answer I can give is, "In the long run, we're going to need all the specialties we have here on Earth, including, very specifically, the artists, writers, musicians, and poets. If there's any one of these things you're good at, then do it, and try to do it very well indeed." The only other thing you'll need is to be able to get along with people, not only to be a good worker, but to be someone who other people enjoy working with. I suspect that what will look good on an employment application for someone who wants to go into space is a record that shows you've held down a job and done well, and that your fellow workers think you're a good person to work with.

The drive to go into space in the long run will be as fundamental as the freedom to move in three dimensions rather than in two. It's not just another job.

Gerard O'Neill

Why would people want to live in space?

Human habitats will be built in space for probably all the wrong reasons. If we look at the way our own country was settled, it was for what many of us like to think of as altruistic motives; but we look back and see the worst possible reasons. It was for the basest kind of economic gain. However, there were other settlers who came later on, who were spiritually motivated: their reasons were religious, and they wanted freedom. This country was settled for all sorts of reasons, some right and some wrong. In space, the early colonies will be there for strictly economic reasons, which is not necessarily bad. If you're providing cheap energy at the surface of the Earth in unlimited quantities, for every nation, you may be doing more in the long run for the betterment of humanity than you could by almost any other method.

Later on, there will come a time when there isn't that compelling drive to make every person-hour count, but instead people will have the leisure to begin to build for the sake of having some room, or some physical and psychological freedom. I think the experiments in new social structures are not going to come in the first generation of space habitats, but that the second generation may follow the first in ten or fifteen years.

If you gave me a choice between eighteen different types of space habitats, I would pick the most democratic one to go to: the one where I would have the least fear that I was going to be controlled by some kind of Big Brother. If you ask me what I suspect is going to be the government of space habitats, I suspect we'll find every form of government we've had on the surface of the Earth, including the bad ones.

One of the most appealing things to me about the possibilities of space habitats is that a relatively small number of people, like five or ten thousand, could be really independent in the way of food, energy, and all of the essentials, and, therefore, be able to govern themselves with leaders that were close enough to pass them on the sidewalks every day, rather like the old city-state concept. There is a lot to be learned from some of the commune experiences of the past few years, and it's my hope that the space habitats, because of these unique possibilities for independence, will be able to continue that social exploration and will perhaps be able to learn things that will benefit many of us back here on Earth.

Can microwaves be used as weapons? Are they dangerous?

They can't be very effective as a weapon. One reason is that the beam intensity is very low; the energy density is less than that of sunshine, and if that sounds strange, the reason is that it's there all the time. Sunshine is there, on the average about one-sixth of the time.

Not enough research has been done on the long-term effects of microwaves. Even though the serious dangers are probably not very great, I feel we should do extensive research, very intensively, and as soon as possible, to understand and prevent any problems before we begin using microwaves in large quantity.

I spent ages 17 to 19 as a radar technician in the Navy. The problem, I think, is not that microwaves are so inherently dangerous, but that for many years we didn't think they were dangerous at all. That is not true. There is an enormous difference between the ionizing radiations in a nuclear reactor, which take many feet of iron and concrete shielding to stop, and which you can't shut off, and microwave radiation, which you can kill by throwing a switch, and where all it takes to completely block out the beam is a layer of household aluminum foil. It's a very different level of risk. I still feel we ought to explore it in great detail, and, above all, not commit the error of the early nuclear technologists, who tended to speak only to each other, assuring each other that there were no problems, without ever turning the problem over to outside groups.

What are the advantages of space colonies?

Many astronauts, looking back on Earth, have picked out with telescopes tiny places where warring nations were arguing over bits of territory since time immemorial. If we had a human habitat in space with people from many different nations, including those warring nations, and they were to look back with the same telescopes, how compelling it would be to think, "What were we fighting about when there is the possibility of almost limitless expansion? Why do we continue to fight over the same tiny boundaries?"

This brings up the fact that the territorial imperative is very deep-seated in all of us. One of the most important effects of human habitation in space will be to make all of us reexamine the whole idea: what is the meaning of territory? Especially when you're in a situation where territory can be extended almost without limit? There's enough unused material floating around in relatively nearby space to build attractive land area that's 3,000 times the land area of the Earth. What happens to the notion of territory when territory is moveable, when two groups who can't get along with each other can actually move their territories apart at very slight cost?

What is it that drives one for this sort of thing? I'm sure, deep down, it's the same thing that would have made me try to jump into Columbus' ship, if I'd been a Spaniard back in the 1400s and there was a new world to be discovered. There is this drive which is in a great many human beings, to try to explore, to go out into new dimensions, both of space and of consciousness.

Looking back from a hundred years in the future, what people will then perceive as the important thing about breakout into space will be not so much the immediate energy benefits, but the much deeper effects on our consciousness and our sense of what we are as a race, what we are as a people, what it is that we're here for, if for any purpose. Those are the things which I think it will take a hundred to three hundred years even to think about properly. Still, if we remain forever confined on a very limited planetary surface, if we cut ourselves off from the possibility of going out into space, I'm afraid we are likely to limit ourselves very much psychologically as well as physically.

Sequence 10
The Third Industrial Revolution
G. HARRY STINE

In his book The Third Industrial Revolution, *G. Harry Stine calculates that the number of technical processes that can be done more efficiently in the gravity-free vacuum of space may exceed 1 googol. (A "googol" is a number represented by 1 with 100 zeros following it.) It seems like a preposterous supposition; yet this is the kind of enthusiasm that accompanies projections about space industrialization. One can only "hide and watch" as this new adventure unfolds.*

The prospect of breaking out of the closed system (Spaceship Earth) and plugging into the total system (our universe) will undoubtedly release new energies in the human spirit and create new consequences in our conceptions of our environment.

The first industrial revolution was the substitution of mechanical power for human muscle power. It freed us to do a lot of things, but it also caused problems. The second industrial revolution was the substitution of computer-like elements to handle the repetitive jobs that the human brain was doing to run machinery. It freed us to do even more things, and it too caused some problems. The third industrial revolution is based on these two: the eventual movement of industry off the Earth, to make things out in the solar system that either cannot be made here in the ground or can be better made in space.

By moving heavy industry off the Earth, particularly the heavy-polluting industries, we can go about our job of basically returning the Earth to an environment much like that of the late

Pleistocene period, when we evolved. We all yearn for this environment. In other words, what the third industrial revolution should do, during the next 100 or 150 years, is return Earth to a garden planet. That's environmentalism from a different point of view. We don't need to give up what we've got. We can have our cake and eat it too.

Right now, we're just talking about it, and sharing ideas and information. The next step in the process is to quit talking to ourselves, and to get out and talk to financiers and bankers who can eventually bankroll this undertaking. As soon as possible, we have to learn to talk their language; we have to learn how to present our ideas to them in such a way that they can understand them and become willing to undertake the risk. There's always risk involved, and there's a very high risk at this point in space industrialization.

Moving industry off the Earth is a long-range goal; it's way down the line. The first thing we have to do is get up there and make some things in space—in orbit around the Earth—that we can't make down here on the ground, or that we can make better up there, bring them back to Earth, and sell them. The whole system has to start paying for itself; it can no longer be supported by tax dollars. To be absolutely crude about it, we've got to figure out how to make a buck in space so that we can have space. It's absolutely imperative that we do so.

If we don't go into space, we are trapped forever on this little planet, essentially in a closed cage, chasing our tails from now until eternity. We know that men can walk other worlds; we know men can live in space. I want to open up the system so that we are not caught in a "limits to growth" syndrome.

The Space Pioneers

Space colonization comes about as a consequence of space industrialization, because if you put ten thousand people out there, what are they going to do? There has to be a reason for them to be there. In the first place, there's got to be a reason for them to *go*—other than the dream of perhaps creating a new Garden of Eden out there. There's got to be something to do, besides survive, and there's going to be the question of who's going to pay the bill for doing it. Our ancestors came to the North American continent for many reasons. They were running from tax collectors, or they were running from the police, or they were looking for something better for themselves and their children. There was a promise here.

It took a lot of hard work. I don't think the inhabitation of space is going to be any less difficult, or any more benign, than the settlement of this country was, or the settlement of Australia. Many people forget about the Mormon Trek and other pioneer movements. Many came in pushcarts, pulled by human power, a thousand miles across the great American desert. *Most of them didn't make it.* I don't think space colonization is going to be very much different.

The first people to come to this hemisphere, the explorers, were basically under government subsidy to do so, and the first

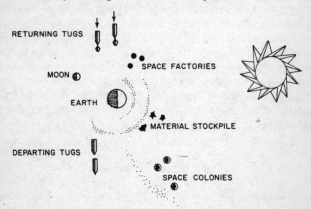

Near the colonies at the Trojan points of the Earth's orbit, space tugs come and go, bringing back mineral-rich asteroids from beyond the orbit of Mars.

settlers that came over here had signed contracts with the new form of social institution known as a corporation. Even as late as the 1900s, when a lot of immigrants came to the United States, they paid their own way. They had to pretty much strike out for themselves when they got here, too.

It's early yet to talk about individuals going into space. We probably will not see this before the 1990s, because the costs are so high for getting a pound of payload into orbit. They will come down; historically, the trend shows they will. If we can get the cost of payload down to $10 per pound, we immediately have space tourism made possible: at least 5,000 people per year capable of buying tickets for a round trip. If it comes down to $5 per pound, you have massive space tourism: 50,000 to 100,000 people per year capable of making a flight into orbit for fun, for a vacation, for a different experience. When the costs are down that far, that's when you start talking about going into space to live. Unfortunately, it's not quite like coming to the United States, where you at least had air to breathe and water to drink: you've got to take a world with you when you go, a microworld; and you have to build a microworld out there. It's not going to be a place for dummies.

It's also going to be a very deadly place if you don't follow the rules—that is, the rules of the universe. It's going to be an exceedingly difficult life, deadly and dangerous, initially. But eventually, I would say within a hundred years, the Moon, or the L-5 points, will be pretty comfortable. Then the frontier, of course, will move out elsewhere, out to the planetoid belt, if not to the stars.

Selling Space Technology

I'm a consultant in high-technology marketing. I'm applying marketing techniques to space industrialization, because I believe that this is what's going to happen in space over the next ten to fifteen years, as we build up our capability in space.

Industry is the sum total of human effort that goes into converting energy into social structure: that's the anthropologist's definition. The idea that a company is going to do something to make itself bankrupt, or give itself a bad image, is ridiculous. It may make foolish mistakes from time to time. If it makes too many of them, it goes out of business very quickly. I wish I could say the same for some governments.

I don't think we are going to be replaced by robots, or 'droids. I don't believe that we are going to become automatons. As a matter of fact, I believe that the expansion of the human race into space, even though it is a small fraction of the human race, is going to set off—in fact, already has set off—the damnedest explosion in the areas of creativity and the arts and the humanities that we've ever seen. For the first time, we're seeing that we're a people on a planet; we've seen our planet as one thing. We're beginning to understand ourselves more and better. The humanities are catching up very fast as a result.

Technology is only a tool. What you want to do with that tool is up to you. We're certainly not going to throw it away. We're going to try to make it better.

Sequence 11

Commercial Possibilities in Space

GARY C. HUDSON

Gary Charles Hudson is Chancellor and Acting Executive Director of Foundation, Inc., a Minnesota nonprofit corporation formed in 1971 to promote the development of space technology. As a director of Foundation, he is directly responsible for its astronautics research.

Educated at the University of Minnesota in microbiology, physics, and astronomy, he has directed a research project in ultraviolet astronomy at the university and taught in its College of Biological Sciences. He has worked as an engineering and design consultant in the medical-device field, and is currently on a team developing a major government/industrial space payload.

Mr. Hudson is responsible for the basic systems concepts that underlie all of Foundation's launch-vehicle designs and systems for commercial utilization of space. These include the Phoenix series of single-stage orbital vehicles, the Windjammer and other launch vehicles, and the Eyrie habitat modules. He is the inventor of the microbomb pulsed fission/fusion rocket engine.

He is a member of many professional associations, including the British Interplanetary Society, the AAAS, and the AIAA, and has presented numerous papers before professional conventions and governmental hearings, in addition to his public lectures and interviews on both British and American public radio.

In this sequence, Mr. Hudson explains the public benefits that may result from commercial, as opposed to governmental, development of our space capabilities.

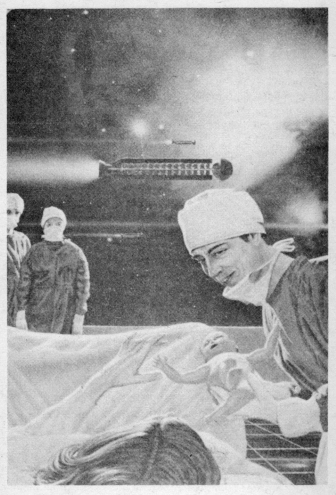

Gary Hudson, envisioned as a doctor in a maternity room aboard a colony starship 300 lightyears from Earth. The Great Nebula of Orion is visible in the viewscreen.

The Foundation Institute's basic, general emphasis is to develop advanced technologies of various kinds in a private mode, as opposed to a government-funded activity. Our specific interest for most of these last seven years has been the field of commercial space industry of one sort or another.

Basically, we've found that the cost of space transportation is the most important single factor in determining the feasibility of any of the space-industrialization prospects, now or in the near future. I personally believe that the space shuttle, which has been heralded as the next advance in low-cost space operations, is relatively inadequate to the task—at $350 per pound to low-Earth orbit. I would prefer to see a broad spectrum of reusable, low-cost commercial launch vehicles developed. That's our basic orientation, and a basic direction now. We must do that before we can get to the stage where we can interest nonaerospace companies with adequate capital who might invest in any space project—such as manufacturing in space, or satellite solar power, or producing synthetic crystals.

Our studies show that space transportation must be very expensive, but fortunately there are several ways of lowering the cost. You can take existing, relatively primitive technologies, developed in the '50s and '60s (for example liquid-oxygen/kerosene engines), and modify them with new materials to build a launch vehicle in much the same way that we now build a commercial airliner. You would have more of a general-purpose light aircraft than something like a NASA spacecraft, an Apollo spacecraft, or a shuttle. For example, the space shuttle costs around $3,000 per pound to build, whereas a DC-10 is on the order of $100 per pound, and a light aircraft, a propeller-driven aircraft, can cost as little as $20 or $25 per pound.

We must change the aerospace mentality, and develop a low-cost industrial approach to getting into space, if we're going to do it any time soon.

If the private sector goes into space, clearly the profit motive will be the most important thing. We will first see profits, I suspect, in the fabrication or manufacture of biologicals, and of certain electronic components. It's most likely because, first off, it can be done with very small payloads—under a thousand pounds—which our original launch vehicles will be able to handle quite inexpensively. Secondly, energy and power requirements for biologicals are very low; consequently the systems can be built compactly and relatively cheaply. Of course, space power always costs you money, whether it be nuclear or solar cells. However, research lead times in this area are very short, so that you might set out to do a project that would run for six or eight months before you start to see some economic return.

The Only Real Last Frontier

I think space is the only real last frontier. The other frontiers that have been talked about—the oceans, the human mind, and so on—are research frontiers, not political ones. Space offers a political frontier, where people can live as they like, do as they like. Our surly cousins, the curmudgeons, the creative minority, or whatever they may be called, all of them together can move off-planet, to habitats on the surface of the Moon, or on Mars, or in free space. They can find a place to be free, fully free. They can have access to an enormous wealth of energy, resources, and technology, which always frees people, rather than enslaving them. Space will be a place where they can make truly enormous amounts of money.

Let's look at some statistics. If in the year 2000 there was a space settlement, with a space population of about 10,000 people, you might think of it as an independent nation-state, a republic in orbit. How much money would this space community generate for itself? Some of the best estimates from NASA and other research organizations indicate that, by the year 2000, easily $50 billion per year in space-based products could be generated, exclusive of satellite solar power. A per-capita income of $5,000,000 per person in space is not bad, and that's wealth that can be used by individuals for individual goals. The more power

© 1978 Foundation. Inc. Painting by David Egge.

Mining an asteroid in Earth orbit at 6,000 miles altitude. A factory ship closes in on its 35,000-ton orbiting target, whose raw materials are worth about $200 million.

you put in the hands of individuals, the less you put in the hands of organizations, institutions, or governments. I'm all for individual initiative.

It's possible that such a settlement might itself be a corporate enterprise. Someone might try that, but their likelihood of success, over a long period of time, might be limited.

The Strategic Advantages of Space

You have certain strategic advantages when you're in space. You're on the "high ground." You don't necessarily have to worry about Earth opinion of your activities. It's going to be a very fascinating place.

Timothy Leary recently commented that space technology has passed, to a large degree, out of the hands of the engineers. It's starting to move into the hands of the sociologists and anthropologists and businessmen. However, the engineers will have one or two last "blows against the empire." The next developments will involve transportation advances like matter/anti-matter-annihilation engines about the turn of the century, and a couple of developments in communication and life support. When an individual can invest perhaps a few tens of thousands of dollars—as much as a person going out to buy a home—then we're going to see a lot of diversity in space.

Freeman Dyson, the Princeton physicist at the Institute for Advanced Studies, once had calculated for him the cost per person, in present-time dollars, of the Mayflower expedition. Each one of those passengers on the trip to the original Plymouth Colony represented $200,000 in investment. (The investments came from other people.) If, in the year 2000 or 2010, we invest that same amount (again in the equivalent of 1975 dollars), I suspect we will be able to live very, very comfortable lives in space.

As for the O'Neill cylinders, the large habitats, I see some possibility, but I would not expect it to happen much before about 2025 or so. Things will probably have to get a little bit worse on Earth before people will leave our relatively benign environment in great numbers.

Elitism, Social Welfare, and Tyranny

At times, I'm accused of being an elitist. I've tried to develop a lot of different answers to that. One is that maybe I am. I'd like to divorce myself from the space program, because frankly I don't approve of government funding in this; I don't approve of taking taxpayers' money to do it. But, on the other hand, the space program is the thing that America will be remembered for. Clearly, in a thousand years, we will be remembered, if at all, for only the Apollo project, and nothing else. Someone has made the point that the space program is our only positive development during the last twenty years.

You know, if you go out and tell the engineers, "Do this," they almost always do it, even with severe constraints on money and time. I don't think the space program is a luxury at all. I think it's an absolutely clear necessity; because, if we don't have it, we will encounter what Isaac Asimov has called the "slow withering on the planetary vine." I don't want to be part of the decline of the human race. I want to be part of its evolution and advancement.

It's a specious argument to say that the money invested in the space program should go into attempts to solve problems on Earth. It's very easy for people to criticize the amount of money that goes into the NASA budget, but it's trivial. In a period of nine days, the Department of Health, Education, and Welfare spends the entire equivalent of the NASA budget. Nine more days of HEW spending would not produce anything new. They've had nearly a decade to prove that they don't do a very good job in spending money on essential programs. They don't create jobs. They don't improve people's lives very much, and in many cases they make them far more miserable—by adding bureaucracy and red tape and humiliation to a disadvantaged person.

Bureaucracies are inflexible monsters. They are a great form of tyranny. I think that technology is a great freer of human beings.

Technology, Bureaucracy, and Monopoly

There's even the possibility that technology will free us from bureaucracy. An example in the short term is the CB radio. The bureaucracy of the Federal Communications Commission was so overwhelmed that they couldn't even take paid license applications any more. The five- or ten-dollar license fee was made free. Now all you have to do is fill out a form and add your ZIP code to it.

Communications, a very monopolistic field, will radically change in fifteen years, with the advent of the hand-held communicator, which operates at a quarter of the legal minimum-power level for licensing by the FCC, about 25 milliwatts. It will contain almost no metal parts, so it will be very difficult to detect; so you can smuggle it anywhere you want. It will be about the

Mining the atmosphere of Jupiter for hydrogen and helium using nuclear-powered ram scoop ships.

size of a pack of cigarettes, and it will cost perhaps $50 per year to run it. Every call you make on it will be a long-distance call, because it will have to go up to the satellite and down, whether it be across the street or across the world. Therefore all rates will be adjusted to be equivalent.

Many different people could put up such satellites. All they have to do is standardize the frequency. That's been done, of course, many times in the past; standardization doesn't require a government. All of a sudden the communications monopoly is completely wiped out. In the year 2000, I'm willing to bet, AT&T will not exist as a viable communications entity; or, if it does, it will be competing in the marketplace with a dozen other companies.

Making Money in Space

To date, the only successful commercial space-related venture from the private sector is the communications satellite. Of course, it has been extremely successful. There are a couple of very large American corporations (which every week spend the equivalent of the NASA budget in their capital spending) who are interested in providing electric power with satellite solar-power stations by some time in the 1990s. This is encouraging, because if these monoliths move forward in a field like satellite solar power, the hanger-on industries that would be necessary—dozens of different small companies that would supply space-suits, or communications equipment, or fabrication equipment, or whatever—would enlarge our potential and our options in space.

The only one that's made money so far is COMSAT. In the next five years, maybe nothing will make money. In ten years, a lot of small manufacturing will make money. Certainly the launch-vehicle business itself will be profitable. We have our own under design at the moment. There are a couple of other organizations, around the United States and the world, who are thinking of getting into the private launch-vehicle business.

At the moment, we're engaged in developing a low-cost unmanned commercial launch vehicle that has a capability of about 5,000 pounds in low-Earth orbit. The development costs are on the order of a few million dollars, and the development time is about two to two-and-a-half years.

I understand the Japanese are planning to have a shuttle of their own in the next 20 years. Once we have a semisuccessful first flight—or perhaps a fully successful first flight—we might make some arrangements with them to demonstrate our capability, with the hope that they would be more interested in acquiring our systems than developing their own. The other developed and developing nations are prime markets for our vehicle system.

I think Foundation offers the public a little bit of hope, because we're thinking about the individual. Since the general public obviously is composed of individuals, those who are oriented toward the future that's going to be required here should be encouraged by the fact that someone is going out and spending their own money and taking the risks for the past couple of years, and is going to take them in the future, to get people off-planet into space.

Sequence 12

The L-5 Society

KEITH AND CAROLYN HENSON

Keith Henson is an electrical engineer and computer scientist, and is President of an electronics company, Analog Precision, Inc. He is the author of many space-related publications and patents, and is a leading researcher in space science. In 1977 he participated in the NASA Summer Study Program at Ames Research Center, which focused on the use of extraterrestrial resources.

Carolyn Henson's parents, Aden and Marjorie Meinel, are both astronomers and solar-power researchers. She grew up around observatories, reading the science fiction that the astronomers left lying around, and at age 17, in collaboration with her father, she published her first scientific paper in Science, the prestigious journal of the AAAS; the paper proved that certain mysterious low-latitude noctilucent clouds were actually vapor trails left by rockets launched from Vandenberg Air Force Base. Her involvement in a broad array of political, civil-rights, and other movements during and since college eventually led to Carolyn's interest in space colonization.

In 1975 Keith and Carolyn presented a paper on space farming at the Princeton Space-Manufacturing Facilities Conference, and in July 1975, with the help of about 30 others, they founded the L-5 Society, which is based in Tucson, Arizona. The Society functions as an information service on space settlements, space industry, and solar-power satellites. (The term "L-5" refers to one of the five Lagrangian points, where the gravitational attractions of the Earth and the Moon are equal.) Carolyn now works fulltime for the Society as its President and as Editor of its monthly magazine, the L-5 News, the first publication to be devoted to the social and technological issues surrounding human migration into space.

The Hensons also have three children, Gale, Windy, and Valerie, live on a small farm with Saanen goats and Polish chickens, and keep up other activities in what Carolyn calls their copious free time.

The L-5 Society is a group of people who want to live and work in space, and we plan to actually get out there. In order to accomplish this, we have an information service: we put out a monthly magazine, the *L-5 News*, which carries the latest news, articles,

Courtesy of Space Age Review

Keith and Carolyn Henson

speculations, and debate; it's a forum for discussing the most significant issues of the twentieth century. We have the biggest well-defined group of people interested in this adventure. There are college students, members of the military, a lot of researchers; we have people with occupations ranging from housewife to Zen Buddhist monk—nearly everybody.

L-5 is mainly an information-exchange organization for the people who are concerned with space industrialization, colonization, and solar power from space. Our goal is to get tens of thousands of people living and working in space as soon as possible. When that happens, we consider ourselves to be a temporary organization, and we will disband the Society.

How the L-5 Society Came to Be

The L-5 Society started partly because of Morris Udall. He was a very early supporter of the whole concept. Since he was running for President at the time, he asked us to tell our people that he was supporting it. He wrote a very nice letter to Dr. Seamans, who was then the head of the Energy Research and Development Administration, suggesting that they ought to put some money into looking at solar-power satellites that might be constructed from lunar materials or other extraterrestrial materials. As a result, we had to start a newsletter to tell people about Udall's support.

Udall's interest arose from a meeting that Carolyn set up for Dr. O'Neill to give a presentation to Udall. We'd gotten involved with Dr. O'Neill partly through publication and partly through, of all things, raising rabbits. O'Neill's original publication, the first time this went public, was September 1974, with an article in *Physics Today*. For a long time the general subject of getting people off the surface of the planet had interested us, and we were long-term students of limits-to-growth concepts. Even in those days, it was fairly obvious to us that the solutions to some of the problems we face do not lie on this planet.

Space Agriculture as Comic Relief

About the same time, in an interview in *Mercury*, O'Neill mentioned that a conference on space colonization would be held at Princeton. We wanted to attend the conference. It was very difficult; that first conference in May of 1975 was not at all well-publicized. We made an effort to contact Dr. O'Neill and finally managed to do so, in a letter explaining that we were running a small business and growing a lot of our own food at home. It so happened that the person who was going to give a space-agriculture talk at the conference could not attend. So, on very short notice, we put a talk together on how you would go about raising vegetables, grain, rabbits, and goats in space. The talk was hardly based on scholarly research at the time, although we put enough effort into referencing it later to nail down the ideas as best we could.

Our talk was enormously successful, because everybody thought it was very funny. In fact, there was one really interesting question asked at the end of it: you could get the rabbit, but what about the wine for *Hasenpfeffer*? The guy was absolutely deadpan, and he was asking whether you could grow grapes up there. You can certainly grow grapes in a space colony, although we were concerned with agriculture for a very early space habitat, a very small one being used primarily for the construction workers. Anyway, though, [Keith] said, "Yes, you can, though grapes require seasons. However, I can think of another recreational plant which you could grow rather easily up there." It brought down the house, but Dr. O'Neill asked us never to say anything like that again.

The primary function of the L-5 Society is to keep people informed. If you want to get more active, there are any number of different ways you can do it. You can begin studying and contributing. Even people who are relatively uneducated — even people at the high-school level — have contributed important elements in this over-all program. It's so new that you needn't be an expert in any field to think about it and consider new ways of doing things. Eventually, it will become a used-up subject, and you'll have to study a lifetime before you can add an iota of knowledge to it, but it's nowhere near like that now. One of the prime contributors in it started just a few years ago, when he was just out of high school, and is one of the largest contributors to the whole business.

Life in Outer Space in the Early Days of Space Settlement

Pioneering might be kind of difficult. There won't be a great deal to do, although there will be some really unique recreational opportunities—three-dimensional tennis, or handball (you might get killed in such a thing). There's always, of course, zero-G sex: there was a paper given on that.

Generally speaking, there will be a unique opportunity among the early people for a lot of comradeship, a lot of sense of accomplishment, because they will be doing things very rapidly. If you're going to do this thing at all, it turns out that you have to double on a scale that is very short, like a couple of years. That means whatever you have in Year One, you'd have twice as much of in Year Two. Actually, the whole set of facilities takes a little bit longer to double than that, but the idea is that in the early days, the effort would be concentrated very heavily on growth.

People will need to work very hard in order to do this. There are lots of self-motivated people willing to go up there, whether high wages are paid or not. However, I'm sure very high wages will be paid for people who are very competent and stable, have good working records, and are capable of handling multiple skills.

A Rich White Man's Game?

Some investigators have charged that most of the people who are going to make it in space are going to be white men from an Occidental industrialized civilization, who can afford the luxury of flying into space, who have the mental ability and the training which is offered only to an elite in this world, and that the rest of the world will not have this chance to investigate outer space.

I would say that the chances are excellent for the average citizen of this planet to make it into space, because this doubling phenomenon is very short in comparison with human life spans. When we dig into what actually makes for wealth, the materials and the labor and the other things that are involved with what we can do up there, the length of time needed to process enough materials to reproduce the entire industrial base, we get numbers that are almost absurdly short. Some run down as short as six months. It's awesome. With an almost certain prediction that the project will double in less than three years, the growth rate becomes very large, very rapidly.

In all seriousness, the one thing that cannot reproduce anything close to that fast is the people. In the not-too-distant future, but at least a good distance into the next century, you're going to have problems with the Earth being drained of population. This doesn't mean just the engineer types, because they are not going to need a whole lot of engineers, even in the early stages of it. The bulk of the space population will be construction people, mid-level technicians.

Relatively few engineers will be required to supervise and to make engineering decisions; most of the engineering and scientific work will be done on Earth. We doubt that it's going to be a highly elite group, because the elite are not going to be butchering rabbits and doing the gardening work, or sweeping the floors, or cooking the food, or maintaining the habitat. A substantial fraction of the total work that has to be done is of that category.

What Real Wealth Is

What is wealth? Wealth is control over the environment. It's air conditioning when it's too hot; it's heating when it's too cold. It's a roof over your head to keep the rain off; it's nice, comfortable, fancy clothes. The ultimate in wealth is room service. You don't even have to cook your food. While it's conceivable that everyone could get such things here, the basics needed for all this, the energy and the materials, are out there. They're not down here.

Many of the problems that we have today may not have solutions on Earth. The solutions may lie only in leaving the planet behind. There's no way we can avoid tearing up the countryside for ores, for fuel, for raw materials here on Earth—short of everybody dying off.

If you want to live in a forest in a space colony, there certainly is no reason that you can't. The potential for building land out there in space is at least on the scale of ten thousand times the land area of the Earth. You can build it—every bit of it, if you want to—just like the most desirable parts of the Earth. This is not in the immediate future: not in the next ten years, say. But in the long range, we can go in that direction.

The Role of Government in Space Migration

It's really difficult, perhaps nearly impossible, to put up any barriers in space. I suspect that government may become very sensitive to what the people are thinking about it, because if they don't like it, they may just leave. When you're talking about people with a great deal of wealth and the ability to buy the means to go out to the asteroid belt, or to do any number of different things, it may be very difficult for a coercive government to keep them under its thumb.

For Earth, I see a transition time that will be very hard. I see restrictive laws, perhaps prohibiting people from leaving until they've posted a half-million-dollar bond, or worked for 15 or 20 years and paid into the Social Security system. I see a number of possibilities: stealing people from other countries; the United States opening its borders surreptitiously; conditions in the whole world improving very rapidly, because you cannot maintain a population that is sneaking out everywhere, trying to get into a country that's welcoming them just to maintain its own population. I can see terrible things, the entire world covered with Berlin Walls for a while.

And then I see people giving up on it, and the Earth probably becoming very much a park.

It's been proposed that the colonies be chartered as parts of states in the United States, which has the advantage of making use of the existing law systems, but there is certainly no reason that you couldn't have colonies chartered as counties, or perhaps provinces, of different countries. I could easily see that occurring.

Advice for the Potential Space Colonist

Be good at whatever you're doing. Inform yourself. The more knowledge you have about it, the more chances there are that you will be one of the people who are in demand. But don't despair if you're not picked among the very first people. No matter how far down the list you are, when the people who are half that far down the list are taken, then, within the next doubling, which is very soon, you'll go too.

There's more than enough room out there for everybody. It's not an elitist thing. The chances are excellent for virtually everyone who wants to go to be able to go, if you're at all reasonably young. Who knows, with life extension, even if you're rather old, you may well have a chance to go if you want to. And if you're one of those who want to stay here, we're going to need a lot of people to stay and maintain the historical monuments and turn the entire Earth into a very large tourist trap.

Financing Space Colonies

Space colonization, financed for its own sake, I believe would be prohibitively expensive for anyone but ten thousand multi-millionaires. It is simply too expensive to build a space habitat for

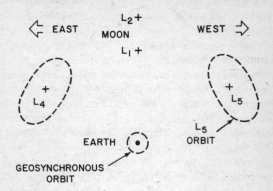

The Lagrangian (L-5) point.

its own sake. It must be piggybacked onto space industrialization, and a way must be found to finance space industrialization, or there are not going to be any space colonies.

The total cost of space industrialization will be somewhere between $60 and $100 billion. It could run as high as $200 billion. Research and development might cost $10 billion or more. All of the aerospace companies in the United States together don't have much more than that. It's just beyond their capabilities unless they get outside financing. They can't get outside financing, because with their present structure they would have to suspend their payment of dividends from their earnings. Also, they can't join together without violating the antitrust laws if they're going to divide the work in some cost-effective way. A new corporation has even less of a chance. There's just no chance for a new corporation, conventionally organized, to raise this kind of money.

So what you need is a totally new business structure. One way that business structure might be organized would be a closed-end management investment company that converts itself into an operating company after its research and development has minimized the economic risk of full-scale space industrialization. Christian Basler, a Wall Street lawyer who thought up this idea, calls it a "staging company." It's like a staging area, in that the company accumulates the capital necessary for a risky assault, in relative safety. An investment company that invests in stocks of companies likely to benefit from space industrialization is a pretty safe investment. You might attract a lot of money that way, which you couldn't attract to something as risky as a direct space-industrialization company.

I'm sure that the people who passed the laws never had any idea that the Investment Act of 1940 could be used for something this strange, and yet it's completely up front: it doesn't endanger people's capital to speak of, in that their capital is safe; they're only risking the interest on it. What it amounts to is a way to accumulate a lot of capital in the investment company, whose function, initially, is to buy stock in other companies. But this would be an unusual investment company, in that its dividends, the money that it receives from the stock it owns in other companies, would not be distributed to the stockholders who own it, or used to increase the value of the fund, but would be used to finance the research that's necessary to get to the stage where we can say, "It's going to cost us $29,543,000,000.29 to do the job." At that point, a majority vote of stockholders, who have spent only the interest on their money during the staging period, converts this fund into an operating company which builds the space industries, and space colonies develop out of the need to house the workers.

Sequence 13
Space, the Environment, and Politics
JACQUES-YVES COUSTEAU

Since 1936, Jacques-Yves Cousteau has dedicated his life to the exploration of the seas. Born in St. André de Cubzac (Gironde) in 1910, he entered the French Naval Academy in 1930, and served in the French Navy until 1957, when he retired with the rank of Capitaine de Corvette.

In 1936, in his free time, he began to experiment with various prototypes of underwater breathing apparatus. In 1943, he conceived and realized, with Emile Gagnan, the Aqua-Lung, an invention which gave humanity, for the first time, the ability to explore the ocean freely in three dimensions.

During World War II, Captain Cousteau actively participated in the Resistance. Soon after the liberation of France, he helped to create, within the framework of the French Navy, an "Experimental Diving Unit" in Toulon. He participated in demining the ports of Toulon, Sète, and the Lion Gulf, and commanded the Navy diving tender Ingéniere Elie Monnier.

In 1950, in Malta, Captain Cousteau acquired the Calypso, *a minesweeper of American construction, which was transformed into an oceanographic research vessel. On board* Calypso, *he accomplished numerous scientific expeditions, including the archaeological excavations at the site of an antique wreck (third century B.C.) at Grand Congloue, near Marseille, France.*

In 1951, in collaboration with André Laban, he perfected the first practical underwater television camera. One year later, he created CEMA, an engineering organization for the design and development of underwater instrumentation. The U.S. Divers Company was formed as well, to manufacture and distribute Aqua-Lungs and other diving equipment and accessories. In 1957 he was elected Director of the Musée Océanographique of Monaco.

The "Diving Saucer" was developed in 1959, the product of a collaboration between engineers Jean Mollard, André Laban, and Jacques Cousteau. The Saucer, a revolutionary concept, is a round, highly maneuverable, jet-propelled submarine, capable of diving to a depth of 1,200 feet, permitting a crew of two to observe, photograph, and film the depths, and even to take samples. This was the first of an entire series of submarine devices, including the Westinghouse "Deepstar."

At the same time, he continued his saturation diving experiments with the so-called "Houses Under the Sea": his Conshelf III (1965) permitted six men, breathing a helium-oxygen mixture, to live and work for three weeks at depths between 330 and 380 feet.

Since 1967, the Calypso team has engaged in a long and fascinating journey from the Red Sea to the Indian Ocean, to the Atlantic and Pacific Oceans, as well as in the Antarctic. Throughout these voyages, a cinemagraphic documentation without precedent has produced 47 films, so far, on such subjects as coral, whales, sea elephants, and so on, which have been shown on television throughout the world.

Jacques Cousteau has also filmed since 1943 more than twenty documentaries for theater release, which have received critical and popular acclaim, including three Oscars. He is author of 32 books, and was awarded the "Chevalier de la Légion d'Honneur" by the French government for his Resistance activities; then was promoted to "Officier" and to "Commandeur" for scientific accomplishments.

Of all his contributions to mankind as inventor, explorer, filmmaker, scientist, and writer, Cousteau's greatest legacy may be as a philosopher. Since 1959, his eloquent pleas to respect the oceans have moved people the world over to new concern for the water environment. In 1974, to turn his ideas into concrete action, Cousteau organized the Cousteau Society. Since then, he has devoted his full energies and vast experience to helping the goals of the Society become reality.

In this sequence, Captain Cousteau comments on some of the relationships he sees between space industry, ecology, and oceanology.

Courtesy of The Cousteau Society

Jacques Cousteau

In recent years, space flights have given us the perspective we had been lacking so long: a general picture of our planet actually contemplated from outer space. It was not by mere chance that space exploration coincided with the birth of our environmental awareness. Thanks to space research, the new generation realizes that there is one single Earth, and that most of this is covered by one single ocean.

To conserve, to protect, to reuse a clean global water system implies a permanent control of the vitality of the oceans. Unfortunately, decisionmakers, quick to grab an electoral issue, are exceptionally slow in dealing with matters that extend in time beyond their mandate or their retirement. It is a shocking fact that there is yet no substantial national or international project to monitor the oceans. And the oceans are crying for help.

The only real color that creeps into the blue of the sea is the dark brown filth from polluted rivers, from city sewers, from industrial sludge, from landfill, from careless development, from countless marinas, from millions of tourists who feel so happy when they speed their boats and empty their bilges into the sea, throwing anything overboard and having a glorious swim in the contaminated water. However, the day will come when the urgency of controlling the sea internationally will be recognized; and technology is ready to meet the challenge.

Compared with the scale on which we humans are made, the sea is a giant environment, constantly changing and incredibly complex. The vast, whirling sea cannot be truly understood from spot measurements made sporadically with microtools such as thermometers, water samplers, sediment samplers, or current meters lowered from the deck of a ship.

Today, remote sensing and telemeasurements from satellites and aircraft are the only methods of investigation compatible with the scope of the ocean, and with the severeness of its man-made problems. This is the only way for us to sense the pulse of the oceans. We know that the pulse of the oceans is the only symptom from which we can diagnose the degree of health of the pyramid of life that we are privileged to hold at our mercy.

Space colonies will be able to perform, probably, industrial things that we cannot do on Earth, and I am for it. It will be a fantastic platform for research, for chemistry, for biological experiments. However, I do not believe that it's a good thing to try to desert our Earth, to try to live in a space colony. I think that's nonsense. I also think that eventually it will be dangerous to try to collect solar energy from outer space and send it back to Earth for heat.

There is so much natural solar energy on Earth. When you add up all the energy contained in the existing known supplies of fossil fuels—oil, coal, gas—it is equivalent to a little less than the

Courtesy of The Cousteau Society

The filming of "The Birds of Isabella."

energy of 3.6 days of sunlight on the Earth. If we are not able to get a little piece of that, I really don't believe in technology anymore. However, technology is there. It should be able to take one out of every 10,000 calories from the Sun and convert it into energy for us. That's all we need.

Energy from the Sun—clean, inexhaustible—has only one drawback. It is thinly spread over large surfaces. On land, people must build such clumsy concentrators as batteries of mirrors; or we have to spread converters over hundreds of thousands of square miles. But the ocean is a formidable natural concentrator of solar energy. Space monitoring will be essential for the clean, harmless management of a fraction of this energy that falls on the sea and that is equivalent to the output of 54 million nuclear plants. However, there is still one thing more important than food and energy; and that is *life*.

We, as human beings, are part of a complex arena of living creatures which started to spread on Earth perhaps three billion years ago and which has never stopped diversifying. The only life system we know of—and we are part of it—is based on carbon chemistry and cannot develop without water. Even if life exists elsewhere, it is exceedingly sporadic; and very seldom do we find on a celestial body the exceptional and lasting conditions that we have enjoyed on Earth for about three billion years, and are likely to enjoy for another four or five billion years.

The logical conclusion is that, of all priorities, the supreme imperative is to conserve, to protect, to nurse the water system of our planet; because its life is our own life, because its fate is our fate.

In 1967, a United Nations resolution urged the equitable sharing of marine resources among all nations. As a result of this resolution, the U.N. has sponsored the Law of the Sea Conference. At the Law of the Sea Conference, men of the sea have no voice. Instead of sharing resources, representatives at the Conference have endeavored to cut up the sea into pieces as butchers

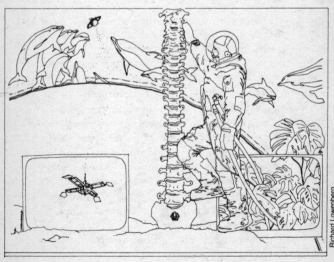

Richard Lowenberg

do with cattle. A trivial incident between representatives of a rich nation and a short-sighted committee could bring about fatal consequences for the world. Having silenced the experts, lawyers and diplomats labor to plant border-crossing signs in the shifting waters.

A good use of the space shuttle might be to offer a one-week trip around the world to the leaders and the top politicians of our time, so that they could realize that there is only one world and only one blue ocean. If, upon their return, they opened their ears to the clamor of their people, they would have to switch to new criteria for priority choices. They would have to get their noses out of the Keynesian mousetraps; they would have to look around them and realize what is happening in this world of rapid and drastic changes.

Today the public wants to have a say in public affairs. Constituents want to be heard through other channels than their official representatives. They no longer accept that a handful of bureaucrats may decide what is good for them. It is high time we all realize that the living water of the oceans is the blood of our planet. It is the same blood for every nation. It is *our* blood.

Sequence 14

Space Law:
An Opportunity for Vision

INA J. RISMAN

Ina J. Risman holds a B.A. in Philosophy from Mills College, and a M.A. in International Relations from San Francisco State University. She is currently Research Assistant to Dr. J. Henry Glazer, Chief Counsel, NASA/Ames Research Center, Moffett Field, California. In the fall of 1978 she will begin law studies.

In this sequence, which is an article specially contributed to this book, Ms. Risman discusses the sources and present nature of laws that affect space colonization and industrialization, and emphasizes the unique opportunity that Space Law gives us to undertake rational decision-making about our future.

My initiation into Space Law began with meeting Dr. J. Henry Glazer, Chief Counsel at the NASA/Ames Research Center in Moffett Field, California. I met with Dr. Glazer to discuss international law, with the focus on energy and arms control. The discussion turned toward Space Law as the logical extension of international law. Before Dr. Glazer's presentation, I had never considered energy and arms-control problems from this perspective. As we continued our discussion, the concept seemed both plausible and necessary. This was my first step toward a new field of inquiry.

Soon thereafter, I became Dr. Glazer's research assistant. Independent projects considered energy questions in terms of Space Law, and methods of propulsion for "Space Cabotage." This term, coined by Dr. Glazer, refers to "the carriage of goods

Ina J. Risman

and persons in space,'' and is borrowed from the maritime model.

My fascinations mounted, and I began reading everything I could get my hands on: from scholarly journals to the L-5 Society magazine. I was hooked.

Without question, my undergraduate work in philosophy, and graduate work in international relations, helped my extension into Space Law. The field is absolutely wide open, and soon to come of age, despite the lag behind the technology. Although institutional sources for the study of Space Law are rare, it is the newest and most ripe area of law on the horizon.

Perspective

Space Law is a new field of inquiry. Right now it is a collection of questions that have been dealt with only in a limited or isolated fashion. However, because existing technology makes it feasible for mankind to venture into space and to become permanent inhabitants of space, we must begin to create a more comprehensive and responsive legal model to deal with such a situation. Not only must our present attempts at juridical modeling for space consider the obvious realities of today, but they must be flexible enough to accomodate whatever interests and priorities the people who go into space may have—and we do not know now who those people may be. The legal regime for space, initiated by Earth-based inhabitants, must not deny future Space-based inhabitants access to materials which *they* deem vital to *their* existence. Space Law must therefore: (1) be equitable; (2) allow for the future interests of permanent Space inhabitants; and (3) be expansive enough to accommodate a wide range of activities, from lunar and asteroidal mining to regulation of the microwave transmission frequencies of solar power satellites. Some legal scholars have noted that the second provision would have no discernable cost to Earth-based interests. Basically, all that is needed for a workable international legal regime for space is vision and expertise.

As people venture into space as inhabitors, entrepreneurs, scientists, etc., they will need to have all facets of their existence be equitably managed. Therefore, every area of law here on Earth will eventually find some application in space. It is not difficult to imagine the complexity of human relations in space; they will cover everything from assignment of liability for damages to persons or equipment, to the property settlement between two space inhabitants bound in marriage. In fact, even the concept of "property," as we know it, will have new meaning in Space Law. Moreover, the legal concept of "domicile" (the notion of permanent residence, with the intent to stay or return) takes on new meanings in space, because "intent" to stay is an insufficient criterion in a totally man-made environment, in which inhabitability depends on the proper functioning of an artificial environment. In sum, because of the extensiveness of human relations, the forward-thinking Space Lawyer will never lack for exciting areas of inquiry.

Sources

In general, Space Law has addressed such issues as establishing the boundaries between air space and outer space (and thus establishing the upper limits of sovereignty), providing standards for safety, registering vehicles in outer space, and regulating satellite communications frequencies. Most interestingly, though, the roots of Space Law are found in the areas of national security, arms control and disarmament, and law of the sea. Because of this connection, lack of progress on measures such as the Third United Nations Conference on the Law of the Sea can hamper the development of any Space Law that is not narrowly tied to the political ambitions of states here on Earth. The striking similarities between Law of the Sea and Space Law have prompted legal thinkers to strive for responsiveness in the Law of the Sea negotiations, in the hope that successes will pave the way for less-restrictive Space Laws. In addition to being plagued by shortsightedness, Space Law has always lagged behind the pace of technological achievements; we have not been able to recognize problems or set up legal means to deal with them until after they have arisen.

Right now, the primary source of space law is the international treaty "On Principles Governing the Activities of States in the Exploration and Use of Outer Space, Including the Moon and Other Celestial Bodies," also known as the "Outer Space Treaty." The treaty was opened for signature in 1967, and 89 countries are now party to it. However, since there have been many significant technological advances during the last decade, either revision of the treaty or additional international accords are now needed.

The Outer Space Treaty was modeled after its predecessor, the Antarctic Treaty. The Antarctic Treaty prohibits both national appropriation of the region and emplacement of nuclear or other weapons of mass destruction there. Rather than being "disarmament" treaties, both the Antarctic and Outer Space treaties are "prevention of armaments" treaties. A prevention of armaments treaty rests on the premise that it is infinitely easier to prohibit activities (such as nuclear-weapons emplacement) before they are begun than it is to convince states to give up something after the fact. In this way the international community is demonstrating a committed belief that we must prevent weapons of mass destruction from ever entering transnational space.

Negotiations for the treaty were initially threatened by a rift in Soviet-American relations, but tensions eventually dissipated. In 1963 the General Assembly of the United Nations unanimously approved a resolution to establish outer space as the domain of all mankind, and to prevent it from being used for military purposes. After considerable debate on versions proposed by the United States and the USSR, the final treaty entered into force on October 10, 1967.

Article I of the treaty contains some of the most significant assertions: that the Moon and other celestial bodies shall be the province of all mankind, without regard for economic or scientific development. Princeton physics professor Gerard K. O'Neill's plan for "mining the Moon" for valuable metals and oxygen could be thwarted by the treaty provisions, were the U.S. to go it alone. Other states may interpret the emplacement of a "mass driver," some two miles in length, as *de facto* appropriation of the lunar surface it occupies. The U.S. could possibly counter the claim by contending that she is within the treaty provisions for "use," as a bonafide member of "mankind" who is not prohibiting or discouraging similar mining operations by other states.

J. Henry Glazer, a foremost scholar in Space Law, has even suggested that a space settlement, located in a fixed orbit, might be construed as a national appropriation of a segment of outer space. However, the problem could be averted by having the settlement be under international or multistate auspices. In addi-

In the nineteenth century, space exploration was conceived in jingoistic terms, as in this illustration for Jules Verne's *From the Earth to the Moon*.

tion, if space settlement openly encouraged a disparate group of interests, including free enterprise, no one nation could be accused of "appropriation." At present, the treaties do not seek to regulate multinational corporations or other nongovernmental entities which could conceivably engage in these activities. However, time limits, such as thirty years, have been proposed as the transition point between "use" and "appropriation."

Present Paths

Probably the single most important piece of international legislation that could adversely affect the progress of large-scale space industrialization and settlement is a restrictive Moon Treaty. Basic treaty provisions, already being debated in the United Nations, might bar both substantial removal of lunar materials and permanent installations there. Should this occur, the Lagrangian habitats envisioned by O'Neill and others would become infeasible, because they could only be built by using lunar and asteroidal materials. Clearly, one of the major "selling points" of the idea of space settlements is that, once underway, they would not rely on Earth for raw materials. If lunar and asteroidal materials were made unavailable by international treaty, the whole concept would become economically (if not technologically) infeasible. For these reasons, we must encourage passage of a nonrestrictive Moon Treaty.

The second imminent problem of Space Law which could impede progress is territorial appropriations of geostationary orbit. Geostationary orbit is 22,800 miles above the equator of the Earth in space. All communication and weather satellites are located there because of the stability of the orbit. If—and, one may hope, when—solar-power satellites are constructed as a source of abundant, ecologically sound energy, they too would be located in geostationary orbit. Most unfortunately, some equatorial states such as Ecuador have already attempted to extend their sovereign borders 22,800 miles into space! It is very unlikely that such a nation could ever enforce such an assertion, but we would still be faced with difficult international political problems. Logically, the international system should look toward the precedents of Law of the Sea (and its attempts at regulating fishing limits) as guidelines for adjudication of conflicts; but, as I have already noted, progress in this area has been at a snail's pace as well.

Future Directions

Clearly, space exploration will present innumerable challenges to Space Lawyers. Possible legal structures range from those of a space "colony" controlled by an Earth state to a Free City in space modeled in part on Danzig. The critical and tangible link that will enable space habitats to be built is the space shuttle, scheduled to begin missions by 1979. The shuttle, or vehicles like it, will be able to bring materials and persons into space, as well as return them, and to perform operations in space that are impossible under the gravitational acceleration on the surface of our planet.

The coming reality of the space shuttle makes the idea of habitats at the L-5 points much more than an idle fancy. The options opened up by such habitats are endless; for example, the Earth could be made a preserve, a pleasant place to visit for vacations, but not a permanent place of inhabitation. The rapidly depleting Earth would have an opportunity to recover from centuries of exploitation, and human beings could literally explore "new frontiers."

Shorter-term benefits to both Earth and humankind will also result from space settlements. Settlements, built as commercial ventures, to provide microwave transmission of solar energy to Earth, could radically reshape international politics. Imagine what may happen if energy, the backbone of modern industrialized society, ceases to be a politically controlled finite resource, and becomes abundant because of international *cooperation*.

Surely such a radical change in the technological basis of the world economy would begin to substitute international trust for mistrust, cooperation for rigorous competition. The developing and developed nations alike could benefit from such a switch in the dynamics of international relations. International cooperation on communications frequencies already exists; the existing apparatus could perhaps be adapted to new and more extensive functions.

It is, however, extremely important that space dwellers be well-protected by Earth laws; for if the Earth comes to rely heavily on the resources provided us by space, we must guarantee space dwellers enough legal flexibility to accomplish their tasks. A "Free City" could easily be protected by a combination of international treaty provisions and municipal rules, and be accountable to Earth only when truly necessary. Issues unrelated to Earth, such as laws needed to safeguard survival or prevent homicide under circumstances that are totally alien to us, should be regulated by *their* standards. The fundamental concept of "reasonable man" will evolve in Space Law until it becomes workable in that environment.

George S. Robinson has elegantly suggested that Space Law be grounded in the biological foundations of *"homo alterios"* (Spacekind) and in the unique social-value scheme that will emerge because of actual physiological alterations in the human body in space. The concepts of "family" and personal responsibility will take new form for these beings if they become markedly different from ourselves. Indeed, he points out the possibility that *homo alterios* may be unable to readapt to Earth environment, and, in that sense, will be a true alien.

Conclusion

Juridical modeling for space is ripe for attention and represents a unique opportunity in the law: an opportunity to plan consciously for interests and situations that we cannot foresee. The sensitive modeler must first be able to acknowledge the limits of his or her present perspective, must be able to separate his or her gravity-based clay feet from the zero-G, free-floating world of outer space. Given such an acknowledgment, we can begin to create a system acceptable to us here on Earth, and flexible enough to accommodate the interests of *homo alterios*. Apart from that, all we can do is maintain our optimism, our vision, that the expansion of *homo sapiens* into space will not be into oblivion, but rather into a realm of renewed hope and opportunity for all of us.

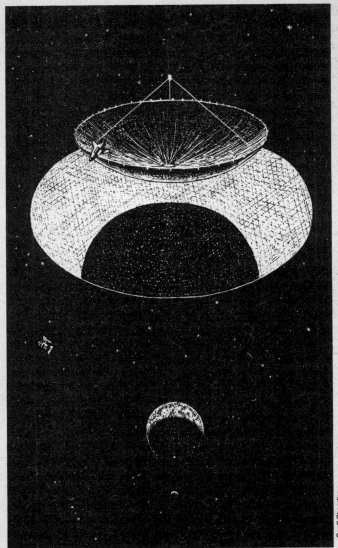

Geoff Chandler

Phase Three
Extraterrestrial Life
The Scientific Search

G. Harry Stine

Prolog
Meeting Extraterrestrial Life
G. HARRY STINE

"I work for myself. I'm an author, a consulting engineer, a marketing man, a model rocketeer, a pilot. I also play the role of a 'hair shirt,' a Devil's Advocate, and an unstuffer of stuffed shirts. I believe in Robert Heinlein's dictum that specialization is for insects."

Harry Stine

I am almost certain we are going to find extraterrestrial life, and we may already have done so. The indications from the Viking landers are very ambiguous; it is our first experience with exobiology. If those Viking landers had been any place on Earth and had given that data, it would have been incontrovertible proof that there was life on Earth. Unfortunately, we were dealing with another planet, and the investigators are not quite willing to commit themselves yet. Remember, it's a totally alien environment that we landed in up there.

As for extraterrestrial intelligence, there is probably a very good chance that we are going to run into it at some time in the future. It may be tomorrow, it may be in fifty centuries, but the chances are better that we will run into it than that we will not. We have no proof today of either, of course, but I don't think we are alone in the universe. It remains a major question to be answered. I would like to be able to look up at the stars at night, and no longer be afraid.

Extraterrestrial Life — *There is a lack of detail that has always frustrated humankind when we gaze longingly at the stars. Space colonies are one thing, but other developments in science are, in many ways, even more profound.*

Buckminster Fuller has pointed out elsewhere (World Magazine, Mar. 27, 1973, p. 23) that "up to the twentieth century, 'reality' was everything humans could touch, smell, see, and hear. Since the initial publication of the chart of the electromagnetic spectrum . . . humans have learned that what they can touch, smell, see, and hear is less than one millionth of reality; 99 per cent of all that is going to affect our tomorrows is being developed by humans using instruments and working in ranges of reality that are nonhumanly sensible."

This phase of our survey deals with attempts to learn more about the universe by use of sophisticated tools that extend the range of our senses to new limits. The following Sequences of information focus on various attempts to learn more about our solar system and those beyond. The current and future probes going out to Jupiter, Saturn, and beyond will not be specifically designed to look for other existing life forms, as the Viking landers did on Mars. They should, however, increase our knowledge of these alien environments and could indicate where to concentrate new searches for intelligent life "out there."

L.G.

Sequence 15
Planetary Probes in the Near Future
NORMAN HAYNES

Norman Haynes, Ph.D., is Director of Advanced Space Projects at the Jet Propulsion Laboratory of the California Institute of Technology in Pasadena.

In this sequence, Dr. Haynes explains the deep-space probe projects that are currently underway and that are planned for the future.

In the near future, we are planning a project called the Solar Polar Mission, using dual European and American spacecraft. It will be launched off the space shuttle, first flying out to the planet Jupiter. One spacecraft will orbit over the top of Jupiter while the other transits the bottom. They will use the gravity field of Jupiter to deflect their orbits out of the plane of the ecliptic, the plane in which all the planets orbit the Sun. We want to get out of the plane of the ecliptic in order to observe phenomena and radiation coming out of the Sun in those regions that the Earth doesn't pass through.

These two craft will come back from Jupiter and circulate around the Sun, outside the plane of the ecliptic, repeating the Jupiter maneuvers, passing over the Sun's north and south poles. There will be no cameras; we can see the Sun just fine from the Earth. Other kinds of instruments will be used to detect the kinds of radiation coming out from the Sun.

Venus Orbiter

Following that is a Venus-orbiting imaging-radar mission, which we hope to launch in mid-1983. The idea of that mission is to fly a spacecraft to Venus and into orbit around Venus. We want to map the surface of Venus, get pictures of the surface, which is very hard to do, since Venus is perpetually covered with clouds, eliminating the use of cameras or any other optical systems. However, a radar signal can penetrate the clouds, and by using a device called a synthetic-aperture radar, we hope to construct a map of the surface of Venus, much as we did for the first time on Mars with Mariner 9 back in 1971. We hope to end up with a globe of Venus completely covered with pictures which show what the surface is like, to a resolution of perhaps a few hundred meters.

Earth-Oriented Missions

We're also working on two Earth-based missions. One is a follow-on to SEASAT. SEASAT is a satellite we're launching in about four months, which will go into orbit around the Earth. It will study the oceans and return information on what's happening: the temperatures, the currents, the wave heights, and so forth. We're preparing a follow-on mission to the SEASAT mission, which we would hope to launch in about 1983 also. It will involve either a satellite or a set of satellites, whose function will be to further monitor the oceans.

The other Earth-oriented project we're working on is called an upper-atmosphere research satellite. The idea behind this mission comes from the recent interest in what's happening with the Earth's upper atmosphere, particularly the ozone layer. In order to actually tell whether chemicals are adversely affecting the ozone layer, we have to understand what's going on at that level in the atmosphere routinely, as a base. A satellite, or a set of satellites, will study the upper atmosphere and try to characterize the dynamics and the chemistry of that region. Once we've done that, then, hopefully, we can begin to tell whether anything is changing and, if possible, whether it's caused by man-made devices or not.

What's Ahead for Mars

The next mission to Mars will probably be either what we call a sample-return mission, where a piece of Mars is brought back to the Earth for analysis, or an orbiting mission with either one or two roving vehicles on the surface. It has proven very difficult to build a set of instruments that are capable and accurate enough to answer the kind of questions we have about Mars, and that we can *send* to Mars. The experiments must be packaged in very small boxes and operate self-contained, on their own, at great distances. It might be easier, and we might get better answers, if we actually bring Mars back to the instruments, rather than sending instruments to Mars.

We will fly a mission to Mars and land on the surface. In one way or another, we will select a portion of the surface, put it in the canisters, seal it up, and bring it back to Earth, breaking it down for further analysis here. Even though we can do a much better analysis with the instruments back here, the mission itself is more complex. It requires more vehicles; it takes longer; therefore it's more expensive. The problem becomes finding some creative way we can do that mission for a price that is reasonable, which the U.S. people are willing to pay.

We were limited, with Viking's landers, by the fact that they landed in one spot. After we had analyzed what was at that spot, and photographed that spot, we had this undying curiosity about what was over the next hump in the hill. Of course, we'd really like to do a survey. In a way, it's been likened to the situation of a geologist, commencing a study of a particular area of the Earth. One of the first things he'd do is just get out and walk around. A roving vehicle can autonomously move around from place to place and study different areas, different terrain, to see how it changes from place to place.

Courtesy of NASA

This spectacular picture of the Martian landscape, taken by the Viking I lander, shows a dune field remarkably similar to those in Earth deserts such as Kelso, Death Valley, and Yuma.

Saturn Orbiter Dual-Probe Mission

Another landing mission we're talking about aims at one of the outer planets. Saturn has a very large satellite called Titan, nearly the size of some of the inner planets in the solar system. One of the missions we're working on is called the Saturn Orbiter Dual-Probe Mission. We want to fly a spacecraft to Saturn and put it in orbit around the planet. The orbiter will study the planet, take pictures and other kinds of instrumental data, and send them back. We will also drop off a probe, which is an entry vehicle that we do not expect to survive. It will enter the atmosphere and eventually disappear or burn up. The probe will eventually get so deep within the atmosphere of Saturn that we can no longer communicate with it, which is why we call it a probe rather than a lander. We're not even sure there's a surface to land on. If there were, we're not sure we could communicate with it from down there.

A second probe would go into Titan. Titan, as a satellite, is a very unusual body. Being of planetary size, it also has an atmosphere. It's the only satellite in the solar system that has one, and we think that atmosphere is at least as big as that of Mars, and may be the size of the Earth's. A planetary-sized body with a substantial atmosphere is a very interesting body to study. It also turns out to be one of the easiest bodies in the solar system to land on, because there's enough atmosphere to slow you down.

One of the problems that makes it difficult to land on Mars, for instance, is that the atmosphere is rather thin. It will slow you down some, but not enough so that you can just come in and land. You still need retro rockets and all that to land. However, Mars is a big enough body to compact its atmosphere enough that, when you go through it, even though it doesn't slow you down enough to land, it heats you up enough that you have to have a heat shield. You need a complex heat-protection system for coming through the atmosphere, then parachutes, and finally rockets to land.

On Titan, we think the atmosphere is as thick, but it's stretched out to a much higher altitude; in other words, it changes much more slowly. As a consequence, landing may be very easy (we think). However, we're not sure what the surface of Titan is like. There are a lot of models: one actually projects a liquid, tar-like surface, rather than a solid surface. Therefore, it's very difficult right now to say that we could land on the surface and survive.

A Glimpse of Titan

On the other hand, after a mission now in progress, we may know more. That mission, flying to both Jupiter and Saturn right now, is called Voyager. It will briefly fly by Titan without going into orbit and take some measurements, which should help to determine whether there's a solid surface or a liquid surface, or some other kind of surface. Presuming it to be solid, we would hope that eventually we could build a lander: something that we could depend on to land, survive, and operate on the surface. Landing on a satellite of an outer planet should be quite exciting.

Titan has been described as a possible body on which humans could live. I haven't thought about it too much, but one of the

Painting of how Voyage spacecraft will fly behind the rings of Saturn in 1980 and 1981 to measure the effect of the ring particles on sunlight.

problems with Titan is that it's cold, being so far from the Sun. And it's quite far from Earth, making it very expensive to transport large amounts of mass that far out.

If you were looking for a planetary body to settle on, there's always Mars, which does have an atmosphere, at least. Presumably, you could live on the Moon as well, if you wanted to build a city and manufacture your own atmosphere, provided the materials on the Moon were proper for making your own atmosphere.

Titan's atmosphere is quite different from the Earth's; it's made of methane and hydrogen—some of the gases, as a matter of fact, that we think were probably present in the primordial Earth's atmosphere. It's certainly not the kind of atmosphere you could enter and comfortably breathe. On the other hand, all of those molecules are made up of hydrogen and nitrogen and so forth; so it's possible, if you took along the proper kind of apparatus, to break down the atmosphere and reconstruct it into other things. I've never looked into what it would take to convert Titan's atmosphere into something a person could live in or breathe in, but it's certainly a candidate. It's as much a candidate as any other planet, which is not very strong at the moment.

I think of planetary exploration as being largely knowledge that's gained about the solar system itself. We're beginning to prove that all the planets evolved out of the same initial soup. Therefore the similarities between the planets and the way they developed can teach us things about our own Earth. We can compare the way the Earth operates with the way other planets operate. From the scientific standpoint, there are good reasons for looking at all the planets.

Asteroid Mines

People are now making arguments that the asteroids, and possibly even the Moon, are filled with valuable materials which could be mined and brought back to Earth. That's still very long-range thinking, because the asteroids are a long distance away, in orbits between Mars and the Earth. You'd have to look very seriously at the transportation costs of flying all the way out there, mining an asteroid, and bringing it all the way back here. People have come up with very inventive ideas on how to do that: maybe not practical ideas, but at least inventive ones.

A mass driver, for instance, is not impractical, but it's not the kind of thing that we could turn around and begin to build tomorrow. We couldn't say, "Sure, for the next mission, we'll go out to an asteroid and drive it back to Earth by using a mass driver." It's a kind of technology that would require not a long, but a fairly large, amount of research and technology to do properly. Also, no matter how you slice it, it would be a very costly mission. Before you undertake a mission like that, you want to be certain that what you're bringing back is worth the effort. Naturally, there must be some amount of research done on the composition of the asteroid. Is it going to be valuable? You'd hate to spend billions of dollars, and go out and bring an asteroid back, and find that there was nothing there to use.

That's why we're doing many of these probes. As a matter of fact, one of the missions we're looking at also, a little further downstream, is a multiple asteroid-rendezvous mission, where we fly a spacecraft out using low-thrust propulsion. The rendezvous—which means to pull up alongside and fly in formation—will be done with several different kinds of asteroids, allowing measurements of what the asteroid is made out of, including possibly picking up a sample of the surface to bring back. In other words, the first thing, before anyone sinks a mine shaft, he wants to go out and pick around on the ground and take something back, and assay it in a laboratory to see if it's worth drilling a mine. You can see the purpose behind an asteroid-rendezvous mission.

Another reason for going to the asteroids is that they seem to be made out of the original "stuff" of our solar system. People argue that, by understanding more about asteroids, you can tell more about what the original solar system was like.

The same techniques can be applied to a comet mission, to rendezvous with a comet. Both these missions would use a new kind of propulsion, which we call solar-electric propulsion.*

The Cost of Unmanned Exploration

Generally speaking, the planetary missions, and even the Earth-orbiting missions, cost in the neighborhood of $100 to $500 million each, depending on which mission it is and how much development has to go on in it. That's in today's dollars, which may be inflated somewhat. They all tend to fall in that region, as opposed to the billion-dollar region. The only mission we have on the books that would probably get into the billion-dollar region would be the sample-return mission from Mars.

---

* See Sequence 16, by Dr. Atkins. Ed.

In the solar system, of course, we made a major expenditure in
trying to look for life with the Viking mission. Nobody has
seriously hypothesized that life might exist anywhere else.
A few people have taken a wild shot and said that it's conceivable
that something like that could happen on Titan. Nobody's pre-
dicting that that's what would happen. From that standpoint,
we would certainly like to investigate Titan's biological possibilities, but I don't think you would predicate the mission on going
there to look for life. As for life on other places within the solar
system, outside of Mars, I think probably the only viable option
is Titan, and that's probably not very substantial.

I certainly don't foresee people moving in large quantities off
the Earth within my lifetime. But then that's a fairly limited
period of time. Whether people will ever leave the Earth and
colonize other planets, I certainly would not want to say now.
I think it's a long way in the future. In order to pick up stakes and
go somewhere else, you have to have some incentive. Either
things have to be very bad where you are, or there has to be
promise of a much greater life somewhere else. It's a very expensive transportation process, going to another planet, especially
delivering people, with their life-support systems. It would
involve almost a commitment of the whole human race on the
Earth to do that. I'm sure a single country, or group of countries,
could afford to send a few people to a planet, but to do it on any
large scale would require enormous expenditure.

Sequence 16

Solar-Powered Ion Propulsion: The Ion Drive

KEN ATKINS

Ken Atkins, Ph.D. in Aeronautical and Astronautical Engineering, is manager of the Comet/Ion Drive Development Project at the Jet Propulsion Laboratories in Pasadena, California. He is the author of several technical papers on solar-electric propulsion (the ion drive) and its various mission applications.

In this sequence Dr. Atkins discusses some of the new propulsion systems that are currently being designed for deep-space exploration.

We are rapidly moving beyond the "easy" missions, which require relatively little propulsive energy, such as trips to Mars and Venus, and flybys of Mercury. They're sort of like walking down to the corner. If we begin to move out and accomplish landings on other planets, it's more like going to another town. Moving farther and farther out, orbiting distant planets, will require steadily increasing amounts of propulsive energy.

I think that can be made clear by looking back to the Viking, which was a very ambitious mission to put a lander on the surface of Mars. It took a certain amount of energy to do that. The propulsion system for actually putting the machine into orbit about Mars was fairly big compared to the systems needed for flybys; and it required still more energy to take a machine from orbit down to the surface of Mars. With chemical rockets, as the energy requirements increase, the fuel masses rapidly become exorbitant. That's why we're now considering using a low-thrust or ion drive.

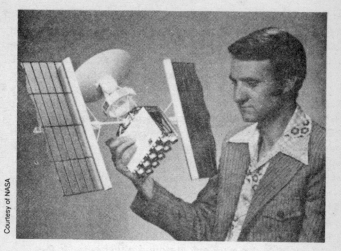

Courtesy of NASA

Dr. Ken Atkins with a one-twentieth scale model of an ion-rocket spacecraft.

It sounds like a contradiction to talk about getting a lot of energy from low thrust. But even though ion drive is very low-thrust, it's attractive to us because of its fuel economy—the "miles per gallon" that we can get. From a device like this, we can improve fuel efficiency by a factor of ten or more. That is, although we might be pushing with a very small force, we can push for a very long time, and do it for a very low cost in the amount of fuel that we have to carry. And, of course, if you push on something for a long period of time, eventually you will have delivered a large amount of energy. For an analogy, walking twenty miles takes a lot more total energy than running a 100-yard dash, but it doesn't generate the excitement of the sprint. So we are looking to the ion rockets as the next generation of propulsive capability for accomplishing these high-energy missions.

We've found that some of the most interesting missions in the solar system demand energies that can be supplied only by this technology. Coming up and flying in formation with a comet;

putting an orbiter about the planet Mercury; going as far out as Saturn and providing an orbiter at Saturn; stopping at several asteroids; returning samples from some of these bodies: all of these are remote-sensing missions, where we would need the ion rocket, in combination with some small chemical rockets for occasional high thrust. That is, we wouldn't do everything with low thrust; we would use it for the long haul, then use the chemical rockets for the brief periods when we need high thrust. It's analogous to the way we might use a diesel train to go from New York to Los Angeles, and then drop off sportscars or freight trucks to deliver the goods at different stores.

The ion rocket itself offers us a very fuel-efficient high-energy system, and it is deceptively simple. It sounds like Buck Rogers, but it's very similar to the way your television tube operates, or even a vacuum tube in an old radio set. The best way to describe it is to imagine a coffee can, empty, and at the base of the coffee can, in the center, we would introduce a fuel vapor: in this case, liquid mercury, the same as you find in your thermometer at home. Mercury is an easily ionizable element, meaning we can charge it electrically with relative ease; we don't need to put much energy into charging it.

We introduce the vapor of mercury into the can or reaction chamber; and over the open top of the can, instead of a lid, we would put two screens, separated by a very small gap. Between the screens, we would maintain a very high electrical voltage drop or potential difference.

In the reaction chamber we would begin to bombard the vapor with a beam of electrons. It's extremely easy to get an electron gun; you can find one in almost any laboratory around. We use it in clever ways, so that we maximize the chance of a collision between the electron and a floating neutral mercury atom in the vapor. When one of these collisions occurs, that makes the mercury atom become charged: it becomes a positive ion.

These positive ions, formed by the collision of the electrons and the mercury vapor, drift up toward the screen. We drift them up there by applying some magnetic fields on the coffee can. As the mercury-vapor ions come to the screen, they pass through the ground screen and fall into the high potential drop. That causes them to be accelerated to a very high speed. We exhaust them from the engine at more than ten times the speed that we can exhaust particles from a conventional chemical rocket like a Saturn V or an Atlas Centaur.

These "coffee can" engines are then clustered. Each of them is not very big, about fifteen inches across and about eight or ten inches deep. Each engine processes some three kilowatts of electric power in order to accelerate the fuel. We would make our ship by clustering these engines on one end of it, to get enough power to process something on the order of 25 to 35 kilowatts of power, which would allow us to accelerate the ship to very high speeds during several years in space.

Essentially, the engine has no moving parts; so, as I've said, it's deceptively simple.

The amount of mercury vapor depends on what mission you're doing. If you're going very far away, or if you're putting in a huge amount of energy, which would depend on the mission target, of course you'd require more fuel than if you were just going to fire for a year or so. The typical fuel load for the rendezvous with a comet, which we're now considering, is somewhere around 3,000 pounds (or 1,500 kilograms) or less. In contrast with chemical rockets, the ion rocket can deliver more than four times the total impulse with less than half the fuel.

There's a point I think should be made: this process can only be used in space. Since the engines process and emit particles on the atomic scale, an air particle would be very large compared to an atomic-size ion. If you tried to operate such an engine in the air around our planet, you would flood the reaction chamber with air molecules, and you'd never be able to get the ionization process to work. Therefore these engines are not useful for launch or recovery. They work only in the vacuum of space.

Once they're in space, we use large panels, covered with conventional solar cells, to convert clean sunlight into electricity. The engines don't care where they get the electricity; so eventually we can consider nuclear sources. The engines are also not necessarily particular about what size they are. In fact, at Lewis

Courtesy of NASA

Artist's concept of the solar-powered ion-drive spacecraft that has been proposed for chasing and studying Halley's Comet when it approaches Earth in 1986.

Research Center, engineers built an ion-rocket engine that was about five feet in diameter. It handled about a megawatt of power. The idea was to use engines of that size, in combination with nuclear-electric power sources, to drive manned ships throughout the solar system. But that possibility seems to lie far in the future.

It's usually a shock for people to realize that ion engines are in space right now. The Lewis Research Center, working with the Office of Space and Aeronautical Technology, launched fifteen-centimeter engines (about half the size that we'll be using in our primary space-exploration mission) into Earth orbit in 1969 and 1970, in a series of experiments to test the electric rocket engine's operation in space. We called that the Space Electric Rocket Test Series, or SERT, and we had both SERT I and SERT II. We experienced some minor problems with them at that time, because they were a relatively early version. By working with them, we were able to clear the problems up, but by that time the Sun had moved to a position where it could no longer supply enough power; so we've had to operate these engines only intermittently since then. But they're still up there, and they're still operable. Late this year, the Sun will arrive in a position where it will be synchronous with the satellite again. There's a plan to start these engines up at that time and bring them to full power, and continue to operate them for as long as they'll operate.

Solar Sails: A Competing Technology?

Solar sailing is another low-thrust technique. There was an intense competition in NASA during 1977, to compare solar sailing and electric propulsion, and to decide which of these two represented a greater benefit for future space exploration. Solar sailing is a very romantic idea—clipper ships of space—and it got a lot of press. I can't deny that it's majestic in concept. However, it's instructive to consider what happened to the old sailing ships here on Earth. We remember that when man first began to explore on Earth, he used sailing vessels. During that time he found, of course, that he was subject to the vagaries of the wind: he had to tack, he had to reach, he couldn't go around storms, he was driven before the winds in many ways: It was one way to do commerce, but it wasn't a very efficient one. The ships were magnificent, they were beautiful. Everyone loved the Age of Sail.

Then along came Fulton with his steam engine. They began to mount these things on ships. They puffed black smoke, and they didn't add much to the appearance of the vessel. However, when the captains and the navies and the people in commerce found that they could drive a ship straight into the wind, and could get from Point A to Point B much more quickly when they ceased to be subject to the vagaries of the wind, and that this new efficiency made money for them, well, then sails disappeared from ships.

When you compare solar sailing with an ion rocket, you are in effect comparing a sailing vessel with a motorized one. The motorized machine will win every time. The solar sail would have to tack; and it would have to be huge in order to develop enough thrust to do the jobs; and it would have to stay very close to the Sun in order to pick up enough radiation to become effective. When it gets far from the Sun, it loses the light and becomes much less effective as a propulsion source. When you contrast that with an electric system, you find an important difference. Even though we also use solar power, and collect electricity by converting sunlight (and, of course, the Sun gets dimmer as our ships get further from it too), there are techniques of putting mirrors (we call them concentrators) along the sides of the solar arrays, so that they collect the sunlight and focus it, much like a magnifying glass; and that makes it possible to take all the available sunlight and intensify it. In this way we can fool the solar cells into thinking they're closer to the Sun than they really are. So the effect on the solar-electric system is not nearly as drastic.

In the competition last year, the ion rocket that we were proposing to send to Halley's Comet was (from wingtip to wing-tip) a football-field-and-a-half wide. That's fairly big. But the solar-sail device that was proposed was over nine miles from tip to tip. That should convey some idea of the magnitude of the engineering job that would have been required to build a solar sailer to do this kind of mission.

For the future, I think we need to look beyond electric propul-sion. I don't think it's the interstellar propulsion system that we will eventually be looking for. We'll need a higher thrust density. That means we'll probably need some kind of device that uses a heat technique, for example, hydrogen gas-core nuclear reac-tors, to get high thrust and high acceleration for long periods of time. I don't see a clear path to a high-energy propulsion system beyond electric propulsion right now, but I'm convinced that there is one. I don't know whether I'll be accused of being a UFOlogist, but's let's suppose that we are actually seeing, at least in several cases, some interstellar or interplanetary devices made by other civilizations. If there are beings who can do this, that must mean there's some fundamental principle in the uni-verse that we are completely ignorant of, because obviously they're able to propel themselves quickly over large distances with small amounts of fuel. That's something we'd like to learn more about.

Sequence 17
Signals from the Stars
ROBERT E. EDELSON

Robert E. Edelson is the Project Manager of SETI (Search for Extraterrestrial Intelligence) and Manager of the Telecommunications Systems section at Caltech's Jet Propulsion Laboratory. He has been actively involved in the design and development of many of the deep-space probes.

In this sequence, Mr. Edelson discusses the JPL effort, and sets forth some of his personal speculations about interstellar communication.

We are embarking upon a search for evidence of the existence of extraterrestrial intelligence by examining the sky for radio signals of a kind that would be particularly good for seeking out interstellar contact. We know that the most straightforward way to conduct communication over the vast distances between stars is by using radio waves. Furthermore, certain frequencies are especially applicable to such signaling.

We will examine the sky with highly sensitive radio equipment, to see if certain kinds of signals are present. There have already been a dozen or more examinations of the radio sky for extraterrestrial radio signals, but the work in this area has been limited, primarily because the technology required to do a search of this kind has not been available, and because the facilities used have basically been radioastronomical instruments, and not really appropriate for conducting a search. We plan to apply existing antennas and very new, highly sensitive, electronic equipment to search for particularly interesting signals — signals that would

Courtesy of NASA

Robert Edelson

be intended for detection by civilizations, such as our own, which have only recently arrived at radio technology.

Existing Earth antennas are actually quite capable of detecting signals that were sent from very far away. The best radio telescope on Earth, the facility at Arecibo, Puerto Rico, has an enormous antenna surface and a powerful transmitter. If we built Arecibo's twin and moved it out to the stars, we'd be able to detect it in Puerto Rico up to 4,000 lightyears away. Now, within 4,000 lightyears there are about 100 million stars that are similar to our Sun, and perhaps 400 million stars altogether.

Our technology, which developed the ability to use radio signals only about 50 years ago, is thus capable of transmitting and receiving signals over a vast region of space. The civilizations which we might detect are probably a great deal older than our own, and superior to us in technology; so we are not at all familiar with the capabilities that they might have. That's why I emphasize that even our own technology is capable of this kind of achievement.

A Million Radio Receivers

We will use small existing antennas to survey the sky for signals from other beings. The key to this is a receiving system which is, in essence, a million separate radio receivers, operating simultaneously, and all tuned to different frequencies. (It doesn't actually work like that, but functionally, that's what it does.) Four such devices will be used, each one occupying a space about seven feet high and perhaps two feet on a side—two feet square—as opposed to the acres of equipment that would have been required, say, twenty or thirty years ago. It is this microelectronic technology that will permit us to conduct a rather comprehensive search.

The frequency regime that we will look at is about one-quarter of the most likely regime for interstellar signaling. It is the quarter that is readily observable from the surface of the Earth. Reception in the higher-frequency three-quarters of that regime is severely degraded by the atmosphere. We cannot test our hypotheses easily in that part of the regime. Still, from the surface of the Earth, we can see the lower quarter, which is perhaps the best part of the region. We will conduct the search over the entire sky.

Many people have hypothesized that transmitters would be found close to nearby Sunlike stars. Although that is a reasonable approach, there are several alternatives that suggest we need to examine broader regions; so we will observe the entire sky, looking for any signals that are of a character called "narrow band." These kinds of signals are generated for many human uses, and are particularly easy to detect. In fact, the greatest

Courtesy of NASA

Two parabolic antennas, forming the research and development site of NASA's worldwide Deep Space Network, stand out vividly against the primitive beauty of southern California's Mojave Desert. The dish diameters are 26 m (85 ft.) and 9 m (30 ft.). These antennas will be used for sky and frequency SETI surveys.

obstacle in conducting a search is that our civilization put out so many of these signals. The system that we use will be automated to distinguish between man-made signals and signals that are of extraterrestrial origin. Any likely candidates identified by the computers will then be subjected to further detailed study. Among them, we hope, will be an artificially generated signal that does not originate from any man-made device.

There are reasons for choosing radio waves as the medium in which to look for extraterrestrial communications. The physics that we know of says that there are a certain number of ways to conduct communications over interstellar distances. These include: sending material vehicles, either with life-forms aboard or simply as automated spacecraft; sending streams of elementary particles; and sending photons or electromagnetic waves. The sending of physically large objects—things big enough to contain life forms or things that are big enough to be automated—involves an enormous energy expenditure.

High Cost of Interstellar Travel

As Oliver has pointed out, sending a dozen people on a journey to the nearest star, using the theoretically perfect rocket, which is thousands of times better than anything we have now, and traveling at 7/10 the velocity of light (which is not a very high velocity as far as getting between stars goes), would require the expenditure of about 500,000 times the annual electrical usage of the United States for a round trip. That's a very large cost to send a few people to a star which is extremely unlikely to have intelligent life circling it.

If you try sending elementary particles, things like electrons or protons, you find that you can't aim them. The magnetic fields in space will change their trajectories, and you have no way of knowing where they're going to end up. With neutrinos, which are an alternative to photons, this does not happen. However, neutrinos are extremely difficult to generate and, even worse, they're extremely difficult to detect. For the same energy expenditure, you can send far more information with electromagnetic waves. They're very easy to generate and very easy to detect.

Electromagnetic waves include everything from low-frequency radio waves up to gamma rays. However, the noise or static that is introduced by the galactic environment, and the noise introduced inevitably by receiving devices, will interfere *least* with a transmitted signal in the radio regime between one and 100 gigaHertz: one billion and 100 billion cycles per second. This is a portion of the microwave region. The equipment needed to detect and transmit a detectable signal here is far simpler and far less costly—in the sense of size and ease of building—than in any other region.

Tachyons—Faster Than Light

There have been hypotheses that there may exist some sort of particles, called tachyons, that travel faster than light. Obviously, the faster the communication can be accomplished, the better. However, there is absolutely no evidence whatsoever of their existence. We could say, "Let's wait, because we may come across a better means of conducting communication in a physics that we are currently unaware of, or by means of a physical phenomenon we're unaware of." But such a phenomenon may not exist at all. If it does exist, then the same argument applies to it as to anything else. You can just as easily say, "Well, these particles only travel at twice the speed of light. Let's see if we can find some that travel at ten times that." It's an essentially nihilistic argument, always waiting for a better system. We've got a good

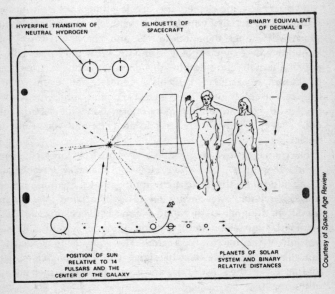

CETI plaque placed on Pioneer 10 and 11.

system now. We've proposed a feasible method by which other societies may be talking between the stars now, and it's the best one we can identify at present.

Leaving aside the technology for the moment, let's look at the fascinating question of what we might say to these hypothetical extraterrestrials. The point has been raised that if they are far more advanced than we are, they might be no more interested in talking with us than the average American would be in getting involved with the Indians on the Amazon—beyond watching a half-hour documentary on them. Even if this is true, that half-hour film may have taken weeks or months to make, by people who *were* interested. And the study that went into understanding enough to make that documentary in the first place probably took many years. There were people interested in the Indian culture, and our culture is enriched by understanding it. That is one reason why these other societies, even if they are technologically far more advanced than we are, might be interested in communicating with us. I restrict my expectations to technological superiority simply because I don't know how to measure cultural superiority. They might be enriched by studying us; we certainly would be enriched by studying them.

Whales and Dolphins

It has been suggested that whales and dolphins have their own cultures, which are a great deal more accessible to us physically, and that our efforts might be better spent in trying to make better contact with them. We're not really sure that the animals are as intelligent as perhaps their brain-to-body weight ratio would indicate. But there's another problem, in that the environment and the experience of those animals are totally foreign to us. We cannot really share the kind of experiences that go into making up the way they think. The primary difference in my mind is that dolphins and whales are not tool-makers. They do not do the thing that is primarily human, the thing that is really our distinguishing quality. I know that chimpanzees use tools and so forth, but I think that merely makes them closer relations to us than dolphins—and we can talk to chimpanzees to some extent, although we have been unsuccessful, really, in communicating with dolphins.

The creatures that we will attempt to contact are those who can build devices that emanate radio waves. In order for us to detect them, they must be tool-makers, and they must use the same kind of tools that we do. That's a common bond, and it might make them closer mental relatives to us than we are to the dolphins on our own planet. The possibilities of communication with such beings, I think, are greater than those of communicating with these creatures on our own world, even if we grant that the cetaceans are our intellectual equals, an hypothesis which has certainly not been established.

What Can We Say to Them?

We have sent out, to my knowledge, five messages into space that were ostensibly intended for aliens to detect. Four of those were physical objects: two plaques, one each on Pioneers 10 and 11; and the two phonograph records on Voyagers I and II. The fifth was a radio transmission from Arecibo, which was basically symbolic; we cannot really expect it to be detected, because the transmission time was so short. Deciding what to send, even in those three messages, I think, was fairly difficult, particularly in the most recent one, the Voyager, where the message was two hours in length.

If we were sending information back to a society that we had detected—and it would be a long time before we were ready to do that—I really don't know what we would want to send, beyond some information on biology and perhaps some Bach. In any case, it would be a political or sociological decision, not a technical one; engineers and scientists *as such* should not decide how we should best represent our society.

When we're talking about a message that would go on for years, deciding on content is a difficult problem. When the time comes for us to do that, and I hope it will come, there will undoubtedly be a very vigorous debate at some organization like the United Nations.

One of the most basic questions, and one of the most difficult to answer, is *why* are we attempting to make contact with extra-terrestrial civilizations? The cultural and biological information from another civilization would be of enormous value. It would be of enormous benefit particularly to biology, where we now have only one example of the way in which life is created—and basically all life on Earth is from a single mold. Beyond the scientific and perhaps the cultural benefits, the philosophical interest is of course enormous. Some philosophies even predict that there will *be* no other life.

The social implications of an interstellar contact are probably best left to be considered in the century after it's achieved. When Columbus discovered the Western Hemisphere, the writers of his time had no inkling of the impact that his find would have on their world. The contact we're talking about is of so much greater importance for human philosophy that its effects probably could not be assessed by those of us who live amidst them.

Sequence 18
Seeking
Extraterrestrial Life
JOHN BILLINGHAM

John Billingham, Ph.D., is Chief of the Extraterrestrial Biology Division at the NASA/Ames Research Center, and is Director of Project Cyclops.

In this sequence he discusses the use of radio astronomy in the search for extraterrestrial intelligence, and the possible benefits to us of contacts with alien intelligence.

If you believe that there are other planetary civilizations, what would be the best way to actually detect their existence? We believe it would be to try to pick up signals that they were giving off, in the same way as we are giving off signals from the Earth: TV, radio, radar, and so on. To do this, you have to build a system of radio telescopes which can pick up and detect those signals.

Project Cyclops

Cyclops, our project concept, is an array, or orchard, of radio telescopes. You can't build one huge one, because it would collapse under its own weight. You have to build lots of them, each one the size of a football field, and then swing them all around and point them in the same direction. Then you take all the signals together, and feed them into the data-processing system.

The original concept of Cyclops was to start not with a whole orchard of antennae, but with one. That other civilization might

John Billingham

be close; it might be far away and signaling with tremendous power; it might even be beaming the signal directly at us. Therefore it is possible, although unlikely, that the signal is already here and is strong. If that is the case, you don't want to spend tremendous amounts of money, time, and energy building that huge orchard of radio telescopes if, in fact, you can do the job with one. What you do, therefore, is to build just one first, connected to a sophisticated data-processing system, and listen with that. Then, if you need to, you build perhaps ten more, which makes it much more sensitive. Then ten more, and so on.

So there is no one Cyclops system. You *might* need as many as a dozen of the Cyclops dishes to detect a signal from another civilization; you might be able to detect it even with dishes that we have right now. Or you might need a very large number, if the signal turned out to be very faint. This makes the Cyclops system necessarily something of variable size.

Let's say we have to develop it to 1,500 antennae, each one the size of a football field; that would be a very large Cyclops system. With that system we could detect the Earth from 50 lightyears away. That is, such a Cyclops system, situated on some other planet 50 lightyears from Earth, could detect our current radio and radar and aircraft guidance signals—after a lag of 50 years, of course. Within a 50-lightyear radius of the Earth, there are about a thousand solar systems.

At present, with the best radio telescope that exists, our range is only about one lightyear for Earth-type signals. Since the nearest star system is four lightyears away, we wouldn't be able to detect anything unless it was broadcasting with a lot more power than we use here, or unless it was some artifact, like an unmanned transmitter aboard some sort of probe.

What Signals Will We Hear?

If we were to conduct a thoroughgoing search for signals emanating from other civilizations, we would look for two different sorts of signals. The first would be signals intended for home consumption on the other planet (or used by inhabitants of the other planet for communicating with their own spacecraft, and so on). The second would be signals which are deliberately beamed with the goal of establishing contact with another civilization. It is conceivable that civilizations in our galaxy are engaged in this sort of project. Of course, we could hypothesize forever without getting anywhere, because the other civilizations would have to be more advanced than ours to be doing this. Therefore we find ourselves in the realm of pure conjecture.

If someone is trying to establish contact with us by sending out messages, these would be sent in a way that was as easy as possible to decode. The senders would do the opposite of what cryptographers do when making codes. It's very easy to construct a language based on fundamental principles which are the same everywhere in the galaxy: principles of mathematics, physics, and chemistry which we know are the same, because we can look at those other stars and find out their physics and chemistry. Freudenthal at Stanford spent two or three years putting together such a language, based on mathematics, physics, and chemistry entirely; it could very easily be decoded. We think it's more likely that we would detect a deliberately transmitted signal, than it is that we would be able to eavesdrop on another civilization's internal signals. In the first instance, the problem of decoding and understanding the new language, and then beginning to understand the message (which would be the most difficult part), would be quite straightforward—although I would fully expect to be surprised.

Project Ozma

Project Ozma was, I think it's fair to say, the first search ever undertaken for signals from other civilizations out in the galaxy. It was done by Frank Drake, who is a sort of father of the SETI project, an astronomer at Cornell University. This effort was stimulated by an article in the journal *Nature* by Morrison in 1959, which suggested that if people wanted to talk to each other across interstellar distances, it would be best for them to talk on one of the commonest frequencies in the whole spectrum, which is the hydrogen line. Hydrogen is abundant everywhere in the universe; therefore it's a common thing. Why not choose a frequency close to the frequency of the hydrogen atom, about 1400 megaHertz, or megacycles, for communication?

Drake was stimulated by this, and listened for two months with a comparatively small radiotelescope at Green Bank in West Virginia, with a very simple data-processing system, to two nearby stars, rather like our own sun and therefore, perhaps, good candidates. The odds of his finding anything, as he knew, were incredibly small because he could only listen to one frequency, and we don't know what their frequency is going to be. His integrating system was not very powerful; his dish was not very powerful; he didn't do it for very long; and he had to listen to nearby stars.

When we did the Cyclops study, we calculated all these probabilities, and one of our goals was to be quite sure that if we went ahead and designed a really comprehensive system, it should be

Courtesy of NASA

Artist's concept of a very large (three-kilometer) spherical SETI antenna, showing feed spacecraft, relay satellite, and radio-frequency interference shield. Located in geosynchronous orbit or beyond.

able to listen across a lot of frequencies in a promising region of the spectrum (which turns out to be the low end of the microwave window) and be able to collect the signal in large quantities, which means it has to have a large surface area; so you have to have lots of big dishes, and, of course, a very powerful data-processing system which would recognize a very faint signal. In fact, the Cyclops system was just such a system; it's still only a design concept, though. Nobody's built it. But it would be billions of times more sensitive than Ozma.

What Radiotelescopes Exist Now?

There is a Western one in the shape of a Y. They use railroad tracks to move the telescopes, of which there are 27. They are quite small; their total collecting area is equivalent to only one of our large modern radiotelescopes. If you're trying to collect very faint signals which come from civilizations far away, that system (which is considered a very large array) would be a waste. You'd be better off to go and use the big dish at Arecibo, in Puerto Rico, where Frank Drake now does a lot of his work; or the one at Green Bank, or the one at Bonn, Germany, or a few others.

When we refer to a large array, it is not because of the size of the dish, but because of the ground area it covers. The reason for all those different telescopes is to use them in a way that tries to measure the distance between the fringes of the light waves and, therefore, can very accurately detect the *position* of objects in space. This is entirely different from trying to pick up *signals,* for which you need a very sensitive receiver in terms of intensity.

Input 18.1
The Space Telescope
ROBERT STEGMAN

Robert Stegman is Project Development Manager for NASA, currently working on the Space Telescope Project.

The space telescope proposed by NASA is so sensitive that any person even breathing on board would totally destroy the image quality. It's an extremely sensitive instrument, and the stability is beyond anything that we've ever done to date. It's such a stable instrument that if the telescope were over Washington, D.C., its area of focus would be within a dime over Boston, Massachusetts.

It's so sensitive that, once again, if it were looking from over Washington, and a truck was coming down the road in Moscow, it would be able to detect both headlights. It will be able to see something like seven times further into space than you can see from the ground, because of the absence of the atmosphere. Looking at nearby galaxies, you'll be able to see individual stars. You'll be able to detect what the

Input 18.1 (Cont.)

core structure of galaxies is like. We can't even see the core of our own galaxy because it's obscured by dust. So we don't really know what our galaxy looks like, except by looking at other, similar galaxies.

We'll be able to detect planets up to thirty lightyears away from us, and there are something like ten solar-type stars within thirty lightyears of us. We'll be able to detect some of the larger planets, actually see the planets themselves. We'll be able to tell whether planetary systems are normal for stars, or what percentage occurs on different stars, or whether we are unique in the universe—which we really don't think we are.

Later on, there will be a larger X-ray mirror, which will be able to pinpoint X-ray sources. There will also be a gamma-ray observatory, and eventually, perhaps, a cosmic-ray observatory.

Finding Extraterrestrial Signals

There is a problem in separating out an extraterrestrial signal from something produced in some way on this planet. Much depends on the characteristics of the signal received. Under certain circumstances, we could identify it fairly quickly as being of probable extraterrestrial origin. However, you have to be terribly careful if you are to rule out the possibility it came from an Earth transmitter. We would conduct an exhaustive analysis of the signal to find out if, indeed, it was coming from a local taxicab, or a passing ship, or an airplane; or if, on the other hand, it had such characteristics that it could only be coming from another civilization very far away.

Hoaxes

We shouldn't overlook the possibility of hoaxes. Under circumstances where there's intense interest, some ingenious minds will go to work trying to spoof the system, and will construct a transmitter which produces some sort of signal which, at least initially, might be misinterpreted. In fact, the Soviets, who are very interested in this whole area of extraterrestrial intelligence, and who are probably doing more about it than we are, have twice so far announced the discovery of signals from other civilizations; in each case, it turned out that they had detected a satellite, one of ours. But there may be deliberate hoaxes, as I say, so you have to be extremely careful in your analysis of the signal. I can't help thinking about hoaxes in the area of UFOs. I'm reminded of the fact that some eminent scientists, in the past, have carried out some of the most perfect hoaxes, which have challenged other scientists for many years afterward. The Piltdown Man was dug up in the early twentieth century in England by an amateur anthropologist named Charles Dawson, who was well-respected, who discovered a strange cranium and tooth and jaw which didn't fit together at all well. So a new species of early man was promptly invented, called the Piltdown Man. In the 1950s, radioisotope dating showed that these remains belonged to fairly modern species of monkeys of different types, and had been very carefully doctored. The hoax question is a real problem.

NASA and UFOs

Based on scientific findings over the last 20 or 30 years, we do not believe we have any proof that extraterrestrial intelligence actually exists; it's just a very strong suspicion. It would be very surprising if, in this huge galaxy in which we live, and in the even huger universe, we were alone. It's probable that out of the billions of planets in our galaxy, there are millions like our own Earth. The conditions which allow life to begin must have been present billions of times in the past, and must be present now in many places. That being the case, it's likely that life *has* begun elsewhere; and in at least a fair fraction of cases, since the galaxy has been around for billions of years, some of that life should have evolved, as we did here on this planet, to the stage of intelligence. If that's the case, it's natural to ask: "Is there any way we can detect the existence of other intelligent species in our own galaxy or outside it?"

You have to be thorough. What we usually do at NASA is to go back to Square One and ask some very fundamental questions. During the past two years we have obtained a little funding to ask these fundamental questions and do a feasibility study. In other words: "Is a search for extraterrestrial intelligence in fact feasible?" When you do that, you look first at the underlying scientific arguments. Do they make sense? How solid are they? What sorts of proofs do you have, or not have? What sorts of proofs should you still search out? If you believe the underlying science is reasonable, you examine alternative approaches, and try to decide how you would go about your search. Finally, and this is very important, you ask, "What is the impact of such a search?" And even more important, "What would be the impact of the successful discovery of the existence of another civilization?"

Contact With Extraterrestrial Intelligence

We've found, in these last few years, that everybody gets confused when we talk about contact or communication. For some years, this whole business has been called *CETI*, or *Communication with Extraterrestrial Intelligence*. That was the name we used when we began. But we found that when we used the word "communication," some people thought that we were already meeting the others across the table, or that it was at least a two-way communication across space. We didn't intend any of this, of course; what we were after was a *search*. Our initial step was an attempt to establish that there was something real in all this. The fundamental question—"Do other civilizations, other intelligent beings, exist out in space?"—that's tough enough. We have to wait until we've answered that one before we even start talking about two-way communication, let alone visiting each other. It's still only a search; it's only one-way.

If a signal were detected, just that fact alone would probably constitute one of the major historical events of our civilization. It would change our whole philosophy and our whole view of ourselves. Just as the pictures the astronauts took brought home to us that we are a small fragile planet in a vast and dangerous universe, in the same way, the simple knowledge that there was somebody out there would make us look anew at ourselves, and might even bind us a little closer together. We are not alone, we are an intelligent species, and there are others! This would motivate people to go on to ask a hundred thousand other questions.

On the other hand, I've also been intrigued by the many doomsayers today: the many people who say we are imperiled, that our own Earth is in great danger because of our own activities, that our species is in danger, and that we will not last very long—fifty years, a hundred years—before some catastrophe overtakes us; because we will not use our heads, and will still behave in an aggressive and emotional fashion.

Benefits of Contact

Any signal that we detected would have to come from a civilization that was millions or even billions of years older than ourselves. It couldn't come from a younger civilization, because they wouldn't have any transmitters. In fact, we're the youngest civilization in the universe. Therefore the ones we heard from would have to be much older; and, therefore, at some point they must have gone through the stage we're going through now. Not identically, of course, but something like it, where they ran into problems of dwindling resources, shortages of food, population problems, disease and war and famine—but here it is, 50 million years later, or two billion years later, and they are still there. That would instantly change our view of things, in that we would then know that it is possible for a civilization which has science and technology to last a very long time. To know about that would be a very fascinating thing—and a very encouraging one.

UFO Reports

The UFO thing, as far as we're concerned, is a completely separate entity. There's no question about the reality of the phenomenon. There are a lot of people who see UFOs and believe they are visitations from outer space. You've got to separate those two major factors very carefully. Many sightings are strange lights in the atmosphere, balloons or aircraft with strange lighting. There may be phenomena in the eye itself: as a physiologist, I know of several things that can happen in the eyeball which give you the impression that there are circular objects moving across the sky. One example is the "floater" phenomenon, which anyone can see after looking at blank pages or down a microscope, for a long time. You see little circular objects and concentric circles, which move about very rapidly. This was all laid to rest about five years ago by a physicist who was hospitalized, and who had to spend a lot of time in his hospital bed looking at the ceiling, which was blank. He figured out that they were diffraction patterns around tiny remnants of old structures in the back of the eyeball from before he was born, in the vitreous humor, which is the liquid inside the eye. My own feeling is that the majority of these things are real in the sense that they are *seen*, and could be explained if the person had access to more information. They don't necessarily have anything to do with outer space.

Our contemporary astronomers may be opening the lid of a new Pandora's box, as their highly sensitive instruments on orbiting satellites detect the existence of quasi-stellar objects (quasars) and giant pulsating, beacon-like energy sources (pulsars). Quasars seem to be no larger than large stars, yet they pour forth unbelievable amounts of energy at all wavelengths—energy equivalent to that of a thousand galaxies!

Then there are the marvelously mysterious "black holes," first discovered by the Uhuru satellite in 1972. Believed to be the remnants of collapsed stars, their gravitational field is so strong that no energy escapes, not even light. We only know they are there because their vacuum-cleaner effect creates X-ray emissions as mass is converted into energy, a process more efficient than any other mechanism known to physics, except for matter-antimatter annihilation.

With each new discovery, the existing assumptions of physics are brought into question, and the ancient quest goes on. Is there anyone out there? Do they know we are here? Is there a force or intelligence that is designing, controlling, managing these seemingly violent energies streaming through space? One begins to wonder if phenomena like pulsars are themselves signals from intelligent beings of an order so far advanced that we poor humans, with limited mental capacities, simply fail to comprehend the magnitude of their existence. As a child, I often wondered, as I stood over an anthill, if those busy oblivious creatures had any comprehension of my existence at all.

We may or may not be like the ants, for we human beings have evolved to the point where we have some idea about what is "out there," even though much of the speculation grows out of statistical probability and projected attitudes. Yet some of our speculation is based on a phenomenon that has refused to go away, the UFOs, and on the possibility that these objects may contain observers from elsewhere in our universe.

L.G.

Geoff Chandler

Phase Four
The UFO Phenomenon
The Enigma of Our Time

J. Allen Hynek

Prolog

Another Exercise in Perspective

J. ALLEN HYNEK

J. Allen Hynek, Ph.D., is widely recognized as the planet's leading expert on the UFO phenomenon, and has pioneered research and writing on the subject for the past 30 years. He is Professor of Astronomy at Northwestern University, and Director of the Center for UFO Studies in Evanston, Illinois. He is Editor-in-chief of the International UFO Reporter, *a monthly journal of UFO news and developments. Professor Hynek was the scientific consultant to the Air Force on UFO's during their Project Blue Book study. He recently served as technical advisor on Columbia Pictures' science-fiction epic, "Close Encounters of the Third Kind." He is author of* The UFO Experience *and co-author of* The Edge of Reality. *His most recent work is titled* The Hynek Report on UFOs: The Inside Story of Project Bluebook.

Suppose we were to make a model which would incorporate everything that our astronomers of today can actually detect with their most sophisticated telescopes. Let's suppose we will make that model as large as the continental United States itself. We here on our planet Earth would be positioned somewhere in the neighborhood of Kansas, looking out in all directions.

On a scale such as that, our Earth would not be visible, even with the most powerful electron microscope known. If we are that much smaller than a particle of dust, relative to the size of everything else in the universe, how can we be so preposterous to think we are the only life in the universe?

The UFO Phenomenon — *In a recent speech, Dr. J. Allen Hynek, who consulted with the Air Force's Project Bluebook for 20 years and who is considered the leading scientific authority on UFOs, likened himself to an explorer who has returned from strange and exotic lands, now giving us a travelogue.*

Dr. Hynek is convinced that we are on the verge of a profound and sweeping change in the scientific belief system. The times are ripe, he believes, for another revolution of the type that occurred in 1543, when an obscure Polish priest, Nicholas Copernicus, asserted that the Earth revolves around the Sun. This information dealt a crushing blow to the dogma that because man was created in the image of God, his place must be at the center of the universe.

The fantastic surge of scientific development during the last 150 years has virtually annihilated the nearly absolute power that once belonged to organized religion. Inadvertently, however, science and religion have taken opposing positions, and many scientists have created their own form of inflexible, dogmatic establishment, interested only in facts: measurable, quantifiable things. The things being discovered these days would make Copernicus's head spin. Quasars and black holes, quarks and subatomic particles that exhibit qualities of "grace" and "charm," constantly boggle the mind.

The new establishment has itself calcified and become afflicted with another malady, "temporal provincialism" (again Dr. Hynek's term), which is the inability to allow for the things not yet known. There is hardly a subject that is more controversial than the study of UFOs. It is here that scientists quickly part company, question credibility, and begin calling names.

Movies and television programs are beginning to create a new atmosphere of social acceptability. Many people who have had experiences are now willing to talk about them without fearing ridicule. Nevertheless, willingness even to examine the data is rare among professional scientists. The information sequences here are from some of the open-minded scientists who have looked at the data and are convinced that it cannot be wished away.

The scientists and researchers represented in the fourth phase of our survey constantly battle against the limitations of the human imagination. They are all convinced that something is going on that deserves serious study. To them, UFO is not a dirty word. They have risked their careers, their reputations, to search for answers to phenomena they feel remain unexplained.

L.G.

Sequence 19

A College Course
in UFOlogy

TOM GATES

Tom Gates is director of the Space Science Center at De Anza and Foothill Colleges, located in the communities of Los Altos and Cupertino on the San Francisco Peninsula. He also serves as a consultant for MUFON (Mutual UFO Network) which is based in Seguin, Texas.

In this sequence Mr. Gates discusses some of the basic ideas, data, and attitudes that he incorporates in his college survey course on UFOlogy.

For about the past four years I've been teaching a course on UFOs, which surveys what the whole thing is about. It looks at UFOs from past history, at what scientific work has gone on in the study of UFOs, and at the people phenomenon, which is perhaps the most interesting. People think they are rational, reasoning creatures, but I think that's a lot of baloney—particularly when it comes to UFOs. We also study the theories about UFOs, and some of the ideas that have been suggested, and there are quite a few of them. The course is well regarded by the school, and a number of other people are teaching courses on UFOs around the country. I've got a publisher asking me to write a book that can be used as a textbook and also for general reading.

Community colleges, as you may know, serve people of all ages. My classes range from teenage high-school students all the way up through people in their fifties and sixties. The reactions have been so good that the demand for the course is increasing tremendously.

Eventually, UFOlogy will probably be taught in the universities like any other subject: the whole field is becoming a pretty serious endeavor. Despite a lot of controversy around the area in the past, it's quite obvious to me that the vast majority of people in this country know there's something going on; they want to know about it; and they want to see a serious study of it. The skeptics continue to dominate the scene—and the question goes on and on, "Do you believe in UFOs?"

It is a ridiculous question. Of course there are UFOs. There are 90,000 cases, representing only 25 per cent of all the reports that have come in. The other 75 per cent have been explained or discarded because there was something unacceptable about the evidence. However, more and more people want to know; and it's already been demonstrated that the number of skeptics now is starting to diminish tremendously.

The Scientific-Skeptic Syndrome

Unfortunately, it's also true that skeptics tend to be those people who hold higher positions in government or in other kinds of organizations, or in the societal fabric. Scientists, who have also arrived at higher reputations, also play a skeptical role. The psychologists who have studied this say, "It's obvious. Who wants to lose reputation? Who wants to lose face with a group of colleagues?" One way to lose face is by getting too far out from the accepted norms of the societal fabric, or of the structural fabric of their discipline. I have yet to meet a single skeptic who can convince me that he's skeptical for anything other than that very reason.

It's strange, but at this point we know pathetically little about UFOs. However, the amount of data is increasing. Circumstantial evidence in the good data certainly seems to suggest that we are in fact dealing with extraterrestrials, but I'm not personally convinced that is indeed what is happening. Many researchers certainly perceive it that way.

The Center for UFO Studies, under the direction of Dr. J. Allen Hynek, is doing a good job of collecting a lot of data. Over 200 scientists are associated with the Center, doing a lot of very good, reasonable work. Some of them are putting together a catalog of what they call "trace landings." The trace landing is where multiple witnesses have seen a UFO on the ground, or very near the ground, and then when they examine the site where the object was located, there is something left behind to study. Normally the evidence amounts to indentations in the ground from assumed landing gear, or rings in the ground, which in some cases have been attributed to radiation which has permeated the soil (soil-analysis laboratories have studied them and have come up with that). Sometimes high winds are generated in which tree branches are broken. That catalog, of just those kinds of cases, now numbers 1,500 cases, a pretty good set of statistics.

Are Aliens Sighted?

There are several profiles, or models, that show up. One of the most common ones is the one that Betty and Barney Hill saw: beings four and five feet tall; hairless; large heads; chalky skin; the teardrop point of the eye going to the back of the head; no external ears. That description has cropped up in so many cases that some of us even call it the Standard Model Zeta Reticulan, which comes from an analysis of the star map which Betty Hill saw in her experience. Other kinds of beings are described as radically different and almost frightening, having the appearance of monsters. Naturally, there are some cases in which it would seem to me that these beings are perhaps projections of the mind; in other words, that it is our projection that is being seen. The being we're dealing with might not be that way at all.

I'd like to make the point that under the main label "UFO phenomenon," we seem to be looking for one answer which solves all UFO sightings, and I'm not sure that's possible. There clearly seem to be different categories of sightings, and this might mean that we have several kinds of phenomena under that one main label of UFOs. Some people get confused and lose sight of that.

Few people are psychologically prepared for an encounter. There are places on this planet where high numbers of sightings take place, such as upper northern California. If one were to just simply go and stay out in one of these areas long enough, some kind of an encounter would probably occur. The greatest difficulty is psychological preparation. People are so absolutely blown away that they have virtually no rational frame of mind left. We see this reaction demonstrated in case after case.

If I were to have such an encounter, I'd of course want to know who they are, what they're about, where they're from, and why they're here. I would want to ask them questions having to do with any sort of advice they could give us. But it could be that we're nothing more than a great scientific specimen to them. Maybe our developmental behavior patterns are being studied from some distance simply to contribute to their own body of knowledge, in the same way that our scientists go and study primitive societies around the Earth. It could be that they don't want to get too involved with us directly, because our behavior patterns would be changed by the mere knowledge of their presence.

Radio Astronomy

The search for extraterrestrial intelligence through radio astronomy is a good program; I think it should be pursued. Of course, the radio astronomers don't want to become involved with UFOs at all. They ignore the field, for good reasons. If they were to agree that there might be extraterrestrials already visiting here, the first thing any congressman would say is, "Well, then, why do you want me to put millions of dollars into something that's going to listen to them way out there? Why don't you ask me for money to study them right here?" They don't want to get shot down. They've got a nice little parade going, and why rain on it?

Their negative comments on UFOs are something they think they have to do, and I can handle that. I'm glad they're around. I'd certainly like to question them, but I don't have any personal desire to force them to change their point of view. Some of my colleagues in the UFO field want to take them to task, and all that leads to is choosing your corners, and coming out fighting at the sound of the bell. Each side is trying to prove to the other who's right; it's a power struggle. I think power struggles are a waste of time and energy. I've got something to say; I have something I know; nobody's going to change what I know.

A Personal Sighting

I've seen a UFO, as a matter of fact. It was a sighting two years ago, when I was on an investigation in one of the "hot spots" in northern California, with another investigator. We had been up in a saddle between two peaks. At 12:30 in the morning we gave up. As we came down to a switchback in the road, we looked back up to the saddle where we'd been. A great big orange object appeared right behind the saddle, about three-quarters of a mile away. It came up and stayed for a couple of seconds. I looked at it through the binoculars. It was an oval-shaped orange light, with a very orange luminous halo around it. It went back down and came out fifteen or twenty seconds later. Still looking through the binoculars, I was able to see orange light all over the ground debris from the logging that had been going on. It shone on the new growth of the grass and the other surroundings, suggesting to me that it was very close to the rim of the hill. We had no good explanation for the presence of that object there.

I was also present at a sighting about twenty years ago, with a group of three other people who were watching the Northern Lights. We saw five oval-shaped lights that went by to the east of us, very slowly. Through the binoculars, each one of the oval lights broke down into a row of lights that looked like portholes. As they neared the north horizon, they all turned a very brilliant white and disappeared over the horizon as they picked up speed.

Sequence 20
Looking at the Evidence
JAMES HARDER

James A. Harder, Ph.D., is a professor of hydraulics at the University of California at Berkeley. As the Director of Research for the Aerial Phenomena Research Organization (APRO), he has considerable experience in researching UFO phenomena. He became a trained hypnotist in order to investigate cases of amnesia, which are often found in individuals who report close encounters with UFOs, and is a leading expert on UFO abduction cases.

In this sequence he presents not only a survey of UFO evidence, but also some of the hypotheses based on that evidence which he is now engaged in testing.

There are about thirty years of continuous evidence of extraterrestrial life. I think the most convincing evidence is that provided by Air Force officers, policemen, and people who have a duty to report unusual things. You don't even have to listen to any civilians; all you have to do is just look at what the Air Force itself has collected in the way of evidence. The problem is not in producing the evidence so much as it is in making people believe the evidence they would readily believe if it were attached to some other subject. The subject itself produces disbelief, rather than the evidence. The evidence is fairly straightforward.

With the testimony "I saw the thing a hundred yards away; it was such-and-such a diameter, made such-and-such a noise; it took off at an enormous speed"—these things are typical reports from really sober official personnel.

Courtesy of J.A. Harder

James Harder

The most highly publicized early sighting was that of Kenneth Arnold in June 1947, about thirty years ago. Of course there have been sightings of UFOs throughout history, notably the miracle at Fatima in Portugal in 1917. There was a great airship observed over the United States in 1896. But the modern era begins at about the time of the Second World War.

Our conclusion is that our planet is under close observation and has been for thirty years. It's almost as if we've excited some kind of concern from elsewhere, starting about the time when atomic energy became available to us. It's only speculation, but between now and the next hundred or two hundred years, the human race may be able to develop interstellar travel itself. If that's the case, we might excite interest or concern elsewhere. After all, the human race perceives itself to be a peace-loving body of individuals, but that might not be the perception from elsewhere.

As far as we know, there has been no official contact. They've come down and talked to various people, usually in rural areas to just ordinary folk, and for the most part they have induced some kind of hypnosis to erase the memory of what actually happened from most of these people. I think the Earth is experiencing a clandestine operation. There doesn't seem to be any policy on the part of the observers of making any overt contact.

Humanoids and Other Intelligent Life Forms

The general aim of the Aerial Phenomena Research Organization, in Tucson, Arizona, is to learn as much as we can about the phenomenon. During the last three years I have been investigating reports of abductions. It's a more polite word than kidnapping, insofar as there is no ransom demanded and people are let go without any permanent harm.

"Close encounter of the third kind" is Dr. Alan Hynek's term for a landing in which humanoids are seen. If the humans are taken on board a UFO and are questioned or examined, you might call that a "close encounter of the fourth kind."

What people report is not uniformly humanoid. The reports that people listen to and hear, of course, are the ones that sound a bit more familiar. I have upwards of twenty or thirty such reports, and although many of them report beings of roughly humanoid shape, some do not.

Look at parallel evolution. Look at the eye of the octopus, one of the mollusks. If it is under dissection, you'd have to be a real expert to tell that it was the eye of an octopus rather than the eye of a mammal. The octopus has an iris, a retina, a means of closing, a lens; it is anatomically almost a perfect match for a mammalian eye. Of course, the mollusca and the vertebrates separated many hundreds of millions of years ago. The parallel evolution is determined by the function required of the eye. There was an evolutionary pressure to develop something to do a certain job. It's not just necessarily true that just because two things look alike, they ultimately had the same origin.

People tend to think that dolphins are extraordinarily intelligent because their brain is more highly convoluted than a human brain. But if you look carefully at the anatomy of the dolphin brain, you'll find that it's all in the area that's devoted to the analysis of hearing. It takes an enormous amount of data processing to convert their sonar echoes into a meaningful picture of the outer world. The shortest wavelength available to a dolphin in sea water is no more than two or three centimeters. To get details about what kind of fish is ahead of it, the dolphin has to make use of all kinds of phase information from the return signal, an enormously complex analysis. That is why his brain is so highly convoluted. It doesn't necessarily mean he's as brainy as an intelligent dog. Our difficulty with dolphins may be that we don't understand as much about the dolphins as extraterrestrials understand about us.

Science fiction, of course, has a wealth of imagination so far as other life forms are concerned. But consider how large an animal has to be to have enough brain cells to develop the kind of thinking machinery that humans now have. We have 1.67 kilograms of brain. If the heads of most of the humanoids that are described are full of brains, they have, per unit of body weight, about three times as much brains as we humans have — which may suggest a reason why they aren't necessarily enthusiastic about coming down to fraternize with us.

Earth as an Anthropological Field Trip

Extraterrestrials may be studying us as we would study a primitive culture. We have Jane Goodall who lived with the chimpanzees. You say, ''Is it possible that extraterrestrials could come and live among us?" They might have a better technology than Jane Goodall. She can't make herself look like a chimpanzee. However, an extraterrestrial she could perhaps make herself look like a human. If we were interested in studying a primitive society in order to learn as much as we could about them in their native habitat, we would do our best to be as secretive and as invisible as we could be in order not to perturb the data we would be gathering. A good anthropologist would rather observe the native group without himself being observed.

I think that to the extent that extraterrestrials are trying to learn something about human beings, they are making a mistake if they are not interacting in some kind of one-to-one relationship. I'm not sure they're motivated to do that, but I think they would learn more if they were.

The reports that I have indicate they can speak many Earth languages. One woman told me, most amusingly, that this alien had a little box at his belt. He was holding what looked like a switch. It was in position one and it made a certain amount of noise; in position two it made a different kind of noise; and in position three, she heard it say, "Do you speak English?" She nodded her head. I said, "What did it say in the first two? Did it say 'Parlez-vous français?' Did it say, 'Sprechen Sie deutsch?' " "Oh, I don't know anything about that," she said.

There are other reports of a humanoid who had landed in South America and, before latching on to the correct language, tried several languages that this particular recipient understood, until he finally settled on Spanish, which he understood the best. Communication may be a problem for us, but apparently it's not a problem for them. After all, they can watch television if they have any trouble with our idiom.

Telepathic Communication

There are many reports of telepathic experiences that people seem to have had in connection with UFOs. In fact, telepathy is reported quite frequently, more often than not. We know it happens between human beings, at least I believe it does, because I have experienced it myself. I don't see why it should be peculiar to us. If you believe that telepathy and clairvoyance rest upon some physical phenomenon of which we're not yet cognizant, you could also hypothesize that the extraterrestrials—if that's what you want to call them—are very wise in the use of that channel of communication. It doesn't necessarily mean that it's something paranormal, in terms of what could be considered commonplace by our own scientists 50 or 100 years from now. It certainly seems to be sufficiently beyond our ability to understand it that everybody feels that he can get into the act, and we have a confused babble of voices. There wasn't the same babble when the special and general theories of relativity were produced.

The Role of Hypnosis in UFO Investigations

It does seem as if most people who have had a close-encounter experience have had a good part of that experience wiped out of their memory in one way or another, at least out of their conscious memory. There seems to be some kind of a hypnotic suggestion; they typically have forgotten something. Through hypnosis, I'm often able to recover something from the unconscious memory that's not normally available to their conscious mind. Afterwards, of course, they do remember it. *Whenever there's been an abduction case that's been authenticated, I've almost invariably been able to develop additional details through hypnosis.*

The event in Pascagoula, Mississippi, was seen by three other groups of people, besides the two men who first reported a UFO sighting, which tends to corroborate their own experience. Apparently it was not an hallucination. They described an object that was "oblong," but I think they meant "oblate." It was about 20 feet wide, and perhaps about a third or half as high as it was wide. I don't believe they got a clear notion of its third dimension. It seems to fit the description of the ordinary, moderate-sized saucer. They were fishing along the river and they heard a swishing noise and turned around and saw it; they didn't see it arrive. Suddenly, it was just there, no more than fifty yards from them. The younger man, Calvin Parker, had an extraordinarily frightening experience.

From the emotional reactions they had during hypnotic regression, I concluded each one of them had a very real subjective experience. However, a person can be regressed back through an hallucination, and the hallucination will seem just as real a second time. The most important thing here was the presence of two witnesses. It is highly unlikely that both men would have a simultaneous hallucination. Both described an objective type of experience.

Information From Other Worlds

Within thirty lightyears of the Sun there are about a hundred stars, perhaps a third of them able to support some kind of life in the planetary systems around them. Life as we know it here may be fairly common in the universe. Within "easy" traveling distance there may be many kinds of intelligent life—if they can persist for millions of years. Radio-astronomer Ron Bracewell postulated that the life of a technical civilization may be so short that they are like fireflies that pass in the night. But the hope is that, after we've solved some of our depressing problems of aggression, overpopulation, becoming able to live in a steady state with our resources, our civilization could last for hundreds of millions of years. If that's true, there may be very advanced civilizations in the immediate galactic neighborhood.

I think it would be very useful if we were willing to pay some attention to information from the extraterrestrial civilizations. It would be enormously useful to know if a civilization has existed for a million years or ten million years. Has it solved the population problem and attained a steady state, with or without too much of a heavy hand from a government limiting individual liberties? Has individual conflict been resolved, so that such a civilization can operate smoothly? Those would be enormously important answers if we really got up the nerve to ask the questions. But we have not really gotten to the point where we're willing to believe that such civilizations exist, let alone try to discover how they operate.

There are those who fear that the extraterrestrials might be hostile to our civilization. That perhaps represents a perception molded from our own attitudes. It is more revealing of human nature than it is of alien nature. If what we have from the reports is at all true, there has been a thirty-year period where they have had the capacity to wipe Earth life out and take over, if that was their motivation. The fact that they haven't done so suggests that they are not intent upon that kind of hostile action. However, they may fear that we would be capable of such hostile action, were we ourselves capable of interstellar travel.

Is It All Just Collective Imagination?

Some people postulate that most UFO sightings are merely "mind phenomena." I don't doubt many people have just imagined things. It's hard to think, though, that an object that returns radar signals, that can be photographed, and the solidity of which is testified to by someone who has walked on its floor, is just something out of the thin air. So I can't go along with the hypothesis that it is *strictly* a "mind phenomenon."

There is a social theory called status inconsistency, which describes people who are extraordinarily intelligent but who live in the poor part of town, or who are well-educated but have a low-paying job, or who are in some way in disparate status situations at a certain point in their lives. Now, a person who is well-educated and reasonably intelligent, has a good job, goes around with people who play golf and watch television, enjoys baseball—that person has a pretty narrow, stable life. A person who bounces around a lot, who has lived in various places, may, just for that reason, have a more open mind to unusual things.

Some studies have suggested that such persons are more likely to report seeing UFOs.

An Idea Is Not Responsible . . .

An idea is not responsible for the people who advocate it. People who are "crazy" can advocate perfectly legitimate causes. Even *if*

The Bettman Archive, Inc.

Victorian nightmares about extraterrestrial contact produced these "Martians."

99 per cent of the people who said UFOs were real came from insane asylums, if you also had 1 per cent who were reasonably sober people and who claimed absolutely, without a doubt, that they had seen them, logically you should believe that 1 per cent. But if we don't really want to look at it purely logically and if we want to believe that 100 per cent of the witnesses are crazy, we have every "logical" reason to do so. It's a part of the human psychological ability to deal with uncertainty.

We have evolved most of our cognitive skills, as well as our ability to perceive things, over millions of years of dealing with a potentially hostile environment. If we perceive that, 99 per cent of the time, something that is yellow and has stripes is a sabre-toothed tiger, we're going to run 100 per cent of the time. That 1 per cent doesn't really matter for our survival. Obviously, we're not very good scientists in our evolutionary development. If we had evolved as scientists, we might be likely to pay a lot of attention to that 1 per cent, because something that is yellow and has stripes and is not a sabre-toothed tiger might be very important to science. But if you're trying to save your life, you're not very concerned about that.

So our psychology, as our human race has evolved, has predisposed us to believe a majority vote, rather than to look at things logically and see that the minority may be right.

They Seem To Disappear

There seems to be a considerable consistency in the form of UFOs. I know that some people believe that there must be some psychic aspect to them, because they seem to disappear. The facts, however, don't necessarily support the idea that they dematerialize, because we have measured, with the help of photography, some accelerations which amount to about 2,000 G. Now something that accelerates away from you doing 2,000 G can get up to essentially 600 meters per second in a thirtieth of a second or less; it would certainly seem to disappear if it were at all close to begin with. So the fact that people see something "disappear" might just mean that it got away before the flicker frequency in their eyes appreciated the fact.

There is the Paul Trent case, from McMinnville, Oregon. There were two photographs taken and exhaustively analyzed by the Condon Committee in Colorado, and they came to the tentative conclusion that they were indeed authentic. I analyzed the photographic evidence, and it was plain that in order for it to be a nearby model (that is to say, a hoax), a whole chain of most unlikely kinds of anticipatory actions would have had to be taken by the hoaxers. They would have had to, for instance, anticipate all of the really sophisticated photometric analysis involving the extinction coefficient of the atmosphere and the calculations made on that basis. It was disc-shaped and determined to be on the order of 30 meters in diameter. There was a very small tower on the upper portion.

The object that was photographed in Oregon was photographically indistinguishable from something that was photographed in France. There are occasions in which exactly the same object or vehicle has been photographed in two different parts of the world. It only requires a few dozen UFOs to have accounted for all the reports and sightings and photographs that we've accumulated over 25 years.

There's a body of relatively expected behavior: they are able to accelerate, to float, and seemingly to defy the laws of gravity—at least what *we* think of as the laws of gravity. There is usually a luminosity observed at night, usually a kind of glow which may be connected with their propulsion system. We also know something about the way polarized light is rotated in the vicinity of UFOs, as if it were being influenced by a magnetic field.

What Are UFOs Made Of?

Dr. Jacques Vallee has an hypothesis that flying saucers are not products of vivid imaginations nor objects, but information sent from another planet. Of course, Vallee is in the communications field, and he's a specialist in computer programming and communications. I lean more toward the viewpoint of physical science. I am perhaps more likely to believe reports that UFOs return radar signals, are photographed, and seem to be solid objects to people who have been very close to them. It's not necessary that we have to choose between the two, because certainly solid objects, people who are perfectly real, can project something that they want us to see, with technology that's beyond us. So I'm not sure there's any disparity between the description that he holds, and that which others hold.

We know very little about what these craft are made of. We do know that there was a piece shot off a UFO over Washington, in 1962, I believe, and it was found to be magnesium orthosilicate, with some tiny round inclusions. Another fragment recovered in Sweden was a chunk of tungsten carbide, one of the hardest materials known, next to the diamond. Some fragments recovered from Brazil were of ultrapure magnesium. Beyond that, people who have been on board describe the floor as being very hard and cold; the materials they encounter are metallic or hard plastic. Of course, they usually haven't any chemical-analysis equipment with them, nor any means to do more than a superficial kind of examination of their surroundings. In general, we still know very little about the material components.

Zero-Mass Matter

The propulsion systems of these craft seem to have some connection with gravity. My friend Dr. Winterberg, Professor of Physics at the University of Nevada, has developed a very interesting theory of how one could produce, with our present knowledge of science, zero-mass matter that is nevertheless solid, and has enormous strength and a high melting point. It's beyond a simple description, but it appears to me to be within the realm of possibility. UFOs may not have any gravitational or inertial mass on the whole, and that would enormously ease the problem of accelerating them to extraordinarily high velocities.

Dr. Winterberg's theory suggests a way in which you could produce material that was just like everything that you see around you, but had no mass, that is, was not influenced by gravity or by inertia. It would float. He's postulated that the fundamental particles out of which protons and neutrons are made, which have been given the name "quarks," have a negative mass. He also postulates that they are magnetically charged. Since they are of opposite magnetic charge, and of negative mass, you might be able to see that the binding energy would be positive. That means that the inherent mass of the particles, plus the binding energy, would have a positive sum, but if you took them apart, the constituent parts might have negative mass. The negative mass particles, then, mixed in some way with ordinary positive matter, could result in something with zero gravitational or inertial mass.

Magnetic Craft Not Feasible

So far as we know, one cannot develop a force from a uniform magnetic field. If you have a magnetic field that has a gradient in it, you can develop a force from a magnetic dipole, but the magnetic field in interstellar space is extraordinarily weak. It seems like an unlikely kind of propulsion system. Also, craft that are seen close to the Earth have not exhibited enormous magnetic fields, although there are some examples of inferred high magnetic fields around craft that are higher in the sky. That may just be something that looks like a magnetic field.

There is also a theory involving some kind of magnetohydrodynamic propulsion system, in which you ionize the air and then propel a craft by some kind of magnetic force. Of course, if you were propelling yourself through air, that might work. It would, however, produce quite a lot of noise, because you'd have the reaction jet of the air leaving behind. The sighted objects don't make that kind of noise. Furthermore, that type of propulsion would depend upon air and would not work in a vacuum. Since

99-plus per cent of the travel is where there is no air, between stars, a system that depends on air would not seem viable.

If this were some kind of local propulsion system, for instance, little ships coming out of a mother ship, I'd say the objection to the ionized-air magnetohydrodynamic theory is that it is not noiseless. Also, it does not produce a thrust in the absence of some kind of backwash or jet, which has not been observed from low-hovering UFOs. Many people have stood under UFOs, and they have not felt any of the down-wash that you would feel if you were standing beneath a helicopter.

Man-Made Flying Saucers

I believe there's someone at the University of California at Davis who has actually constructed a craft in which the levitation or propulsion is developed by certain kinds of propellors within a disc-shaped object. It probably will fly, but it makes an awful lot of noise and produces an awful downwash. These stories of our trying to emulate flying saucers is reminiscent of those "cargo cults" in the South Sea Islands, where the natives were building models of airplanes, hoping they could make something that would fly.

I don't think that isolated mechanics and inventors in far-off parts of the world are going to be able to solve a problem that's beyond the capability of the people down at Moffett Field. I'm not sure they have tried to produce a flying saucer, but if anyone were able to do it, it'd be people in NASA who would have the technical ability to try it.

It is true that an individual like Einstein or Rutherford was able to make some independent breakthroughs on the scientific plane, but it's a lot more difficult nowadays to make scientific break-throughs than it was 75 years ago. Nowadays, in order to do experiments in particle physics, you have to have tens of millions of dollars' worth of equipment. It is hardly possible for an individual to develop something technically useful like a rocket that can go to the Moon. It may be that he can develop an idea, but to put it into technical practice is something that a small group of people will find practically beyond their ability.

Government Policies

There are many things that are tracked on radar regularly that are not reported because of the Air Force policy on such things. The Air Force doesn't recognize the reality of the subject. Anyone who comes to them with any evidence will be faced with one of their public-relations releases, in which they state flatly that there is no evidence that UFOs are real, in spite of several secret documents that they have produced themselves. The CIA Robertson Panel Report of a meeting held on January 14, 1953, stated that the United States public had to be protected from panic that might be perpetrated by the Russians. At that time the Russians were being very quiet about UFOs, and our government thought perhaps this constituted a public policy. Remember, this was the McCarthy era, and the psychology of the time was somewhat different from that of the present.

The government is not all of one mind. Even within the vast reaches of the CIA, there were different points of view expressed back in 1952, when a serious effort was made by people within the CIA to mount an investigation into the physics of the UFO. This investigation was subsequently quashed when Allen Dulles became the director, in the early part of 1953. Allen Dulles knew something that the researchers who were pushing for scientific investigation apparently did not know, that there were policy questions which an investigation would probably upset. Some of those policy questions revolved around the very great interest that the defense community has in certain kinds of things that UFOs were observed doing. This interest continues, and, I believe, constitutes the real nub of why the thing has been kept secret. After all, if indeed we let it be known that we're taking it seriously, it might persuade the Russians that they should take it seriously.

Sequence 21
Flying Saucers Are Real
STANTON T. FRIEDMAN

Stanton T. Friedman has B.S. and M.S. degrees in physics from the University of Chicago, and 14 years of industrial experience as a nuclear physicist working on such far-out programs as the development of nuclear aircraft, fission and fusion rockets for space, and compact nuclear systems for space applications. His past employers include General Electric, General Motors, Westinghouse, and TRW. He has been interested in UFOs since 1958, and since 1970 has earned his living lecturing on the subject "Flying Saucers ARE Real" at more than 400 colleges and professional groups in 47 states and 4 provinces. He belongs to numerous professional groups for space scientists, UFOlogists, and speakers. He claims to be the only space scientist in North America known to be devoting full time to UFOs, and has appeared on hundreds of radio and TV shows across the continent. He lives with his wife and three children in Hayward, California.

In this sequence Mr. Friedman discusses the evidence that has forced him, as a scientist, *to conclude that "flying saucers" are indisputably real phenomena.*

I first became interested in UFOs while I was working as a nuclear physicist for General Electric on nuclear airplanes, back in 1958. I happened to be ordering some books by mail, and there was one for only a dollar: the *Report on Unidentified Flying Objects*, by Edward Ruppelt. In the early '50s, Ruppelt was head of Project Bluebook, an Air Force effort concerned with UFOs. The book stimulated me, so I read another fifteen or so books, and talked with my professional colleagues. It took a couple of years of looking at lots of data, some of it junk, before I was convinced, and I didn't do much about it, other than get newsletters from a couple of big organizations. Finally, I gave my first lecture about UFOs in somebody's living room in 1967.

Since that time, after getting out of living rooms, I've lectured at over 400 colleges in 47 states and four Canadian provinces. The title of my lectures is "Flying Saucers *ARE* Real." For the last

San Francisco Examiner

Stanton Friedman

eight years I've been the only space scientist in North America who is *known* to be devoting full time to flying saucers. In other words, rather than being a hobbyist, like someone who reads two books a year and figures he's an expert, I earn my living lecturing all across the country. That means I have to stay on top of the data, because I have to answer questions all the time.

I have some rather strong and definite views about flying saucers. *I'm convinced, after twenty years of study and investigation, that the evidence is overwhelming that planet Earth is being visited by intelligently controlled vehicles from off the Earth. In other words, SOME UFOs are somebody else's spacecraft. I'm further convinced that there's an enormous amount of public interest, coupled with a distressing amount of public ignorance.* My role is more like being the Ralph Nader of the UFO world, rather than the Billy Graham. My function is to put facts and data and solid information out on the table, rather than to make people believe what I say. I'm not out to make believers out of people, because I hate that word "believer." I am not a believer in flying saucers; I am a scientist who has studied data and has reached certain conclusions from that data.

A Cosmic Watergate

I've also become convinced that we're dealing with a sort of cosmic Watergate when it comes to flying saucers. That is not to say that everybody in the government knows everything and nobody's talking—not at all—but there is an enormous amount of data that's never seen the light of day. I say that for two reasons.

The first is that, in the course of lecturing all over the continent, I've talked to more than 80 former military people who have told me of excellent sightings that occurred while they were in the service. Their data didn't go to the old Project Bluebook, which was ostensibly the only government group concerned with UFOs, but instead typically went to the Aerospace Defense

Command, the National Security Agency, and other such organizations. The security lid was clamped down immediately. When I hear all these stories independently all across the country, I can hardly say that all the witnesses are lying.

Second, let's look dispassionately at the total situation. There was Project Bluebook, which in its heyday had a major, a sergeant, a couple of secretaries, and a bunch of filing cabinets. Compare that to the Aerospace Defense Command, whose role is monitoring the skies. Whether you're looking for a flying saucer or a Russian airplane, the technical problems are exactly the same. ADC has 35,000 employees, the most sophisticated network of computerized radar systems in the Western world, closed communication systems, aircraft ready with instruments to go up after UFOs, direct access to the President, and no need to talk to the press. It turns out that Bluebook had no computers, no radar, no aircraft, no instruments—it didn't even have a "need to know" for the Aerospace Defense Command data.

It seems to me that Bluebook, with its pitifully small staff and lack of real competence or interest, was an unwitting "cover" operation for a much more sophisticated effort elsewhere. I am not saying that they knew what was going on someplace else. I'm saying they were the Public Relations cover. They listened to people. They wrote them letters. Meanwhile, the guys with the data were the Aerospace Defense Command and whatever organization was at the end of the communications channel: the CIA, DIA, NRO, NSA, or any of the many other alphabet-soup places.

Nay-saying Newsmen and Fossilized Physicists

I'm also convinced there isn't a good anti-UFO argument around. There are a lot of people who haven't studied the data. There is a gross tendency for a noisy minority of nay-saying newsmen and fossilized physicists to make proclamations about UFOs: "You know it's a bunch of baloney"; "No scientist believes in UFOs";

"Only little old ladies in tennis shoes believe in UFOs"; "All sightings can be explained"; and other completely false statements.

It's really amazing how the will *not* to believe in flying saucers has spread about so much. This noisy small minority has managed to create a situation in which, although most people do actually accept UFO reality (see Table 21.1), the same people also believe that most other people don't believe in UFOs, and they act on the basis of that belief rather than on their own convictions. People ask me, "Don't you get a hard time at your lectures?" I say, "No, I've had only seven hecklers in over 350 talks; two of them were drunk, and the audience took care of the other five." Most people come to my lecture curious and agnostic. They hear lots of data, and after I point the finger of ridicule at the foolish and stupid arguments of the noisy negativists, they suddenly recognize that they're in good company with many other proponents of UFO reality. There certainly are loads of "closet UFOlogists," whom I'm encouraging to speak out.

Table 21.1. Responses to Gallup Poll question, "In your opinion, are UFOs real or just people's imagination?"

Respondents	Real	Imagination	No opinion
In 1966	46% (61%)[a]	29%	25%
In 1973	51 (65)	28	21
In 1978	57 (68)	27	16
Breakdown of 1978 data:			
Rs with grade-school education	40 (51)	38	22
Rs with high-school education	57 (68)	27	16
Rs with college education	66 (74)	23	11
Rs under age 30	70 (78)	20	10
Rs of ages 30–49	63 (73)	23	14
Rs of age 50 or over	40 (51)	38	22

[a] Numbers in parentheses are the percentage of all those who expressed an opinion.

Who Sees UFOs?

At the end of every lecture I ask, "How many people here believe that they have seen what I would consider to be a flying saucer?" Hands start going up very cautiously as people look around fearfully left and right. As soon as I see a hand, I start counting out loud as fast as I can count. Then the hands on the other side of the room go up much less cautiously. Each one had thought he was the only one who had seen one, and each one is relieved to find that 5 to 10 per cent typically believe they've seen a UFO. Then I ask, "How many of you reported what you saw to some military group?" About 95 to 100 per cent of the hands go down. If there's anybody left, I'll say, "Were you in the military at the time?" And if there are any people who were in the service when they had their sightings and reported it to a military group, I'll ask, "Do you want to tell us about it?" That's the way I get people to tell some very interesting stories.

The whole point is that the negativists have held sway for such a long time. Carl Sagan and I were classmates at the University of Chicago. Carl is on the Johnny Carson show every so often and says some utterly absurd things about flying saucers. Typical of the false pronouncements, Carl has said, "There are no interesting UFO sightings that are reliable, and there are no reliable UFO sightings that are interesting." That's a rather profound statement, totally contradicted by data that he has. In the largest official study of UFOs ever done—Project Bluebook Special Report #14, completed in 1955—scientists from Battelle Memorial Institute looked at thousands of UFO sightings. They found that the better the quality of the sighting, the greater the reliability, in other words, the more likely it was to be an unidentifiable flying object. That's exactly the opposite of what Dr. Sagan said; and 21.5 per cent of the sightings couldn't be explained, completely separate and distinct from those that were listed as "insufficient information" (see Table 21.2).

Table 21.2. Categorization of UFO sightings.[a]

Category	Number of sightings	Percentage of all sightings
Balloon	450	14.0
Astronomical object	817	25.5
Aircraft	642	20.1
Miscellaneous	257	8.0
Psychological	48	1.5
Insufficient information	298	9.3
Unknown	689	21.5
Total	3,201	100.0

[a] Data are from Project Bluebook Special Report No. 14.

Many of the negativists say, "The only reason the unknowns couldn't be identified was that there wasn't enough data." This statement, which I hear all the time, is totally false! There was a separate category; if there wasn't enough data, the sightings went into that "insufficient information" category.

Radar Sightings and Landings

People ask, "Why aren't they seen on radar?" They *are* seen on radar. If they go to the records, they find lots of radar sightings. So they ask, "Why don't they land?" Ted Phillips in Sedalia, Missouri, has collected reports of more than 1,100 landings of UFOs in which physical traces were found or changes were produced in the environment, and the data comes from 57 countries. Frankly, it's dull after the first 300 accounts; the same things keep happening all over the world. About a quarter of those reports involve creatures associated with the craft. There are many abduction cases on file, good ones, and more than a dozen involve investigations by professional people trying to ferret out what really happened. Therefore, we are not dealing only with lights in the sky. There are lots of poor sightings like that, but they're not the ones that concern any scientist who wants to get to the truth about flying saucers.

The basketball coach is quick to recognize that, although the average person is 5'9", there are some seven-footers. With flying saucers, most sightings can be identified, but let's forget them. I'm only interested in the others. That's where the paydirt is. You have to have the horse sense of a gold miner, who knows that, if there's an ounce of gold in a ton of ore, it's worth mining. He doesn't say, "It's 99.99 per cent junk; so I'm not going to mine it." He says, "There's an ounce of gold there; I'm gonna get rich." You have to do the same with flying saucer reports: mine the gold.

History of Project Bluebook

Project Bluebook was a study set up by the Air Force at Wright-Patterson Air Force Base, near Dayton, Ohio. It was under the aegis originally of the Air-Technical Intelligence Center, whose title was later changed to Aerospace Technical Intelligence Center, then to the Foreign Technology Division. Their job was to look at foreign technology. The original concern of the Air Force, quite legitimately, in 1947, was to find out who on this planet was making these things, because if they were going to attack us, we would get clobbered. Obviously, we couldn't keep up with them.

Apparently by 1952 or 1953 it was determined that the most interesting UFOs weren't from Earth, and that we didn't need to worry about being attacked, because they were alien. Now we wanted to find out about them so we could duplicate their technology in military systems.

Obviously, anybody who was able to build a fleet of flying saucers could rule the planet. They could literally fly circles around anything we had in the air. At that point Bluebook became an ineffectual public-relations outfit with a monthly visit from a guest astronomer. It was run by people who really didn't care, and didn't have much technical competence even if they had cared.

Meanwhile, the Aerospace Defense Command uses their radar systems, and they detect and monitor UFOs. They have airplanes with radar, and they photograph the radar screens. They get the good data that can be used by some (as yet unknown) group to try to figure out how these things work. A few measurements are worth an awful lot of eyewitness reports.

Bluebook went through a whole succession of project monitors. It was closed in 1969 by the Air Force, partly because of the University of Colorado recommendations at the completion of their study in early 1969. It's interesting to note that the Air Force did *not* say, when Bluebook was closed in December 1969, "There are no flying saucers." They made a very carefully worded statement, which has been extrapolated by the press and the nonbelievers to indicate something that the original statement didn't say at all. The USAF said that "no sighting investigated, reported, or evaluated by the United States Air Force gives any evidence of being a security threat to the United States." Let's analyze that. What does it mean? It means that if any one of those three functions (investigating, evaluating, or reporting) was done by the Navy, the Coast Guard, the CIA, or any other agencies, the statement could still be true, but essentially meaningless. In the second place, the penguins in Antarctica, for example, aren't a threat to the security of the United States; they're certainly real, though. The first statement doesn't tell us anything whatsoever about whether there are or are not flying saucers.

The second statement they made is, "There's no evidence of technology beyond our knowledge." I don't know what that's *supposed* to mean, but, as I point out in my lectures, trips to the stars aren't beyond our knowledge. We just haven't done them yet. If we want to spend the money, we know which way to go: staged fusion or fission propulsion systems. I've worked on them. Right-angle turns? Sure; not with a jet, but with a magneto-aerodynamic craft. So the second statement doesn't mean anything either.

The third statement indicates that the Air Force has no physical artifacts which indicate that flying saucers are somebody's spacecraft. I don't know what that means either, because, again, if the Navy or anybody else had the artifacts, it would still be a true statement, but meaningless.

So when you boil it all down, they haven't *said* anything. A lot of people *think* that they said, "There are no flying saucers." That is *not* what the Air Force has said; it didn't say it in 1969, and it doesn't say it now.

"They Violate the Laws of Physics; They Can't Be Real."

As a physicist, I really get irked when I hear someone say, "UFOs violate the laws of physics. What people claim to have observed is obviously impossible; so they can't have observed it." Those nay-sayers, in their infinite ignorance, are probably not aware of ways and means that might be used to perform some of the feats that are observed. It's very hard to build a pocket calculator with gears and wheels and cogs; it's very easy with microintegrated circuits. You can't get to the Moon very easily if you're walking or on a bicycle, but you can get there in a rocket.

Another objection, one you hear from the astronomers, is, "You can't get here from there." They do all of these stupid computations of trying to figure out how many civilizations there are in the galaxy. And they come up with an average distance between advanced civilizations in the galaxy. It's a totally absurd calculation; one might just as well throw a dart at a dart board. In the first place, they leave out colonization and migration, which are obviously very significant aspects of population distribution on planet Earth. Most Californians didn't have their ancestors living here 20 generations ago either, much less two million years ago. Second, averages don't mean anything. A six-foot man can drown in a pool whose average depth is three feet if he falls in at the deep end.

What we should really be concerned about is what's going on in our neighborhood. The stars aren't distributed uniformly, and one can assume planetary civilizations aren't either. But the biggest drawback about all these calculations, besides making silly assumptions, is that we only have data on one "civilization"—our own. It's like a one-point graph: you can draw a line in any direction. There is no way to accurately theorize on how many civilizations are out there.

Martian Microbes or Project Cyclops

We spent a billion dollars to land the Viking spacecraft on Mars, a very technologically sophisticated venture. We wanted to find out about Martian microbes, if we're lucky, but remember we had no data on Martian microbes. It's a little hard to design instrumentation to look for them. Why not just stay down here on the surface of the planet and look into the flying-saucer data? Those data should tell us something about *intelligent* beings coming here from somewhere. It seems like enormously more significant data than Martian microbes.

The radio astronomers write papers and go to conferences at the taxpayers' expense in order to search with radiotelescopes. Now they want society to spend huge amounts of money: ten billion was the last cost figure for Project Cyclops. However, I must admire the radiotelescope users union. I've belonged to two unions: Hotel, Restaurant, and Bartenders when I was working my way through college, and now I belong to AFTRA; so I can't knock unions. It's great for job security for radiotelescope astronomers to set up a radiotelescope. "Hi, out there!" Forty years later you get back an answer, "Oh, what can we do for ya?" You pass your job on to your kid, and he passes it on to his kid. But in terms of sense, as a taxpayer, I must strenuously object on several levels.

One is the assumption that radio is the ultimate means of communication. Any study of technological development during the last 50 or 100 years immediately tells any thinking person that technological progress almost invariably comes from doing things differently, in an unpredictable way. The future is not an extrapolation of the past. You have to change the way you do things. The laser is not just a better light bulb. A microintegrated circuit is not just a better vacuum tube, or even a better transistor: it requires new physics and new technology. So to assume that everybody out there is stuck with radio is absurd. If everybody's communicating with laser beams, for example, you obviously can't pick it up with a radiotelescope.

The second assumption is that somebody's got a beacon out there broadcasting in our direction to attract our attention, waiting for us to respond so we can join the galactic radio network. That's absurd. No advanced civilization is trying to attract the attention of a primitive one with radio; when you can travel there, you monitor.

The next assumption, which, believe it or not, some physics professors have stated, is that as soon as we latch on to this beacon, they'll send us a means for translating what they send to us—one of the those mathematical languages that these guys love playing games with—and then the aliens will transmit to us the wisdom of 10,000 books a year, all the secrets of the universe! That's absurd too. No civilization gives its technology to a primitive one, any more than I would give my ten-month-old daughter a gun to play with.

You do not hand technology to primitives whose major activity is tribal warfare, especially when you can check them out. I say "primitives" simply because we are not able to move into space yet. We will be, and that's one reason for their coming here.

"They Can't Be Extraterrestrials"

Some scientists make the stupid argument that there are *too many* visits to planet Earth for these things to be extraterrestrial. "If these flying saucers are really somebody's spacecraft, there are just too many of them." In an article in *The New Scientist*, and in several other places, unfortunately, a scientist says, "We can prove it. We'll assume there are a million civilizations sending out starships. There *must be* ten billion interesting places to visit, so therefore we've got to have 10,000 starships per civilization launched per year, and that's an awful lot." You'd think that was written in a comic strip; it's so ludicrous. Why not assume there are ten billion places *sending out* craft and only a *million* interesting places to go? That would give you only one in 10,000 coming here every year. We really don't have any data on those things.

But we do know something about airlines. I know of no airline that makes 10,000 times as many flights from a civilized place like San Francisco to an uncivilized place like the North Pole: it goes to *other* civilized places. You don't fly at random; you don't land out in the desert (you can't with a 747 anyway). So the whole notion that they can calculate these things and rule out flying saucers by such absurd means is just funny—except that they're looking for taxpayer money to support their games.

Are We a Typical Planet?

There's another level here, too. These guys assume that our solar system is typical of all solar systems. They further assume there's been no "colonization"; they assume wherever there's life, it has to have originated wherever it *is*, which is nonsense, because it leaves out migration. Our situation is not necessarily typical. The nearest star to our Sun is a little over four lightyears away. There are only 46 stars like the Sun within 55 lightyears, although there are about a thousand stars altogether in that volume of space.

We're isolated; but take a look at Zeta One and Zeta Two Reticuli, two stars in the constellation of Reticulum, easily observable only from the southern hemisphere. Rather than being isolated several lightyears apart, they are only three light*weeks* apart. They're a hundred times closer to each other than we are to our nearest neighbor. So from a planet on Zeta One Reticuli looking over toward Zeta Two, that star is a hundred times brighter than Venus is to us; it's visible all day long—which would be rather shocking—and with a reasonable-sized telescope you could directly observe planets around the other star. We have no hope of doing that from the surface of planet Earth. We're out in the boonies; we can't even see the smoke from the next guy's chimney. These guys have next-door neighbors! So you can imagine a Zeta Reticulan going to his Congress and saying, "We'd like to take a little interstellar jaunt."

Congress says, "Where will you go?"

"Oh, just over to the neighbors."

"How do you know there's anybody there?"

"Oh, we can see six planets, and on their television they're advertising stuff that we don't have. Besides, the trip's only going to take a few months. It's only three lightweeks—no big deal."

Zeta One and Zeta Two Reticuli are only 37 lightyears distant from us. Our galaxy contains roughly 150 billion stars. Certainly we don't just happen to have the place with the closest-together Sunlike pair of stars in the whole galaxy. There are probably places where the distance is only a few light*days*. That type of environment would change one's perspective enormously. On top of that, we've only had a technological civilization for a few hundred years. In a system that's five billion years old, that's not very long. You could reasonably expect that some civilizations started before we did on their technological kick. It's doubtful we would be able to predict what their technology will consist of— only that it will be different and more sophisticated than ours.

A Scientific Ego Problem

If one accepts, as a given, the notion that there is other life in the galaxy, what should we do, as taxpayers and scientists, in order to make contact? Looking at the total picture, the only data we have, and can use right away, are the data on UFOs: clear data that other intelligent beings are coming *here*.

Part of the problem is an ego problem. The researchers looking for life in outer space inherently feel that if anybody was coming here, they'd want to talk to them. A Harvard astronomer, one of the noisiest and nastiest of the sceptics, who wrote three anti-UFO books—Dr. Donald Menzel (now deceased)—once said, "If aliens were visiting Earth, they'd certainly wish to talk to the National Academy of Sciences," of which he and Dr. Condon, of the University of Colorado, were members. His attitude was, if they haven't asked for an appointment, they must not be coming here. It's inconceivable to the Menzelians that somebody might come here and not want to talk to them.

We all know of the "Take me to your leader" jokes. What's funny about them is that there isn't any leader to be *taken* to. There's nobody who speaks for planet Earth. Menzel also suggested that if they didn't talk to the National Academy, they'd land on the White House lawn. The President of the United States certainly does not speak for four billion Earthlings; he often doesn't even speak for our 220 million Americans.

The most virulently anti-UFO people are almost uniformly those who took great pride in their knowledge of all that's important, especially in the scientific realm. They seem to use this kind of reasoning: "If flying saucers were indeed intelligently controlled extraterrestrial vehicles, that would be very important. If it was very important, people like me and the *New York Times*, who keep up with the important things, would *know* about it. We *don't* know about it; so there is no basis for saying these things are important, and therefore anybody who thinks flying saucers are real must be crazy. We don't need to look at any data, because there's no data to be looked at; because if there was, we'd know about it, and we don't; so there isn't." I would find this kind of reasoning fascinating if I were a psychologist, which I'm not; but as a physicist I must stand up and proclaim that it's nonsense. An ego-kick is not the way to arrive at the truth.

Primitives Engaged in Tribal Warfare

How do we look to the aliens? From an alien viewpoint we're a primitive society whose major activity is tribal warfare. Listen to the six o'clock news for a week and you'll see. "Why don't they want to talk to us?" What in the world for? That raises the bigger question: What are they doing here? What's so fascinating about this unimportant place out in the boondocks? There is one thing, usually ignored by the exobiologists, that must be of prime significance to others in the neighborhood, about what is happening on planet Earth right now. For the first time, we've given an indication that we'll be able to move out from our own planet to bother people on other planets in our neighborhood.

You would naturally assume that every civilization is concerned about its own survival and security. Certainly, you would expect them to keep tabs on the local primitives. As long as a society only makes a mess of its own planet, it would only have to be checked out once in a while. However, as soon as it becomes the potential Genghis Khan of the neighborhood, as we are . . . Thirty years into the future we will be heading out to the stars. That would be of interest to any Galactic Federation, or to anybody else in the neighborhood.

They must find out enough about this place before we put up the "No Parking" signs. They may want to be able to negotiate at some future time. Until we become a space-faring civilization, there's no point in negotiating with us; but if they let the thirty years go by, they won't have as much data about us as they'd like to have before they do any negotiating.

For a million years we may have been a sort of pastoral civilization here: a nice place to visit, a good place for a honeymoon, great for hunting and fishing, you don't need a license. Yet, since the Second World War, we've loudly proclaimed—not by what we said, but by what we did—that we Earthlings (a) are nasty creatures, and (b) are going to the stars. The combination of nuclear weapons, rockets, and sophisticated electronics, like the radar signals now leaving the planet in great numbers, has alerted some sensible watchman going by. He broadcasts, "Whoops! Let's get the data now; bring your field trips here." And the GFIA—that's the Galactic Federation Intelligence Agency—gets on the stick.

It really is funny that, with all that's been written by these exobiologists, they have never once suggested that anything special is happening here. If we make a mess out of our planet, it probably wouldn't matter much to another planetary civilization. However, the fact that we will be able to make a mess out of *their* planet—and, judging by our past, we would once we got there— would be of concern, regardless of the form of their civilization.

We need a broader perspective. The kind of nonsense that gets into the *New York Times* and *Time* and on the "Tonight" show about this whole subject of extraterrestrial life is shameful. It's a game being played by the people who apparently have nothing better to do.

How Do the Aliens Look?

We cannot generalize from the data reported by the people who have *seen* them. We can't say that 1 per cent or 15 per cent or 99 per cent of the creatures out there are like us, humanoid. We can't say that at all. Certainly if you were a police officer sending a cop to quell a riot in an area where only Spanish was spoken, you'd send in a Spanish-speaking police officer. If you want to go up to the top of a very high mountain, you find a Sherpa who can stand the high altitudes. If you're going to send somebody to Earth, you find somebody who can handle the gravity, the atmosphere, somebody who wouldn't cause panic.

Of course, that leaves out something we should consider: maybe we're somebody's colony; maybe civilization here is the *result* of somebody's colonization or migration or crash-landing. This might, for that matter, be the Devil's Island of the local neighborhood, and they sent all the *bad* boys and girls here. Don't forget, Georgia and Australia got started by convicts.

What data do we have that the aliens apparently, in general, are humanoid in form? A composite drawing done by someone who looked at 200 different eyewitness reports of alien occupants of UFOs comes up with somebody who's under five feet tall, has a relatively large head, relatively skinny body, relatively long arms, and two eyes that are basically more to the side than ours. (Our eyes are very much more to the front than those of most animals, which means that our peripheral vision isn't as good as that of many animals.) In most instances they seem to be able to breathe our atmosphere. The sounds they make are quite foreign, except occasionally one of them seems able to speak English or French or Spanish with a strange accent. It's perfectly logical: they listen to radio and television, run it through the computer, and learn the local language, because somebody's got to tell the specimen—and in the abduction cases that's what we're dealing with—to stand up or sit down or lift your arm or whatever.

Getting a valid composite picture is like watching the vehicles that drive down the highway and taking a look at the people inside the vehicles. You get a broad spectrum of certain features in common, but you practically never see a three-armed individual driving down the highway. There is quite a range of different vehicles, and we don't think much of it. Some people say, "Well, how come there are so many different kinds of flying saucers?" There's General Motors, and Ford, and AMC out there too, I suppose. We can't assume they're all coming from the same place, for the same purpose, or with the same model of craft. Look at our spacecraft: there's an enormous variety.

What Propels the "Flying Saucers"?

We can only speculate on the saucers' propulsion systems. We have a two-part problem: how do you get here from somewhere a long distance away, say many lightyears (although there's no reason to say there aren't bases much closer); and once you're here, how do you flit around in the atmosphere with sharp turns and high speed? The environment is drastically different in outer space; you don't need to make a right-angle turn when you're on a trip of five lightyears; and you don't need to go at the speed of light when you're on the surface of a planet, because you're going to miss your target. There's no need to assume that the same craft are doing both; we might be dealing with Earth-excursion modules carried here aboard a "Starship Enterprise," if you will. It's similar to the nuclear-powered aircraft carrier *Enterprise*, which has many little airplanes on it which don't look at all like the mother ship, don't act like it, and aren't propelled in the same way.

There are a number of published papers which show that staged fission or fusion propulsion systems would be capable of making trips to nearby stars in less than a person's life span. I have worked on both fission and fusion nuclear-propulsion systems. The most powerful nuclear reactor ever tested in the Free World (at the time, at least) was the Phoebus 2-B nuclear-reactor rocket-propulsion system built by Los Alamos Scientific Laboratory. It operated at a power level of 44 hundred million watts. That's 4,400 megawatts, twice the output of the Grand Coulee Dam, and it was something under six feet in diameter, mind you. That's existing hardware, not imagination.

Fusion is even more exciting. I haven't talked about dumb old chemical rockets; they won't do the job, but we're not stuck with them. If you use the fusion process properly, you can kick particles out the back end of a rocket that have ten *million* times as much energy per particle as they can get in a chemical rocket. On a miles-per-gallon basis, fusion is definitely the way to go. Fusion we know something about: H-bombs are fusion devices; the Sun is a fusion factory.

If you want to spend 50 billion dollars in twenty years, we can get to the stars. We know how to do it.

However, I would certainly expect that the aliens use techniques about which we know nothing. Invariably, progress comes from doing things differently in an unpredictable fashion.

We can look at the quasars, quasistellar objects, where you get the energy output of a galaxy in something the size of a star. If we can ever figure the process, we could probably use it for propulsion systems. When we get into the subnuclear world, we can certainly expect that, just as when we moved from the atomic to the nuclear world, we went down in size and way up in energy per particle. When we go from the nuclear world to the subnuclear world, as they're doing at the big accelerators now, we'll go down in size again and up in energy again. When we figure out how to use that energy, we'll be able to make a propulsion system out of that, too.

A Long History of Terrible Calculations

It's interesting to look at past calculations by astronomers about space travel. There's a long history of terrible calculations. About the worst: a Dr. Campbell, President of the Royal Canadian Astronomical Society, in about 1941, published a paper full of equations in which he *showed* convincingly that if you wanted to get a man to the Moon and back, it would take a rocket whose initial launch weight was a million million tons. As it happens, we did it with a rocket that weighed 3,000 tons. He was off by a factor of 300 million; he was *astronomically* in error. So when astronomers say you can't get here from there, don't believe them. They make the wrong assumptions. It's not their bag.

So, to move between the stars, either fission or fusion will do the job. In the atmosphere, an entirely different situation obtains; the craft doesn't even need to carry its own power supply. If you have a magneto-aerodynamic craft, it could be like a golf cart: charge it up on the mother ship, run around for a while, and go back and recharge.

About ten years ago, an electromagnetic submarine was built in California. I believe you could build an analogous airborne system where you create an electrical conducting fluid, similar to the seawater around the submarine, by ionizing the air; when you've got ionized air as opposed to dumb old neutral air, you can get around all the problems of high-speed flight, because you can interact with that electrically conducting fluid, with electric and magnetic fields. You can reduce heating and drag; you can increase lift; you can eliminate sonic-boom production, change your radar profile, do a whole host of things, many of which would be classified, by the way, because that's the nose-cone reentry situation. When a nose cone with an H-bomb on board comes into the atmosphere, it creates this plasma of ionized air. You can try to get the Russians to think (by changing the properties of the plasma, which is what the radar sees) that the real one is phony, that the phony one is the real one, that sort of thing; so that gets you into a classified situation very quickly.

An Entirely Different Approach to Flight

Evidence from a number of UFO sightings certainly suggests we're dealing with ionized air and high magnetic fields: the change in color, the absence of noise (indicating nonmechanical sources of motion), the disappearance from radar screens while the object is still in view to the eye. When the frequency of the radar is changed, it's back on the radar scope.

All of these together suggest an entirely different approach to flight, again consistent with my philosophy that technological progress comes from doing things differently in an unpredictable way. You'd certainly expect that flying saucers capable of 10,000-mile-an-hour velocities and right-angle turns at high speed would not work the way that airplanes do. Airplanes can't do any of those things. We don't need thirtieth-century technology to get to the stars or flit around in the air. I'm not saying that for $10,000 I'll build you one of these in my basement. I worked on multi-hundred-million-dollar-a-year programs. Development doesn't come cheap. On nuclear airplanes we were spending a hundred million a year; for nuclear rockets, about the same amount. So this is not something for a professor and three graduate students. It's also not something they can design to conclude whether it is or isn't feasible. You've got to get access to a lot of classified data and a lot of technological work that's been done in industry, not at the universities.

Clandestine and Classified Research

One of the reasons I bill myself as the only space scientist in the world *known* to be devoting full time to flying saucers—I emphasize the *"known"*—is that I honestly believe there are a number of professional people working at a secret project, using the data input from the Aerospace Defense Command and others, trying their darnedest to build a flying saucer. It might not come easy.

You might have handed Thomas Edison one of today's pocket calculators forty years ago, and there's no way in the world he could have figured out how it worked. So if they have significantly advanced technology, it's going to take a lot of effort for us. Even if we figure out how it works, that doesn't mean we can duplicate it. It's like knowing about A-bombs; without the fissionable material, you can't build them, no matter how much you know about them. So it's a multiprong problem, and one that I don't expect the people working in secret would talk about in public. Because *he who is able to duplicate flying saucers in quantity is going to rule this planet.*

Antigravity and Electromagnetism

There are a number of people looking at gravity and a relationship between gravity and electric and magnetic fields. The term "antigravity" gets thrown about, usually in the wrong fashion. A rocket isn't an antigravity device. I have no doubt that we can use gravity; we do already when we go to the Moon; we use the Moon's gravitational field, and it saves us some payload room. The Pioneer spacecraft zipped around Jupiter and had its velocity tripled. One can conceive that Zeta One Reticulans take advantage of the gravitational field of Zeta Two to give them a free kick on the way by. Dwarf stars and black holes are especially great places for a free launch from a space traveler's viewpoint—if you don't get too close, you will get a lot of acceleration. However, I know of nobody making any real progress on a local antigravity system.

Certain materials, under special conditions, become superconducting. That is, they can conduct an enormous amount of electricity without any resistance to the flow of the current. A magnetic field cannot penetrate into a superconductor—diamagnetism. There is a connection between gravity and electromagnetism, because when light from a star goes past the sun, it's bent; Einstein predicted that. Everybody thought he was crazy, until the careful measurements of the changes in the apparent position of stars near the Sun during a total eclipse of the Sun, when the Moon was between the Sun and the Earth. One can hypothesize that perhaps under some special, peculiar, as-yet-unknown conditions, we can make things diagravitational just as superconductors are diamagnetic; so gravitational fields won't penetrate through them. You can think in terms of a shield against gravity; a little push goes a long way, if gravity isn't holding you back. At present, I haven't the faintest idea how to do that. However, I won't rule it out.

At first, superconductivity was a lab curiosity, but when you learn more about it, it turns out to be relatively common under the right circumstances, meaning very low temperatures. Handbooks have multipage lists of different superconducting compounds. So it may be the same with gravity; what is the gravitational field when the magnetic field is a million million times greater than normal? I don't know.

A Personal Observation

I have never seen what I would consider to be a flying saucer. I've spoken to thousands of people who have. I spent fourteen years in industry as a

nuclear physicist, chasing neutrons and gamma rays, radiation shield-
ing. I have never seen a neutron or a gamma ray; I think they're real too.
I've never even seen Australia, but it's there.

A Twice-Told Tale of Contact

I've heard a story twice—which I'll believe if I hear it a third
time—from two different former military people, one on the
East coast, one in the far West. Each individual was at a military
installation with lots of sophisticated radar and communications
systems, where they got a lock-on with radar on a UFO. Pretty
soon the antennas started getting all kinds of radio communication; the tapes were really whirling and spinning. Suddenly
security personnel come in and grab all the tapes and tell them to
say it never happened. I've now heard similar accounts of that
event happening independently at two different locations. The
implication is that there *has* been communication from the aliens
to us. It wouldn't surprise me.

Politics and UFOs

The big problem with flying saucers is a political one. Suppose
there was an announcement tomorrow by Walter Cronkite and
Henry Kissinger that flying saucers are real and they're neutral.
If you say they're nasty, you've got "War of the Worlds." If you
say they're neutral, what would happen? There would probably
be an immediate push toward a new view of ourselves as Earthlings, instead of Americans or Russians or Chinese, these nationalistic labels we all have. Obviously, from an alien viewpoint we
are all Earthlings, like it or not.

But there's the rub: I don't know of any government on this
planet that's desirous of having its people owe their allegiance to
the *planet* as a whole, as opposed to that nationalistic model.
Nationalism is the cement that holds the nation-bricks of the

planet together. We have a problem: How do you decide who speaks for planet Earth? How do you negotiate as a planet?

It took six months to decide the shape of the table for negotiating about Vietnam. How much longer would it take to figure out who speaks for the planet? Some will say, "Oh, we'll have an election." That'll be the day, when we give the Chinese four times as many votes as we have. Even if all the major powers were quite aware of flying saucers, quite aware that at some point five years hence the aliens were going to come down and say, "Okay, fellows, here's the way it is," you still couldn't just lay it out on the table, because the enormous amount of work that would need to be done would require trust, which is in short supply on this planet. To go from a nationalistic-oriented place to an Earthling-oriented place will not be easy. On the other hand I don't think there's any hope for the future of this planet unless we make that step. There's the great difficulty.

I don't expect them to come down and say "Take me to your leader." I don't expect them in the middle of a World Series game to circle around inside the stadium and say, "Here we are!"

They Know That We Know They're Here

After you've been tracked enough times on radar, shot at enough times, you know that the locals know you're here. I expect we're on a collision course before the end of the century, partly because of the space shuttle and space stations. There will soon be colonies of men in space. Astronomical instruments above the surface of the Earth will be able to see things we can't possibly see from down here.

We're limited, we're at the bottom of the manhole. As we begin moving into space, things will change. Max Planck, the great German physicist, said that new ideas come to be accepted, not because their opponents come to believe in them, but because their opponents die, and a new generation grows up that's accustomed to them. It's fascinating that all the polls show that

Richard Lowenberg

the older the individual, the less likely to believe in life in outer space, and the less likely to believe in flying saucers. *As the young Star Trek generation grows up, we'll have a whole new attitude. For the first time in history, we will have a whole generation alive during whose entire lifetime there has been a space program.*

Sequence 22

UFOs Informally Considered

JEFFREY MISHLOVE Interviews
CHARLES BOWEN & GORDON CREIGHTON

Jeffrey Mishlove is the first student at the University of California at Berkeley to create an interdisciplinary doctoral program in parapsychology. As part of his examination requirements, he authored The Roots of Consciousness, *an excellent survey of the history of psychic phenomena and current trends in scientific research. He has also produced over 300 radio programs on San Francisco Bay Area stations, approaching human consciousness from scientific, social, psychic, experiential, spiritual, and humorous perspectives.*

This selection is based on a conversation recorded in Britain in the summer of 1976 as Jeffrey talked with Charles Bowen, editor of Flying Saucer Review, *an international journal of UFO information. Joining the conversation was Gordon Creighton, a linguistic scholar and former British diplomat who translates the reports which are channeled to the magazine from various parts of the world.*

We're going to consider how UFOs may be affecting the minds and activities of people on this planet. I'm presuming we can talk about UFOs without defining them; the best guess is not that specific.

Some people claim they are interplanetary spaceships; some claim they are psychic phenomena; but there's no clue as to what they are really. A number of the things that we see resulting in UFO reports do give the impression that they could be physical craft coming from somewhere beyond the Earth's atmosphere, or inside the Earth's atmosphere. They also seem to create psychic impressions in human beings. This evidence comes from reports

Jeffrey Mishlove

from all around the world of encounters with strange occupants of these craft.

The pair of us [Bowen and Creighton] have been working together for nearly 12 years. We have processed over 10,000 reports of this kind.

Healings and Parapsychological Phenomena

Some people talk about religious messages and speak of UFO occupants as angels; others get messages that seem totally absurd, nonsensical, like a lot of modern theatre. Other kinds of contacts seem diabolical, monstrous, and painful. Injuries and death are known to occur.

It's difficult to say why this happens, and we've been particularly interested in the "nasty" accounts. There have also been cases of healings. We know of one case in France where a quite remarkable healing occurred. The subject was a doctor who had been wounded in the head while in the service in Algeria. He had also, just previous to this encounter, cut his leg while attempting to fell a tree. During his encounter, no occupants were seen, but he had a light shone on him. His paralysis disappeared, and also his leg healed. After his healing unusual things happened. There were reports of his levitating. He became somewhat of a religious figure, after having a conversion experience. One aspect that was unusual was the appearance of a triangular redness, like a rash, around his navel and also around the navel of his infant child, who was with him. It would reappear simultaneously from time to time on both him and the child, even though they were in different locations.

This is a good example of the psychic effects and the incidence of psychic phenomena that often appear: levitation, poltergeist effects in the house. Whether this is for good or evil, we don't know. The actual healing of the man was obviously a good thing, as far as he was concerned, but what was the purpose behind it? Goode and McCoy, a couple of police officers in the United States, also experienced a healing. One of them had received a bite on his hand from his pet alligator. A UFO came low over their car. His hand was on the door and a light shone on it. Within an hour the wound was completely healed.

The explanation may be as simple as the fact that there are "goodies" and "baddies" up there. There have been later developments in the "Dr. X" case which have caused him to wonder and to be gravely worried about what lies behind it all. And we must never forget the famous story of Dr. Faust, for example. Remember that Faust was promised everything by the Devil, and he had a wonderful time of it, but in the end the Devil came to collect. And I've sometimes wondered about the people being healed in this way. It might not be for their ultimate good. How do we know? We have to be very cautious in attributing any ultimate values to any of these things. In line with the advice of Aimé Michel, the French investigator, we must go on collecting evidence without trying to reach any final conclusion as yet.

Teleportation and Amnesia

We have, for example, many cases of teleportation reported, most of them occurring in South America. But I suspect this is something that is going on everywhere. We have a case reported June 9, 1976: A young man living outside Rio de Janeiro stepped out one evening to go buy a pack of cigarettes at a cafe, where he knew the owner. He had only the clothes on his back, and just enough money for the cigarettes. Apparently, the owner short-changed the young man, and so he hurried after him into the street. To his horror, he saw a UFO hovering over the young man in the street, with a beam of light shining down on him. He tried to rush forward and shout a warning. But suddenly, a force appeared which paralyzed him where he stood, nailed him to the ground, and stopped his ability to speak. He watched his friend disappear around the bend in the road with the light still shining on him. Nothing more was heard from the young man. He vanished. The police and army searched for him without success.

More than a month later, on July 14, a rather confused letter arrived. It said, in essence, "Dear Family, I'm in Rio Grande do Norte [about 2,000 kilometers from Rio, as the crow flies]. I'm here without enough money to get home." When he did get back, he was observed to be having periods of blackout and amnesia. His version of what had happened was that as he was walking along the street, he became aware of a light around him. He felt himself being drawn up into the air. He then blacked out. He had the sensation that his eyesight was failing. (Many people report this same phenomenon of failing eyesight.) He woke up several days later (he doesn't know how many) in a grove of coconut trees, where he was found and taken in by two peasants.

There have been many such cases as this that we have published in the past. Under controlled hypnosis, a very different story emerges from the one remembered by the conscious mind. I'm beginning to ask myself this question: Are we all having these kinds of experiences all the time? We may all be programmed and controlled by something without knowing it.

An Early Sighting in China

Creighton: I have had one or two visual sightings. I don't put much store in such matters, but it is true that I wouldn't be interested in the subject today if I hadn't had them. It was during World War II, in 1941, in China. We were far up the Yangtze River, because the Chinese government had retreated from the Japanese invaders. We had reached the point, not very far from Tibet, where the Chinese made their final stand. And it was there, walking along the south bank of the Yangtze, at about two in the afternoon. There were two other men with me; one was a British diplomat, who has just recently been British Consul General in San Francisco, by the way. We were all three dead sober; we couldn't even get liquor, because the Burma Road had just been closed.

All three of us saw a very strange sight. An object was traveling very fast from the northeast toward the southwest, toward Burma. It was to me a disc-like thing, a very large disc. It was going much faster than the fastest airplane. And we were used to seeing the fastest airplane at the time, the Japanese Zero fighter. What struck me very much was that on the top of it there was a vivid white light, rather bluish, such as you get in arc welding. The light flashed on rhythmically, absolutely regularly, so you could anticipate when it would flash.

Of course, I didn't say, "There goes a flying saucer." (The term hadn't yet been coined.) I was already interested in psychic matters, had been for a number of years. Also, I was deeply interested in Oriental religions. And I did think that I had seen something psychic. A few months later, I went to the States, as British Consul in New Orleans. There I read of similar sightings in the press, during the Allied invasion of Europe.

Dreams, Archetypes of the Unconscious, and Mass Hysteria

Bowen: There is a funny thing about human experience. We are conscious 12 to 16 hours a day, and we sleep eight hours a day. In this sleep we go through many cycles and states of consciousness, hypnagogic awareness, and dreaming. There are enormous numbers of people who report UFO imagery in their dreams, to the extent that Carl Jung, the great psychologist, wrote in his book *Flying Saucers* that UFOs may well be real, may even be physical, and that there is another dimension entirely.

Jung emphasized that this UFO image, this mandala image, seemed to appear frequently in the dreams of his patients. He thought that this was something profound, because it marked an archetypal change in the development of man. He was really filled with foreboding about what it might signify for the future. But I would like to add here something that is not generally known. We have had the opportunity to meet Jung's niece, Fräulein Leuzista, who lives in Basel. She is one of the people in Switzerland most interested in UFOs. She has a rather good collection of UFO photographs. She told me that in his later years he expressed that it was not just a matter of dream images, but that he believed there was quite a solid reality to it.

Creighton: Besides the physical sightings, I have had some extraordinary dreams. In one of them, I was in some hill country, looking over a valley. There below me were two UFOs with large quivering wings. They weren't like discs, as we think of them. They had huge metallic wings, and they were alive! I was filled with cosmic awe and wonder. There have been other dreams where I have apparently met entities from these machines; and some of them seemed very malevolent. In one dream, I was in the subway under Buenos Aires, with my wife and family. I've never been to Buenos Aires and I don't know if they even have a subway. There was a tremendous UFO flying around overhead, and I could see it, even though I was underground. And again, there was an enlargement of consciousness, a cosmic experience. So it may be that these sorts of dreams are very important.

Bowen: The UFO phenomenon is largely a nocturnal phenomenon. There is a considerable body of evidence showing that these things are reported over houses at night, where people are probably sleeping. And one wonders what, precisely, they are doing there. Is this the source of the dreams that Gordon Creighton and others have reported?

Jacques Vallee and Aimé Michel did some interesting surveys during the incredible amount of UFO sightings that occurred over France in the 1950s. People had been offering the theory that the sightings were the result of mass hysteria. Vallee pointed out that this explanation was unlikely, in view of the fact that most UFO sightings were not in the cities or amongst crowds, but were found out in the countryside. It seemed that the UFOs were deliberately following a pattern of appearing when people were not likely to see them.

Government Attitudes and the French Connection

We're intrigued by the discrepancies between individual experience of UFOs and what major institutions of government and business are willing to acknowledge. It seems that the work that the two of us are engaged in may be the bridge between individual experience and institutional recognition. We have an institution, a magazine with many thousands of subscribers, some of whom are government agencies.

However, the English and the Americans would rather not have it known that they even read our stuff. They don't like to consult us. It's all very much under cover in Britain. In France, it's quite a different thing, apparently. We had this incredible series of events in France in late 1973, and in neighboring Spain and Italy, where there were a large number of landings reported. This was preceded by an incident in northern Italy, near the airport at Turin. A young pilot, flying a small plane, was attempting to land. He was warned to keep away from the runway, because there was an object hovering about 400 feet above the far end of the runway. At the same time two airline pilots flying DC-9s also saw it and had to take evasive action. This startling event attracted the attention of a man with French broadcasting, Jean-Claude Bourret. He decided to do a series of radio programs. On the 21st of February 1974, a statement by the French

Minister of Defense, Robert Galley, admitted that the government was interested in these reports and that they were to be channeled through the police to M. Claude Poher, who is the head of such investigations in France. The whole thing was done on an official basis. There was no panic, nothing.

This spectacular series of programs lasted 39 days. It was disclosed by the French Minister of Defense that they had been seriously studying UFOs since 1954—secretly, of course. Jacques Vallee reported over 200 landings in that year, and over forty of them were sightings in which occupants were seen. The minister admitted that landings are now happening, that the phenomenon was somewhat disturbing, and that the gendarmerie had the responsibility of interviewing and collecting information when an incident does occur. He also admitted that 10 per cent of all the French sightings are on radar. Now, this is one thing that the Americans and the British have always tried to deny. We have seen accounts in reputable British papers, eight years ago and more, that Russian astronomers had admitted that huge craft had been sighted over Russia. Some of them were between 400 and 500 feet wide, disc or crescent-shaped, and many of those were also seen on radar.

Sequence 23
The UFO Phenomenon
JACQUES VALLEE

Dr. Jacques Vallee, a major figure in UFOlogy, is considered one of the field's most original thinkers. Dr. Vallee holds a Master's degree in astrophysics from a French university and a Ph.D. in computer science from Northwestern University. Before starting his own computer company, Infomedia, which sets up worldwide scientific activities through computer networks, he served as Manager of Information Systems at Stanford University. A Jules Verne Prize winner for his first science fiction novel in French, Dr. Vallee has published over forty articles in scientific and popular journals. He has written five books on UFOs, the most recent of which is titled The Invisible College, *named after a network of scientists privately studying UFOs. Dr. Vallee has pioneered research in the psychological, social, and psychic aspects of the UFO phenomenon. Jacques Vallee was also the model for the character 'Lacombe' in the film "Close Encounters of the Third Kind."*

In this sequence, Dr. Vallee discusses various approaches to interpreting the data on UFOs.

The first thing we need to do is to differentiate between UFOs and extraterrestrial intelligence. Among the scientists who study UFOs, there is of course a great variety of opinions, and among those who agree that there *is* a UFO phenomenon, there is also a variety of opinions about what that phenomenon really consists of: if you could prove there are UFOs, would you be proving that there is extraterrestrial intelligence? Or could they be something else?

My own interest in this has shifted from just looking at the phenomenon of UFOs to looking at the mythology they gener-

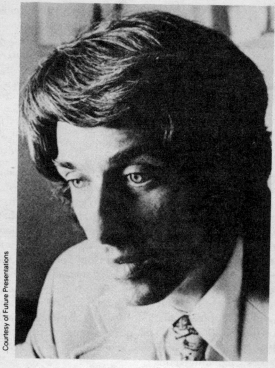

Jacques Vallee

ate. I'm not using the word "mythology" in a negative sense here. I'm not talking about a "myth" as something that doesn't exist. I'm talking about the ideas, the social image, behind something like the UFO problem, and its possible role in a very critical time in human technology.

In the Middle Ages, the Establishment was a religious establishment. It was the Church, and there was a counterculture that centered on observations of little people, devils, witchcraft, and so on. It's ironic that in this day and age—where the Establishment is Science: technology, computers, space stations, and that kind of thing—there is also a counterculture that is largely ignored by both physical and social scientists, which centers on all these strange stories and rumors about contact with strange beings that come out of flying saucers. I've been interested in both aspects of that subject for many years.

Physical Evidence

There are so many claims that physical evidence has been recovered. I want to look at this from the physical point of view and from the cultural-anthropology point of view. From a physical point of view, there are a number of physical parameters that are available regarding UFOs. Most of us scientists who have looked at the UFO phenomenon would agree that the majority of the sightings can be explained away—anywhere between 70 and 80 per cent of them—as balloons, meteors, airplanes seen under strange conditions, and so on. Then you have the residue of maybe 20 or 25 per cent of the thousands of reports that simply resist any attempt at explanation. Those are cases where you had just too many witnesses, too many independent reports, sometimes with radar confirmation and with traces, for the sighting to be explained in natural terms.

Of course, you look immediately for material traces, for physical evidence, and there you have the fact that UFOs can be detected by radar. You have photographs in a few rare cases—*reliable* photographs. You have traces on the ground in the form of imprints or burns or signs of very great pressure in a certain area. In one case, a French Air Force intelligence unit was on the scene very quickly after the sighting, and made an estimate of the total mass of the object, given the dimensions that were reported, and found an estimated mass of something like 20 tons: a very massive object of relatively small dimensions.

The question, then, is: Why don't we have any material residue? Well, in fact, some people have claimed that they did. When I visited Wright-Patterson Air Force Base, which was headquarters of Project Bluebook during the Air Force investigation, they had all kinds of strange things that people reported as UFO residue. Most of these, again, could be explained in perfectly natural terms, including strange things that had been thrown out of airplanes, rocket reentry material, and so on. There are, to my knowledge, only a couple of cases where some really strange material has turned up. One of those cases took place in Brazil, when two men had described an object coming down toward the beach. They observed the object as going through a very strange maneuver and then exploding. As it exploded, there was a shower of strange material that fell on the beach. They picked up some pieces, and this was later determined to be 100 per cent pure magnesium. Well, there is no such thing as 100 per cent pure magnesium. You'd always have some trace of oxidation and impurities. There has been a raging battle ever since about just how pure that magnesium sample was. It has been analyzed by the Air Force and reanalyzed at the University of Colorado, and there is now yet another attempt under way to analyze it. The only thing we know so far is that this material is not quite as pure as the standard for magnesium purity at the time, but it does not contain the *same* impurities that the standard did.

The Argument Against UFOs

There are hoaxes among UFO reports, of course, as John Billingham has pointed out. I've already said that the majority of UFOs could be explained, and the first thing a careful investigator will do is to check as thoroughly as he can for this possibility. Hoaxes fit a certain psychological pattern. You can detect that pattern. Most of the unexplainable UFO material comes from observers who were separated in space, and where, very often, there is some confirmation from outside, and this excludes the possibility of a hoax.

All the arguments that are used against the existence of UFOs are best summarized in a book called the Condon Report. In 1967, the University of Colorado received half a million dollars from the Air Force to do a study to decide, once and for all, whether or not we should investigate UFOs and whether or not the Air Force should continue its project. The conclusion was that science had nothing to learn from UFOs. This was very much based on the same arguments that you've heard here, that there's only a small proportion of sightings that are really intriguing, and that among those there is a large possibility of hoax. I was in Europe when the report was released, and the effect was absolutely devastating. Suddenly there was American science, with all its weight, saying there was no use wasting money on UFO research. What was the use of pursuing our own efforts?

That impression lasted a few years, until there was a sighting in 1973 in Torino [Turin] Airport. What happened was quite simple: a small aircraft was about to land, and it was practically told by the control-tower operators, "Don't land; there's a UFO on the runway." There was a large luminous object that was in the vicinity of the ground, and the control-tower operators were looking at it, and the pilot and other people looked at it for an appreciable time. Then it moved and passed over a military airfield next to Torino Airport, where it was detected on radar, and the commander of the airfield came out with binoculars and also got a good look at it. Then, as if this wasn't enough, this object followed an airliner that was going to Rome. It was seen by the crew and 80 passengers. Within a few hours, every TV and radio station and newspaper in Europe had a reporter on the spot. That really punctured the bubble of the Condon Report.

A lot of people started looking at that Report again, and found that the University of Colorado had taken those sightings that they could explain and explained them—which anyone could have done. But more than a quarter of the observations were still unexplained. These were put aside with a claim like, "If we had more data, we think those too could have been explained." But they did not in fact do that; so they did not go through a really scientific procedure.

Anthropology

At the end of all this, you're left with the same puzzlement you had when you began. It is possible to make a fresh start by looking at all this from an anthropological perspective. I have a friend at UCLA who is very interested in the UFO phenomenon in terms of the question: What happens to a society that is confronted with a technology that it does not understand? In projects like Project Cyclops, we may be faced with that same possibility. If there is another intelligence, does it have to be like us? Does it have to communicate in terms that we can understand? Does it have to be communicating by radio? What about other possibilities? My UCLA friend asked his students to look at every instance they could find of travel reports, reports from sailors, stories, myths, and so on, pointing at instances where a primitive society had been exposed to something like an aircraft, of which they had absolutely no concept. He wanted to know how it was reported by the observer, what the observer believed, and what was the social impact.

They found a primitive group in New Guinea where someone in the jungle saw an aircraft for the first time during World War II, ran to the village, and reported it to the wise men of the tribe. The wise men had *only one question:* "Did it have eyes?" He said no, as far as he could tell. They lost interest. In their culture, if something was to fly — that fast, that high, with so much noise — and it didn't have eyes, it couldn't exist. It was transparent to that culture. Anyway, what would it eat?

We may be faced with the same thing with UFOs: they represent something that runs contrary to all our cultural conditioning. All of us have read science fiction and thought about super-rockets; so we're conditioned to perceiving anything strange coming from the sky as a *spaceship.* Immediately we associate the idea of UFOs with something from outer space. We assume, if they exist, that must mean we're being visited by space people. It might be that we only *perceive* it as a form of technology. I'm very intrigued by what projects like Cyclops might do when faced with communications that were difficult to decipher, or *absurd* communications. What would you do with a thought that someone tried to express in your language, which related to a concept that was beyond your cultural level at the time? I'm more interested in the semantics of the communication represented by UFOs than in the technology itself.

The Psychic Component

My motivation as a scientist to look at UFOs all these years is the realization that we have an amazing problem of scientific methodology here. Science usually evolves in a way that is illustrated by the space-colony project; namely, that we extrapolate from what we already know. We say, "If *this* is true, and we can perform *this* experiment, then we can infer *this;* and then we will build a device that will detect X, Y, and Z." You proceed outward. Science usually works from the inside out. We haven't done that with UFOs; it has posed *itself* as an object of observation. It has chosen to be observed. It's not something we're prepared for.

The observations come in all kinds of shapes and forms, but usually center on a witness who is sincere and reliable, in his or her natural environment (his own backyard, very often), and who suddenly sees something that he's never seen before. That something *seems* to be a machine, sometimes is described as a spacecraft, and it *seems* to have some sort of life associated with it. At that point the evidence stops, because we now have a witness who is close to phenomena that he or she does not understand. We don't understand it either, because it appears to violate what we think of as the laws of physics; it seems to be able to appear and disappear on the spot, and it seems to be able to induce very strange psychic effects. By psychic, I don't necessarily mean telepathy or that sort of thing, but a coupling between the consciousness of the witness and the phenomenon out there.

When I mention the *psychic* aspect of UFOs, people sometimes think that I mean hallucinations. To them, something psychic is something that isn't really there, isn't physical. But think of technology that we already have and which is both physical *and* psychic: television, for instance. Television is a part of physical technology: you can touch it, you can look inside and see electronic hardware. But if you turn it on, you're going to start *seeing things* that will be part of your reality; it's going to do something to your perception of your environment; and you may have the Nobel Prize in physics, but you won't be able to tell whether those things are real or not!

That's the situation UFO witnesses are in: they are close to an object that they've never seen before. They experience psychological effects that are strange; ideas come into their minds that they may be interpreting as messages or revealed truth. There is a whole distortion of their time and space perception. Yet this kind of testimony is the only kind of close observation we have. Does that constitute scientific evidence? That's the question a few of us have to answer, as scientists, when we are concerned with the UFO phenomenon.

Personal Observations

I have seen something that would be classified as unidentified, but it wasn't very spectacular. What originally intrigued me wasn't so much the object itself as the reactions of my colleagues where I was working: my first job, at Paris Observatory, as an astronomer. We were tracking satellites; this was in the early days of the space program. Occasionally we were tracking things that should not have been there.

One night we got eleven observation points on one of those things. We wanted to feed the data into the computer to obtain an orbit and see if we could catch it again, and the man in charge of the project erased the tape. He didn't do that as part of some big cover-up, or because he was instructed to do that by some sinister organization, but simply because he was afraid of ridicule. I asked why we didn't send it to the Smithsonian, since the Smithsonian Observatory at that time was the international center for satellite observation, and he said, "No, we can't send it to the Americans, because the Americans would laugh at us."

You always hear that if there were such things as UFOs, astronomers would see them; therefore, the argument goes, since astronomers never report UFOs, there are no UFOs. Here was a whole team of astronomers, and we were seeing those things, and we were destroying the evidence. It occurred to me that if Paris Observatory was destroying that kind of thing, how many other observatories were doing the same thing? So I started a little private network of underground contacts with my colleagues, and that network we have jokingly named the Invisible College. The Invisible College was the name of the secret society of scientists who were doing science in the days when it was forbidden to do science—during the Middle Ages. And it's ironic that in this day and age there are still scientists who have to work underground on things like UFOs.

There are important changes that take place as more and more sightings are made all over the world. I first became interested in the sightings in France. Then I saw the files of the U.S. Air Force, and spent four years going through those files, and found that the patterns were absolutely identical in America and in Europe.

At that point, you can put aside the question, "Is the problem real? Is there a real object out there?" Mythology doesn't work this way. You can find twenty scholars who will prove to you that Jesus Christ never existed, and you can find twenty scholars who will prove to you that he did; it doesn't make one bit of difference except to those scholars. The phenomenon is here because Christianity is real to enough people. Similarly, to the extent that there are hundreds of thousands, or millions, of people who believe in UFOs, the UFOs are real.

What Are UFOs?

If the UFOs are really there, as described by witnesses, then they are probably not spacecraft. They seem to be a violation of the spacetime continuum, of what we think we know about physical reality. Everything in science is based on a mental model of reality; our model comes from the brain, and we're only beginning to understand a little bit about how that process works. It turns out that reality is a construct; reality is something that we're constructing as we go.

Our view of the physical universe is conditioned by what we see in the first few days or weeks after birth; after that initial period the brain has frozen its mode of perception of reality, and that is the only reality you have agreed to perceive from then on. Such experiments have been done with cats: if the newborn cat looks at the world through goggles with horizontal slits, he will be able to recognize horizontal surfaces; for example, the cat will jump on a table, but will hit the legs of the table, because it has no conception of vertical lines. Similarly, if the slits were vertical, the cat would be able to walk around the legs of that table; but it would never occur to that cat that it could jump onto the table. We are wearing goggles like that. It's important for people to realize that even scientists are wearing goggles like that.

While it is true that we're trying to become more and more clever, and to devise new experiments, and to extend our senses, the basic fact is that we're wearing goggles called culture, education, language ... We're trying to extend our perceptions by devising other languages, like mathematics, to talk about things that are not rational in common sense or describable in normal English, but we still have a long way to go. I think that's the challenge of the UFO, and the search for extraterrestrial intelligence: that it will force us to constantly revise our view of reality.

Geoff Chandler

Phase Five
Space Age Myths
The Future is Now

J. Allen Hynek

Prolog
Another Reality

J. ALLEN HYNEK

Regardless of what else you can say about the thousands of reports of UFO encounters and the plethora of paradoxes associated with them, it is clear that there is some form of intelligence associated with them. What, then, is the source of this intelligence? Is it really extraterrestrial? Is it metaterrestrial, from somewhere here on Earth? Is it coming from another reality, another dimension?

Of course, the idea of "other" or "higher" intelligence is by no means a new concept. All the founders of the great religions, especially the Eastern religions, have maintained that the physical world we see around us is not the sum total of our environment. Jesus said, "In my Father's house are many mansions." The Bible is full of accounts of angels. We may not literally believe these accounts, even though we go to church every Sunday. And yet the prophets, the philosophers, and the great religious teachers have all indicated there is more to life than that which meets the eye.

Space Age Myths — *In C.G. Jung's* Flying Saucers: A Modern Myth of Things Seen in the Skies, *the great psychologist sees these airborne objects as images of redemption. He felt there was some connection with "round things in the sky" depicted in Renaissance and seventeenth-century art. Apparently, the sixteenth and seventeenth centuries were a time of vigorous debate about the "shape" of angels, many contending that angels were not people with wings, but "light beings" nearly spherical in form.*

Dr. James Hillman, a contemporary psychologist and author who spent the last 20 years at the Jung Institute in Switzerland, recently commented on the archetypal parallels in our present-day art form, the Hollywood movie. Already millions have seen the awesome image of the gigantic mother-ship that appears at the climax of "Close Encounters of the Third Kind." As gaping scientists mutter "Jesus!" and "Oh, my God!" it descends from above; it is round; it is light; it is complex; and it speaks in the universal language of music. It offers redemption, especially to the everyman hero Roy Neary, who literally ascends, leaving behind all trappings of the material world: family, home, wife. He looks only ahead to the adventurous promise of unknown worlds beyond.

We are here entering a less-tangible phase in our exploration of the everlasting frontier of space—the realm of myth, of philosophy, of strong feelings and emotions that border on the religious. If we wanted to hypothesize, we might propose that what many people saw and reported as angels were actually UFOs. However, one could just as well propose that what some people see and report as UFOs are nothing more than angels, conveniently ignored by secular science for the last few generations.

In his latest book, The Invisible College, *Jacques Vallee reports fascinating similarities in phenomena associated with appearances of the "Blessed Virgin Mary" at Lourdes in France (1858), Fatima in Portugal (1917), and Guadalupe in Mexico (1531). He notes predictable patterns in these "miracles" that parallel his research in UFO phenomena. The Roman Catholic Church doesn't have a monopoly on miracles, it seems, for there is also the appearance of the Angel Moroni to Joseph Smith. Smith allegedly was directed to find some golden tablets, which he translated into the* Book of Mormon. *Most of us know the story of how those who believed in the revelations were forced into leaving their homes in the Midwest, finally settling in Utah in the 1800s. Today, no longer ostracized, Mormons represent a powerful economic and political force in our society, an example of the "today's crazies are tomorrow's establishment" syndrome.*

On the subject of "unidentified flying angels," we should probably check out an account in the amazing 2,000-plus pages of The URANTIA Book, *first published in 1955. The description on page 438 of the interplanetary departure of a "transport seraphim" contains the familiar characteristics of a common sighting: "Human beings have sometimes been permitted to observe . . . the seraphim grow pointed at both extremities and become enshrouded in a queer light of amber hue" which metamorphoses into "an almost transparent, vibrating, torpedo-shaped outline of glistening luminosity." These "living spaceships," it seems, can reach velocities approaching three times the speed of light! (Unfortunately, it doesn't reveal exactly how that's done.)*

Actually, The URANTIA Book *has practically nothing to do with UFOs, but it does have an enormous amount of information about life elsewhere in the universe. Previous visits to our world from extraterrestrial sources are related in great detail, including the "mission" that originally "implanted" life here. Unlike the* Book of Mormon, *there seems to be no connection with any living person who will take credit for having anything to do with authorship. It purports to be "authored" by a cosmic committee which was commissioned to reveal this information at this particular time by our galactic headquarters. These invisible beings call our planet "Urantia"; and for a bunch of aliens, they certainly seem capable of communicating in elegant, precise English.*

The URANTIA Book *is an example of a cultural artifact that anticipated many of the themes that emerged in popular culture during the late sixties and early seventies. The fascination with gaining higher consciousness shows no sign of waning; rather, the trend continues to proliferate in new techniques, workshops, and seminars, all loosely called the human potential movement. Utopian dreams of a better world for all to inhabit still provide inspiration for replacing destructive patterns with positive alternatives, where cooperation is valued as much as competition.*

We still long to live in a world without violent war, a world where resources are not wasted in pursuit of purposeless practices. We still long for a healing of the wound in the mind/body of the human psyche, where religion and science can cohere in a unified whole. Most of all, we still long to know what lies beyond the portal of death. We long for immortality.

The answers to many of these enigmas may be as much available inside our own beings are they are "out there" in the universe. Perhaps we are just not ready to hear them. Perhaps the massive consciousness changes of the past two decades are only the beginning of a necessary psychological preparation for this next great adventure of humankind, the journey into space.

The selections in this final phase range far and wide across the limitless plains of personal speculation. We have included them because they represent yet another dimension of the search for meaning and values in contemporary thinking. These personal opinions are as important as you make them, no more important than your own.

L.G.

Sequence 24

Neuropolitics:
The Meaning of
Space Migration

TIMOTHY LEARY

Timothy J. Leary, Ph.D., former Professor of Psychology at Harvard, and former resident of various foreign countries and U.S. federal prisons, is easily one of the most controversial figures on the American scene today. Despite criticisms leveled against him, his SMI²LE program (Space Migration, Intelligence Increase, and Life Extension) has gained the respect and often the advocacy of almost all who have examined it carefully. He has authored many books, the most recent being Neuropolitics, Exobiology, *and* What Does WoMan Want?

In this sequence, Dr. Leary discusses space migration as a further unfolding of the human spiritual adventure.

I'm going to present a simple notion which I find extremely amusing. Don't take it seriously; yet, if you think about it, it may change all your political views—at least, for those of you who are flexible enough to allow any change of the slightest nature in your political views. The theory is this: on this particular planet, the evolution of intelligence and the evolution of the human race have moved on a direct trajectory from east to west. That's the time track we're on, the genetic runway. Things started in the East: Babylon, Egypt, then Athens, Rome, the Renaissance, the Spanish and British Empires; and then moved over here. This is the basic generalization, the basic compass orientation point of neuropolitics or geopolitics. Wherever you are, ecological zones east of you are lower in I.Q. or intelligence, and more reactionary in politics. In other words, the farther east you go, the farther

Courtesy of Space Age Review

Timothy Leary speaking at Space Day.

you go back into the past and down in evolution. And by the same token, if you go west, you're going into the future from where you are, toward more liberty, more dynamic interchange, and more possibility of creating new realities.

West to east is a time dimension: Washington is still being run the way it was years ago, when it took two weeks by horseback to go from Bangor, Maine, to Washington. They're still in that era of representative government and caucuses. When you leave Washington, which is 200 years old in its thinking, and go to London ... Now, come on, what's happening in London? Nothing has happened in London in 300 years. When you go to Paris, you're going back to the time of King Louis XIV. Every

Frenchman is tweaking his mustache and opening his wine with a flourish, acting out the fantasy of the Golden King. Now, when you go from Paris to Rome, you're really going back a thousand years. Athens! What, right now, is happening? Or what is going to happen in Athens? Nothing, in the sense of new dimensions for the human future. The farther east you go, the more worship of tradition, the more respect for authority, the less freedom, the less technological and intellectual advance.

I think the most intelligent people alive on the planet today are on the west coast of the United States. It's the last frontier of Earth. There's no question of that. You're simply freer in California; there's more experimentation, more openness, more tolerance of differences, more future orientation in the West than there is in any other place in the world.

You Can't Argue with Chimpanzees

Now, you wouldn't argue with a chimpanzee, would you? Then you can't argue with an Irish Catholic or an Irish Protestant in Belfast; you simply can't. They're 400 years old. The Irish Catholic parents are teaching their kids to kill Protestants, and vice versa. You can't treat those people as members of your species. They're educated chimpanzees, or something.

Now, when you get to Cyprus, the Turks' war against the Greeks is like the conflict between the foxes and the wolves. You can't interfere with it. I don't think we should go back east and exploit these simple creatures and kill them for their pelts. I'm ecologically in favor of sending veterinary medicine to England, Ireland, Africa, and the Middle East, and inviting the smart ones to come over here. But, neurogenetically, you have to realize that the human species is not one. We're exploding in a genetic way into hundreds of new species. Genetics is the key to future philosophy. We're learning a great deal about genetic concepts which have to do with migration, the neurology of mutation, swarming, social castes, gene-pools, neoteny, and terminal adulthood. Now, if I thought there were more intelligent people any place else, I'd be there. The reason I'm in California is because I think this is the place where it's happening. I invite anyone to send me an offer about where they think the *real* frontier and growing edge of the human species is. I'll pack my bag, and Susan and I'll head there tomorrow.

The beautiful thing about space migration and the fabrication of miniworlds is that it's not compulsory. Those that self-select, and want to go, can go. Those that want to go back underwater can do it. *We're* not going to select who goes into space. It's going to be self-selection. At least, that's what the group I'm associated with is working for: self-selection, not civil service, government, bureaucratic selection.

The North American Experiment

I want to repeat something I've said before: the North American experiment is the greatest success in evolutionary history. In 1493, Columbus came back to Spain and said, "Hey, we can *live* over there," just as the astronauts came back and said, "Listen, the Moon and high space are settleable and can be colonized." Now, when the word came back that there was a new continent, a New World, a lot of people said, "Well, how dare you go over there? You're copping out. We should stay back here in Europe and solve the problems. We've got to build the dome of the Vatican; we've got to settle the wars of the Catholics and the Protestants; and any decent Spaniard would want to stay and fight with the Armada in England. You guys are bugging out by going over to the New World."

There were others who said, "Life as we know it now can't exist over there. It's a primitive and terrible place." The migration to North America was self-selective. Each gene-pool sends its seed west. It's always been self-selective. William Penn and his group of dissidents wanted to get out of England, because they couldn't create Quaker reality there. Lord Calvert, the Catholic, led a group over in their spaceships because they were being persecuted by the Church of England. The Pilgrim mothers and fathers fled from England to Holland, mortgaged their possessions, and built the Mayflower, because they wanted a place where they could be free to live out the kooky, freaky reality that they collectively shared.

The North American experiment has always been an experiment self-selected for those that wanted freedom. I'd say that 99.9 per cent of those that come to North America were self-selected. A Jew in a ghetto in Moscow got the message: "Hey! People are freer over there. The Czar won't draft your kids." If you were a starving peasant in Ireland, there was a chance to find land over there. The signal of the New World, the North American continent, was freedom! Those who came over here, our foremothers and fathers, responded to that call because they were genetically designed to be freedom pioneers. And there's no question that the North American experiment is a success. Americans are a freer species than Europeans. And Californians are a new species evolving away from Americans.

H.O.M.E.s in Space

The point is, in space migration, space colonization, any group of people can get together and build a new world cheaper than they could buy individual houses down here. Within 25 years there'll be a H.O.M.E. (High Orbital Mini-Earth) for bisexual vegetarians. There will be a H.O.M.E. for Anita Bryant followers. And there'll be another one for National Rifle Association members; there they can shoot each other up and nobody will care. The main issue in the bisexual vegetarian home will be whether they want a socialist or a free-enterprise state; so they'll divide and build new H.O.M.E.s. There'll be two bisexual vegetarian mini-worlds, one socialist and one free-enterprise.

Human options, the chance to experiment with new social styles, the chance to fabricate *your* vision of a social reality, can be exercised, an authentic vision that you searched for within and found. You have every right, it's your duty, your responsibility, to try to externalize that vision with those who share your vision. And the only way you can do that is in a High Orbital Mini-Earth, because there's going to be a poverty of vision down here as we get more populated and energy decreases.

It will take 15 years to build these new worlds. Fifteen years! I look back at the last 15 years and marvel! I've been through 27 reincarnations and metamorphoses in the last 15 years. It's difficult to imagine today the changes we'll experience in the next 15.

We're going to change faster than we did in the last 15 years, because of what we learned from the great neurological revolution-revelation of the 1960s. We're basically change agents. Permanent neoteny. Enduring adolescence. We won't settle for any adult structure. The only reason we pause in any hive-structure is to get food and fuel to make the next change, or for rest and recreation preparatory for the next movement, the next dramatic high-energy, fast-accelerating precision trip that lies ahead.

I think that within the next 15 years we're going to see many changes in our understanding of human nature. We're going to get so much smarter; we're going to get much more control over our nervous system; we're going to get control over genetic engineering so we will extend the lifespan. There are so many alternatives and possibilities and options developing within the next 15 years that to be specific would be encyclopedic.

You cannot understand the American Revolution of 200 years ago until the next migration begins. Only now can we precisely understand the genetic significance of the American Revolution in providing an ecological niche for the freedom-mobility-intelligence genes of Old World gene-pools.

The Problem with Science

In the past, scientists and engineers—impersonal, abstract, square, crew-cut, and slide rule—have been unable to communicate with poets, psychologists, and the spiritual, emotional people on the other side. Our smartest logical, precise minds were becoming less and less human, and the most human of us turned away from intelligence and systematic thinking.

Gerard O'Neill was rightly concerned with that question. We've all been concerned with that horrid split between hardware and software. C.P. Snow wrote about the Two Cultures, and Robert Pirsig in his magnificent *Zen and the Art of Motorcycle Maintenance* talks about the Romantic versus the Classic perspective. I've been very concerned with this left-brain/right-brain split, and it was my hunch, going back to that Gallup poll 1969, that there was a new generation of physicists and chemists and scientists emerging who were *heads*. (In 1969, polls revealed that 64 per cent of M.I.T. and Caltech students smoked grass.)

So as soon as I got out of prison, I went down to Los Alamos on an anthropological mission to check this out. I performed several dangerous drug experiments there. I got several physicists drunk. It turns out they're closet humanists.

Ecological Puritanism

Now, there are some among us, the ecological puritans who say, "Limit growth!" Well, you can't limit growth. One message we've learned from the DNA code is that population growth is out of our control. Naderites give human beings much too much credit, and also much too much blame. It's not within the power of a domesticated primate race like ours to really change an evolutionary process which is two and a half billion years old, and is expanding throughout the galaxy. It's all this moralism. We're really not that bad; we're really not that good. We're just robot evolutionary agents, programmed to transport sperm-egg cargoes higher and faster and farther.

There are many reasons why you can't limit growth. One is political. The world is now divided into "haves" and "have-nots," both in our country and throughout the world. You're not going to tell the have-nots, "Sorry, brother, but we're not going

to have any more of that industrialization." Every have-not
person in Asia and Africa and our own country and South
America has a right to demand two cars and a color television in
their garages, and skateboards, and snow blowers, because who
are we to tell them they can't have it?

There's a Jimmy Cliff song, "The Harder They Come, The
Harder They Fall," where the Black Man says, "I'm going to get
mine." Trying to stop that ambition has never worked before,
and it's not going to work now. Population is increasing. Within
10 or 15 or 20 years, our volatile situation could explode. Some
dictator, in some small country, totally enraged and flipped out
because there's no hope left, will press a button, and who'd
blame him? Space migration is the escape valve.

The economic situation is this: You're never going to have full
employment in this country. Both parties realized that in the last
Presidential campaign. Everyone ducked the issue. Nobody's
come up with any plan for full employment, and for getting a
growth economy without inflation. The reason is clear (Kennedy
saw it): you're never going to have a growth economy in this
country without a war. Kennedy realized, in the early '60s, that
he couldn't make his promises to the American people stick to
get the country going again unless he moved us up. He said,
"We're going to go to the Moon. We're going to go there in a
decade."

More of the Same?

Space migration is not another cycle of exploration/exploitation.
It's the only way in which a multiplicity of options can be assured
to our species, the only new ecological niche in which the next
series of experiments in human genetics can occur. I go back to
that old theme, "When you mutate, you've got to migrate."
When you've got new ideas, you can't hang around the old hive;
you've got to keep moving out.

The real political issues are not Reds against Whites, not East
against West. The real political issue of the next 15 years is: who

controls space? And you better believe that the Russians are planning space labs. When they send up their crews, I don't think the Russians are going to be doing it to expand the plurality of human options. I don't think the Russian cosmonaut crews, up there, are going to be trying to encourage experiments in lifestyle, or in increasing intelligence.

In our own government, there's this strange notion that NASA and the bureaucrats in Washington control space, or that the military controls space. I'd like to stimulate alertness to the real political scandal of our times. You can worry about multinational corporations, and oil companies and their profits, but that's knee-jerk liberalism. *They're going to steal the whole solar system from us,* unless we're alert.

I'm already getting in trouble with NASA. A lot of people in NASA don't want me going around talking to people about H.O.M.E.s. They don't want you to get interested. They're afraid that you'll put too much pressure on, you'll want it too soon; you'll demand results, and you'll get disappointed if they don't deliver. Still, I don't want to eliminate NASA. Within NASA, there are young heads, space freaks, people who sincerely and deeply want to get this planet moving, and want to provide human beings the increased freedom of space migration. There are plenty of good people in NASA. But democracy and freedom always require total vigilance.

The Key to Space Migration

The key to space migration is this: it must be self-selected. Ethology, sociobiology, behavioral genetics has much to teach us about the demographics of population movements. The advanced technological (i.e., the most intelligent) human gene-pools are now engaged in swarming. Pollution, crowding, and restlessness are the characteristic stimuli for migration.

Studies of social insects, of migrating herd animals, and of human migrations all seem to show that some migrate and some stay put. Some marine creatures climbed out onto the shoreline

The Bettman Archive, Inc.

and some remained underwater. Some paleolithic hunter-gatherers left Africa and Southeast Asia, and moved up to the more demanding and challenging temperate zones; and some remained behind. Some restless gene-carriers left the ghettos of Warsaw and the bogsides of Ireland and came to the New World. Most remained in the Old World where, even to this day, they continue their ancient territorial-totem conflicts.

Self-selection must be the key to space migration. Some are impelled, compelled, obsessed, driven, fired, wired, and sired to move into space. Others are bone-deeply, cell-essence horrified by the idea. We must listen to and respect these strong reactions, both for and against space.

Here is a simple ethological experiment which anyone can perform. Ask the next hundred people you meet if they would like to migrate to and inhabit large High Orbital Mini-Earths. Once they realize that the migration is actually happening (reminded, for example, that the Russians are now manning a permanent station), at least half of those polled will embrace the idea. About 10 per cent will be immediately enthusiastic. The younger the sample, of course, the higher the percentage of aspirants for migration.

Such responses are probably genetic. The idea-signal either does or does not trigger off an "Ah, yes" reaction. We can be sure that the same process has been occurring for centuries. When the idea-signal Migration-to-America was flashed in the sixteenth century, some nervous systems reflexively flashed "Let's go": the William Penns, the Lord Calverts, the Pilgrim mothers and fathers.

Selection of space expeditions should be based upon such genetic sensibilities. Those who are not fired-wired to go should be assured that migration benefits those who stay put in at least two ways:

(1) Migration is an escape valve that rids the home-hive of the restless outcastes; and

(2) Migration allows for new experiments, technological, political, and social, in a new ecological niche far away from the home hive. The stay-puts then benefit from the fallout of the frontier mutational experiments. In this context, America can be seen as an enormous selective-breeding genetic experiment performed by Old World gene-pools. Everyone benefits if the restless-mobile outcastes are allowed to move on.

I find it useful to conclude discussions about space migration with an appeal to women. The hardware-male-macho-militarist phase of space exploration is over. The swashbuckling argonaut-astronaut caste always forms the first wave. Once the mysterious frontier is demonstrated to be safe and inhabitable, then the hive-bureaucrats, religious and economic, move in to exploit. But nothing happens until the women are activated.

Migration involves the movement of gene-pools, families, kiths, kins, clans, totem-collectives. North America had been discovered and explored by scores of male parties in the six centuries before Columbus. But nothing happened until the wives and husbands, daughters and sons, aunts and uncles got involved. Space migration will explode when women realize that the best place to have children, raise children, make love, fabricate new cultures is in a High Orbital Mini-Earth of one's own design.

Sequence 25

Cryonics and Future Perspectives

ROBERT ANTON WILSON AND J.B. WHITE

Robert Anton Wilson is the author of more than nine fiction and nonfiction works, including the Illuminatus *trilogy, which he coauthored with Robert Shea, and* Cosmic Trigger. *He is currently working on a three-volume comedy about quantum theory,* Schrödinger's Cat, *which will be published by Pocket Books.*

J. B. White is President of the Bay Area Cryonics Society, a membership foundation, and a Director of Trans Time, Inc., a commercial firm. These organizations promote and implement the preservation at cryogenic temperatures of the bodies of persons who have died of currently irreversible causes, with the hope that the remaining biological and psychological information may enable future science to restore them to indefinitely prolonged life, health, and youth.

In this sequence, Mr. Wilson and Mr. White explore the spiritual implications of life extension and immortality for our society.

Hope is created out of belief in yourself, which gradually extends to belief in others and belief that there's a sound, sane center to the universe, in spite of appearances. First of all, you've got to make a commitment to the future, a commitment to challenge, a commitment to risk, and be willing to pay the price of taking risks and going far out. And then you find that there are grounds for hope, because there are a lot of other people who are bold, visionary, turned on, and taking risks too. Humanity does not consist only of domesticated drones doing their jobs in the hive. Evolution is made by mutants who have doubt, hope, and charity—these three, and the greatest of these is doubt.

The Cryonics Society

The Prospect of Immortality, by physics professor Robert Ettinger, postulates that people living and dying now have a real, though presently unmeasurable, chance of indefinite life extension. He reasoned that current freezing techniques might preserve the

Courtesy of Future Presentations

Robert Anton Wilson

essential biological and psychological information upon which individual life and personality are based. This is true even with imperfect freezing methods that are applied only to persons who are already medically and legally dead. An advanced future medical science might use the preserved information to restore the individual to active life, health, and youth.

Once participants in the Cryonics program internalize the thesis that indefinite life extension is possible and worthy of attainment, they experience something of a liberation of consciousness. The strictures on awareness and achievement vanish, as if receding away at the speed of light, leaving a panorama of the waiting universe. They conceive this vision as a potential that *will* be actualized if civilization continues to progress. All diseases will be curable or preventable. Aging, the senescence due to the accumulation of years, will be preventable or reversible. Any damage caused by accidents, other than catastrophic destruction of the body, will be repairable. People will be able to live for hundreds, thousands, or millions of years. Perhaps true physical immortality will be realized. Humanity will expand throughout the solar system and the galaxy and the universe; in the process, humanity will become superhumanity. It will improve physiologically; more importantly, it will improve in consciousness, in awareness, in its grasp of facts and of the nature of the boundless reality around it. The Cryonics program for our period in history is a focal point and key link in the evolution of consciousness in the cosmos.

There are grounds for hope; the universe is huge. The immensity out there and the immensity of our ignorance give us reason to believe there are many potentials of which we are not even barely aware. We can tap these potentials to use for our own purposes, to improve ourselves and our achievements. The Cryonics program offers the prospect of participation not only in building our own future evolution but also in realizing its benefits. Ettinger formulated what he calls the First Theorem of Hope: It is always too early to despair.

Also, many of us dare to hope that we will never have to be

cryonically frozen. That is, the present advances in life-extension research, by scientists such as Dr. Bernard Strehler, Dr. Paul Segall, and hundreds of others, give us grounds to believe that a chemical cure for aging will be available in the next 10 to 15 years. There's an excellent chance that the first longevity drugs will come along soon enough to give us each another 100 or 200 years of life, and in that time further research will almost certainly give us much longer—fantastically longer—lifespans.

Despair

Despair is both fashionable and respectable these days; you might even say it's chic. It's the "in" thing these days: contempt for humanity, hopelessness, apocalyptic dread. Any sociologist is aware that a despair program is a self-fulfilling prophecy. It's obvious that if you think that you can't make out with a certain woman, you're not going to make a pass at her. If you think that you can't get the job, you're not going to apply; you're not going to fill out the forms, and so forth. The more despair around, the more causes for despair there are. The extent to which hope is a self-fulfilling prophecy is not quite that obvious, but as long as you have hope, opportunities do open up. You can see chances that you wouldn't see with a despair program.

Life After Death

Early efforts to revive drowning victims were ridiculed and stigmatized as blasphemy for their obviously diabolical attempt to bring people back from the dead when God had chosen otherwise. Everyone knew that when someone cold and blue was hauled from the water, God had called the soul and sent it whithersoever He desired, and that it was not only useless but blasphemous to attempt revival. The resuscitation methods used were inadequate, but they actually began to succeed in reviving drowning victims. The furor eventually subsided, as the concept developed that the victims just weren't really dead. Before, individuals in such conditions were thought to be dead, but obviously the ones revived were actually alive all along.

Similar reactions to medical advances have continued up to the present, even in response to the Cryonics program. If the information on which life and consciousness are based is still present in a cryonically suspended patient, then the individual is in a deep coma and at least potentially alive. If the information is dissipated or destroyed, from whatever cause—whether by a purely physiological process or by God's having severed the essential connection—then the person is dead. Not even the most learned theologian of whatever religion—Buddhist, Christian, Islamic, and so on—who believes in some sort of spiritual existence apart from the body, would claim to know the precise nature of the relation between spirit and body or the conditions under which that relation is dissolved. No one knows exactly when this transition from enough to not enough information may occur, though science gives many grounds for optimism that essential structures may be much more resistent to damage than is usually believed. Our ignorance and the value we have for individual conscious life impel us to behave just as we would if we knew life still to be present but gravely in peril. The cryonic procedures aim to preserve and extend that life.

Some cryonicists believe in the soul and in spiritual life after its dissociation from the body, but they are nonetheless choosing the option of cryonic suspension for themselves. Many religious leaders are favorably inclined toward the Cryonics thesis. They say that physical life is sacred, a gift from God, not to be relinquished unless the reasons are very good indeed. We do not consider the diagnosis of medical death by an attending physician, relative as it is to our continually changing contingencies of time, place, knowledge, and technology, to be sufficient reason to make us give up hope and effort.

The life-extension sciences use the concept of "identity reconstruction" to refer to a hypothesized technique of extending life by reconstructing personality and memory when an individual's physical remains have been so damaged that the usual projected methods of repair would not be applicable. A severely damaged brain, for instance, would not be simply revived, but the personality and memories might be reconstituted by using the intact information. This might involve a transfer of consciousness and personality into a cloned or even artificial brain by means of a causally continuous cybernetic mapping that preserves the quantum relations of information contained in the weave, RNA, and DNA of the original neurons. Just as transistor technology could not have been envisioned even a hundred years ago, so the future will conceive and implement strategies we cannot dream of today.

From another perspective, there are lots of approaches to an identity. It's quite possible that the sort of central galactic computer or the brain of the energy-shunting system can have these personalities on tap, and whenever the genetic roulette wheel spins around to the right place, they come up again on a particular planet. In other words, if the personality is basically information, mathematically considered, that is not very far from the theological term "spirit" or "soul." We're talking about coding, and that can reappear in many ways, so that people who claim to remember past lives may well be remembering the genetic archives. This is what Dr. Leary calls the seventh circuit of the nervous system, the neurogenetic circuit in which you can remember the DNA archives. This information is always potentially available, so that somebody who has been cryonically frozen can reappear in many forms, besides the one in which the cryonic suspension is ended and they're revived. In other words, identity is not that intimately connected with the body.

To put it another way, inside every cell of your body is a very complicated DNA code, which contains all the information that decided how tall you were going to be and what color eyes you would have and so on. This coil appears inside every cell of every living creature on this planet. This is sort of the evolutionary strategy computer that's been operating for the last three and a half billion years. It obviously knows a lot more than any human brain. From a certain perspective, as Mueller, the geneticist, says, we're giant robots created by the DNA to make more DNA. Tim Leary would say, to make better DNA.

Trans Time van.

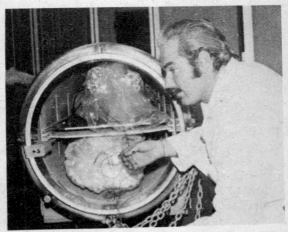

Two patients just placed in cryogenic storage capsule. Trans Time President Art Quaife examines thermocouple leads, used to monitor temperature during further cooling.

The data of mysticism, the data of memories of past lives, can be accounted for by Leary's theory of a loop between the nervous system and the genetic code: that you are capable of remembering things that didn't happen to this nervous system, but actually happened to other nervous systems the genetic code had created. Out-of-body experiences are easily accounted for in terms of Leary's eighth circuit, which is the neuroatomic, metaphysiological circuit. Just because you're out of the body doesn't mean that you're out of physics; you're just metaphysiological, not metaphysical. The same theory has been proposed by such physicists as Dr. Evan Harris Walker, Dr. David Bohm, Dr. Jack Sarfatti, and several others.

Future Prospects

We're all living on a planet that has reached the point where we can no longer afford to have any people who are being oppressed or who even *think* they are being oppressed. The potentials for violence and destructiveness are absolutely shattering. Nobody is safe, not even people with as much money as the Hearsts. There's no place to hide. We've got to face up to our responsibilities, and realize the only remaining options are Utopia or oblivion. Plutonium is missing, for instance. There's a jolly group that calls themselves "The National Committee to Overthrow the Government Next Tuesday After Lunch," who are sending out schematic diagrams on how to make an atomic bomb at home. At the trial of Captain Crunch recently, he got a sentence cut from four years to three months for telling the government how he managed to tap the supposedly fail-safe untappable lines of the White House, the CIA, the FBI, the Pentagon; how to get into bank computers by telephone and shift a million dollars from one account into another; how to fire missiles by telephone and start World War III. He showed them how to build in more fail-safes to prevent the kind of thing he discovered he could do; but, of course, the next one along can find a way over Captain

Crunch's fail-safes. We have got to develop a sense of responsibility, and realize that a just, happy society is not a luxury but a necessity.

A person can realize that all of these things we have discussed are scientifically possible. As long as you're talking religion or metaphysics and so on, people have a chance to ignore it and get off the hook and say, "Well, that's all unproven." We're talking about things that can be done practically. And once you internalize these possibilities, then the enormous stupidity, the enormous waste, and the enormous threat involved in continuing our habitual ways of thinking become obvious. You don't need to take a psychedelic once you have internalized these ideas. You don't need a psychedelic to become aware that every moment is important, that every decision is important, that every human being is important. We are all contributing to the ledger on one side or the other. We're all contributing to the amount of violence, hatred, prejudice, brutality, in the human experiment; or we're contributing to the other side, toward love, intelligence, tolerance, forbearance, and all the traditional works of mercy recommended by Thomas Aquinas. But we're definitely contributing every minute to one side or the other, and within this next decade, or the next five years, very important decisions are going to be made.

We are going to have longevity and eventual immortality; we are going to the stars; we are going to transcend all of our previous levels of consciousness and intelligence. Or we are going to end this experiment on this planet, this life experiment that has produced so many beautiful things, from Beethoven's music to the bluejay that lands on the tree and sings for you. It's an awfully stupid time to blow the whole show when we've got greater potentials than we've ever had before. What's really behind the whole SMI^{2}LE program is making people aware of this. Every person matters; body is unimportant any more. And every living being matters, and every decision matters, and every minute is going to be full of love and hope, if you want it that way, or full of negativity, if you want it that way.

The Baraka

Not only can we no longer afford to have any oppressed people on this planet; but we can no longer afford the childish indulgences of despair and self-pity, even. We have got to be strong individuals. As Lao-tse said, "You can't do good until you feel good." But the converse is equally true: you can't feel good until you do good.

One very simple exercise—it's very basic to Sufism—is putting *Baraka* into things, that is, concentrating on putting good energy into, say, a plant. This has been scientifically verified in the last few years. You can put good energy into a plant and it will grow better. You can start with simple things like that, and deliberately try to put good energy into more and more things, until you begin to realize that the good energy is coming back to you. This is what in alchemy they call "the Multiplication of the First Matter." This is a very simple neurological law: the more good energy you put out, the more good energy comes back to you. And I'm not talking in the simple-minded sense of a system like "positive thinking." There's no guarantee against calamity. But you will find, as you put out more and more Baraka, that if it does happen that tragedy befalls you, you will be surrounded by a network of love and support that will help you get through the pain. This is not at all theoretical; this is based on actual experience.

People don't seem to have any hesitancy about trying negative programs; if they're told, "Everything is hopeless; give up," they accept it very easily. If you tell people, "If you try to become a more loving being, the love will come back to you," they say, "Oh, that sounds sentimental. I'm not going to try that." All you've got to do is try it to find out how true it is. Try it, you'll like it!

Penology

Consider the problem of penology in terms of life extension. How long can you keep people in prisons before everybody thinks it's abominable? Can anybody contemplate a 700-year prison sentence? It's occurred to me that when life extension becomes commonplace, penology is immediately going to go into two extreme schools. One will say, Execute all, right and left; we're not going to support these thieves and murderers through a hundred years, 200 years, 700 years, 1,000 years, or whatever. The other extreme will say, Life is so precious that we can't contemplate destroying it, and certainly we don't want to keep people caged for that long. A thousand years in a cage is an inhuman concept, and it's expensive for us as taxpayers, too. So we've got to find a cure for these problems. The abolition of poverty is the first major step toward solving those problems, but it's not the whole answer, of course.

Tim Leary has suggested that we should abolish all crimes without victims in the first place, which is an ordinary libertarian position which makes sense to everybody except puritanical fanatics who are constantly haunted by the fear that somebody somewhere might be having a good time without being punished for it. And then there's the question, what do you do about crimes against property? Leary and other libertarians say that a criminal should have to repay. Now, if we're talking about a society in which there's still poverty and the criminal can't repay, then the state should pay the victim. And then the criminal literally has a debt to society. He would have to work off his debt to the state; so the person who was ripped off would get back the money to buy whatever was ripped off. And the criminal would have to pay that off to the state by doing socially useful work. We would have a tremendous amount of forest rangers, hospital orderlies, and so on, who would not add to the tax rolls as convicts do. And then comes the question: What about crimes against people? The obvious answer, until we have a cure, is that those people have to be segregated from the rest of society, but they don't have to be put in cages, which only makes them worse.

The cage experience is neurologically punishing and disorienting. Somebody has to be a neurological adept to get something profitable out of the present prison experience. Most people are pretty racked up by it, and come up more crazy-mean than when they went in. Tim Leary says to put them in colonies without cages. Take a whole state that's practically uninhabited and make it a gigantic colony where these people can go, with their girl friends, their wives, their families, or whoever will go with them, and have whatever kinds of lives they can make there, like the pioneers in Australia, who were composed of the criminal classes. Just get them the hell away from the rest of us; so we don't have to be victims of their violence any more. This makes a lot more sense than the current penological system, in which, if somebody rips you off or kills someone you love, you, along with all the other taxpayers, have to support the institutions which will maintain them for five to twenty years—or whatever—and where we murder the murderer on the idiot logic that one plus one equals zero. Capital punishment is no deterrent, it accomplishes nothing, and it just shoves the problem under the rug.

We're on a leaky lifeboat, you might say; every time we shed blood, we attract more sharks. As the Buddha said, "Hatred does not stop by hatred at any time. Hatred stops by love." The amount of violence in our society is directly proportional to the amount of glorification of violence in the media. There's this general idea that the only solution to any problem is to shoot the bad guys. We've got to come to a basic change in philosophy where we recognize that every human life is important. And so, an adherence to life extension, cryonics, and so on, is just an extension of an involvement with pacifism. It's an expression of the same thing. This is a terribly violent society if you compare it with, say, Sweden, for instance. There's nothing innate in human nature that says people have to be as violent as Americans are today.

Universal Perspectives

Let's not forget that one day in 1928 Bucky Fuller stood on the shore of Lake Michigan and planned to throw himself in. He was ready to give up, because he was a failure financially, by the standards of the upper middle class, which he'd been born into. As a construction engineer he hadn't succeeded. And because his daughter had just died of polio, the whole universe didn't make any sense to him, and he was ready to throw himself in. He stopped himself and said, "Wait, I can't be sure. Maybe there is something I can do in this universe that's important." He said, "Well, what can I do? Let's see what a man of average intelligence can do if he starts questioning everything that's taken for granted and starts looking for alternatives." I don't know if he ever was a man of only average intelligence, but by questioning everything, he came to realize, as he said, that when you don't accept anything except that which can be experimentally verified, you are overwhelmed by the inherent integrity and rationality of the universe. The most incomprehensible thing about the universe is that it's comprehensible, as Einstein said. And that gives you faith in the sane, sound center of the universe we mentioned earlier. As Ezra Pound wrote in the death-cells at Pisa, looking at the stars, "Out of all this beauty something must come."

Ever Rethinking
the Lord's Prayer
May 8, 1978
BUCKMINSTER FULLER

Photo by Christopher Wentworth

To be satisfactory to science
all definitions
must be stated
in terms of experience.

By Universe I mean
all of humanity's
in-all-known-time
consciously apprehended
and communicated (to self or others)
experiences.

In using the word God,
I am consciously employing
four clearly differentiated
experience-engendered thoughts.

Firstly:
    predicated upon past successions
    of unexpected human discoveries
    of mathematically incisive,
    physically demonstrable answers
    to what theretofore had been misassumed
    to be forever unanswerable
    cosmic-magnitude questions,
    I now assume it to be
    scientifically manifest,
    ergo experientially reasonable,
    that scientifically explainable answers
    may and probably will eventually
    be given to all questions
    as engendered in all human thoughts
    by the sum total of all human experiences;
    wherefore my first meaning for God is:
    all the experientially explained answers
    to all the questions of all time.

Secondly, I mean:
    the possibly existent
    total comprehension
    of the integrated significance
    of all meanings.

Thirdly, I mean:
    the only intellectually discoverable,
    a priori, intellectual integrity
    indisputably manifest
    as the only mathematically stateable
    family of generalized principles
    —cosmic laws—
    thus far discovered and codified
    and ever physically redemonstrable by scientists
    to be not only unfailingly operative
    but to be in eternal,
    omni-interconsiderate,
    omni-interaccomodative governance
    of the complex
    of everyday, naked-eye experiences
    as well as of the multi-millionsfold greater range
    of only instrumentally explored
    infra- and ultra-tunable
    micro- and macro-Universe events.

Fourthly, I mean:
    all the mystery inherent
    in all human experience,
    which, as a lifetime ratioed to eternity,
    is individually limited
    to almost negligible,
    twixt sleepings, glimpses
    of only a few local episodes
    of one of the infinite myriads
    of concurrently and overlappingly operative

sum-totally never-ending
cosmic-scenario serials.

With these four meanings I now directly
address God.
    "Our God,
since omni-experience is your identity,
You have given us
overwhelming manifestations
of Your complete knowledge,
of Your complete comprehension,
of Your complete concern,
of Your complete coordination,
of Your complete responsibility,
of Your complete capability to cope
in absolute wisdom and effectiveness
with all problems and events,
and of Your eternally unfailing reliability
so to do.

Yours, Dear God,
is the only and complete glory.

By *Glory* I mean
the synergetic totality
of all physical and metaphysical radiation
and of all physical and metaphysical gravity
of this finite
but nonunitarily conceptual
scenario Universe,
in whose synergetic totality
the a priori energy potentials
of both radiation and gravity
are initially equal,
but in which their respective
behavioral patterns are such

that radiation's entropic, redundant disintegrating
is always less effective
than gravity's nonredundant
syntropic integrating.

Radiation is plural and differentiable,
is focusable, beamable, and self-sinusing,
is interceptible, separatist, and biasable,
ergo has shadowed voids and vulnerabilities.

Gravity is unit and undifferentiable,
is comprehensive,
inclusively embracing and permeative,
is nonfocusable and shadowless,
and is omni-integrative,
all of which characteristics of gravity
are also the characteristics of love.
Love is metaphysical gravity.

You, Dear God,
are the totally loving intellect,
ever designing
and ever daring to test,
and thereby irrefutably proving—
to the uncompromising satisfaction
of your own comprehensive and incisive
knowledge of the absolute truth—
that your generalized principles
adequately accommodate any and all
special-case developments,
involvements, and side effects;
wherefore your absolutely courageous,
omnirigorous, and ruthless self-testing
alone can and does absolutely guarantee
total conservation
of the integrity
of this eternally regenerative Universe.

Your eternally regenerative scenario Universe
is the minimum complex
of totally intercomplementary,
totally intertransforming,
nonsimultaneous, differently frequenced,
and differently enduring
feedback closures
of a finite
but nonunitarily conceptual system
in which naught is created
and naught is lost
and all occurs
in optimum efficiency.

Total accountability and total feedback
constitute the minimum and only
perpetual motion system.
Universe is the one and only
eternally regenerative system.

To accomplish your regenerative integrity
You give Yourself the responsibility
of eternal, absolutely continuous,
tirelessly vigilant wisdom.

Wherefore we have absolute faith and trust in you,
and we worship you
awe-inspiredly,
all-thankfully,
rejoicingly,
lovingly.
Amen.

Sequence 27
A Scenario for the Future
BARBARA MARX HUBBARD

Barbara Marx Hubbard, co-founder and President of The Committee for the Future, has long been interested in the relationship between personal growth, transpersonal connectedness, and social/political change. She is the initiator of Syncon, a synergistic convergence process for problem solving and cooperative planning. She authored The Hunger of Eve: A Woman's Odyssey Toward the Future.

In this sequence, Ms. Hubbard explains the techniques by which she helps people learn how to feel and think in the synthesizing, global manner that will be needed for our future growth as a world society. She also sets forth her own spiritual understanding of our unfolding relationship to the universe around us.

I was born into a materialistic, comfortable family. And I had a sense early on in life that material well-being could not be the only purpose of existence, because I had that. Also, there seemed to be this magnetic pull toward another state of being. Of course, in that secular-agnostic world into which I was born, there was virtually no affirmation for this feeling. However, there was this sense of something coming in the future that was deeply attractive to me.

Relatively early on in my life I made a study of world philosophies and world religions. When I read through the world philosophies, I was rather surprised to find few images of the future. Either they looked back to a time when things were better, such as the so-called Golden Age; or they were cyclical, and thought everything was repetitive until you got off the

Barbara Marx Hubbard

Wheel of Life; or they were Stoical, and said you should just get with whatever is; or they were Existential, saying that there is no meaning and you have to assert it yourself; or they were Absurdists, and said it was all hopeless. None of those ideas really corresponded to my sense of magnetic joy.

Then I went through the world religions. I was far more attracted to them, in particular to the Christian vision, promising that a time would come when "we should all not sleep but would all be changed"; that the suffering of the present cannot be compared to the glory that shall be revealed. Because, you see, I felt that sense of glory. But living in Scarsdale, New York... to get from Scarsdale to the glory untold was a leap I couldn't take.

A Lost Sense of Purpose

I was beginning to sense that Western civilization was losing its whole sense of purpose because it had believed solely in progress, had believed that power, knowledge, technology, and science could lead to a better and more satisfying life, and now that philosophy was beginning to be in jeopardy. I found myself in a genuine metaphysical bind: I couldn't see any reason for being. I couldn't seem to get to the religious dimension, and I couldn't work just for more money, more things, or more comfort for myself. Finally I got to the point where I felt it was very hard to live.

My father is of Jewish background, but he, himself, had rejected his own ancestry. And the only thing he ever told us was that we were Americans.

I would ask him, "What does that mean?"

"Well," he used to say, "it means *do your best*."

And I used to say, "At what?"

I guess I really have tried to answer that question, first of all for myself.

A Search for a New Philosophy

In my search I began to develop an evolutionary philosophy which had three key elements. The first was the discovery of Abraham Maslow's *Toward a Psychology of Being*, wherein he postulates that there is a natural desire in us for something more than material and social well-being, and that this urge is normal, not a sickness, but a sign of potential health. It was a real joy to find that this tremendous frustration I had been feeling was simply a desire for growth.

I was 32 at the time. I had five children, and I had tried just about everything I was supposed to do in this culture to be happy and productive—but I was miserable. The misery got worse and worse as I got more and more biologically productive, because with each child the question of meaning came up again.

The second discovery was Teilhard de Chardin. He affirms the expectation of newness. In his philosophy there is a pattern in the evolutionary process (going all the way back to the formation of Earth, cells, and multicellular life) toward greater complexity, higher synthesis, deeper consciousness and transformation. I began to understand that the growth potential I was feeling in me was related to the growth potential in the collective evolutionary process in the whole world.

An Experience of Personal Transcendence

A third element then came along, and it gave me a tremendous insight. It was the Space Program. When I saw John Glenn go up in that space capsule, I had a personal experience of transcendence, just watching it on television. Tears were streaming down my face, my heart was pounding, and the words "freedom, freedom, freedom" were pounding through my being. I would almost call it a cosmic birth experience: the physical body of humanity was piercing into the infinite.

Then I had what I've come to call an expanded reality experience. It was around 1966, when I was taking a walk alone one day in Connecticut. I asked myself a question: "What in our age is comparable to the birth of Christ?" And I went into what I call "autodrive," turned my mind off, and started walking around the beautiful hills of Connecticut. In a flash, something happened. This little blue cocoon of Earth opened up, and I was in the universe; and my mind's eye was on the Moon, looking back at ourselves, here on Earth, and I got an answer. It was: What is going on in our age is a birth. It is our own, the birth of mankind. We are being born!

And with that I felt myself as a cell in the body, the whole planetary body, which was trying to coordinate (itself). I literally felt "us" running out of energy, gasping for breath, reaching into the universe for new sources of energy. I got a sense of the presence of other life, just as a newborn baby probably has a sense of something around it, but is too immature to pick it up.

And with that came an experience of joy, as though all the cells of the "body" of our planet, all the billions of people, were for one instant recognizing their oneness. And the power of that euphoria, that connectedness, on a planetary scale, with the idea of us being part of a universal community, completely flooded me with joy.

A Birth of a New Human Species

We are like a young extraterrestial species, just barely making it with our eyes open, cracking the cosmic egg. On that same hill, in that moment, I had a flash of our evolutionary past as though it were a common gestation. I lived through a sense of the first explosion, of being on the early Earth, of coming up through single-cell life, multi-cell life, the dawn of human consciousness, in order to get to the birth.

Instead of getting mystical at that point, I found we could extend our concreteness by adding our new scientific capacities: our capacities in astronautics, in genetics, and in understanding the potential of our own minds and its purposeful cultivation. I saw the outline of a universal species capable of living beyond this planet, possibly capable of extending its lifespan and transforming its physical body consciously with the aid of computers. This universal species would be able to draw information from its total planetary memory system, and perhaps be able to contact extraterrestial life.

It seemed intuitively clear not only that the religious predictions, (if you want to call them that) were correct, but that the transformation was occurring in our own generation. The new element, science, was part of the mystery that Saint Paul talked about, the same science which, when it began to grow so dramatically, was rejected by the church because of fear of the new knowledge, and has ever since grown separately from the church. It never has been adequately synthesized with the deep religious perceptions of our species. So, because of my own intuition that we are becoming universal physically as well as spiritually, I began to piece it together.

The Committee for the Future

With the birth experience, and with its perception that not only were we becoming one, but we were becoming part of a universal community, John Whiteside and I founded The Committee for the Future in 1970, and searched for a way to test this out with other people. Because if it is true that we're becoming one and that we have new capacities, they're all inherent in our social body right now. So we designed a conference process called Syncon (Synergistic Convergence) that would enable each individual and each function in our society to examine its own growth needs in terms of the capacity of the total growth system.

A Synergistic Convergence

At Southern Illinois University in 1972, we built a large wheel in the school union, and divided it into sections representing the functions of the social environment: the production of food, goods, and services; the governing function; the health, education, and welfare functions; the tool makers; and the technological processes that actually enable us to do things. All the participants were in a people mandala, shaped into task forces. We asked each group to identify its own goals, needs, and resources in little workshops while remaining in the whole wheel. Outside the wheel, in smaller rooms, were the Futurists: workers in the fields of biology, information sciences, and extraterrestrial development; the humanistic and transpersonal psychologists; the physical scientists; and the political-economic theorists who are trying to think of whole-system economics. We asked them all to identify new capacities in their areas.

Gradually we asked the groups to identify their own goals and to report to the whole; and the growing edge groups reported the new capacities. Then we merged them slowly, and asked them to look for common goals, and for matched needs and resources. We asked the growing edge to merge, and to piece together the capacities for the rest of the body.

For example, the psychic people, the computer scientists, and the artists merged. They put together a spectrum of ways of knowing. They had a hard time communicating with each other, because their languages were different, but knowing that they were going to make joint presentations to the whole body helped alleviate the language problem and also the attitudinal dislike. For instance, electronic engineers in 1972 did not like to be in the same room with people who called themselves psychic. It was like the body had an allergic reaction to parts of itself. Each part didn't want to be associated with the other. The conservative economists didn't want to be seen with the radical students; the social-reform people would not be in the same room with the nuclear scientists.

However, because the process was organically structured to seek for commonality before looking for differences, the participants discovered that they began to link up. As they linked, the walls were gradually physically removed, symbolizing the coming together of function. Individual environmentalists and technologists began to find that the distrust they felt toward each other was not necessarily valid, that each was actually concerned with the same problems. The technologists were not antienvironment, and the environmentalists actually needed assistance from the thinking of the technologists.

The Joy of Supra-Sexual Love

Finally, when all the walls were down, we had a musical ceremony, and an amazing thing started happening. People started feeling enormously joyful. Even more amazing, love started being generated between these prickly groups. If you could measure what was happening on a "psychic counter," it was as though a field of force was being established that was drawing people into a synergistic whole body.

Various parts of the body as we met in the whole session were asked if there was any conflict left over that was unresolved, and if so, to bring it up and see if the whole group could solve it in such a manner that no part had to feel excluded or hurt. It began to work so rapidly that people fell in love with each other. These were people who could not stand each other three or four days before.

It was not just a personal love, more like a supra-sexual love, just as sex was actually invented in the evolutionary process along with multicellular life. I got the feeling that our generation is being required to come together, literally, for survival; so an attraction is being exerted which impels us in that direction. The right environmental process can enable us to fuse, to synthesize, in order to create a common future that is greater than the sum of our separate parts.

The Future of the Synergistic Process

Through the SYNCONs and other such opportunites for synergy, the human species is finding its way toward a fusing. We're not doing it just by intellect or even personal intuition alone. If you want to call it the God Force, if you want to call it the evolutionary process or Syntropy, whatever made the atoms cohere into the molecules, and the molecules cohere into cells, is helping us cohere into a whole body. And, as is the tradition of evolution, when you get into a new whole system, you are greater than the sum of your parts. The excitement of our age is that we're getting to that whole system.

SYNCON was a social replay for me of that original birth experience, but the beauty of it was sharing it with others. I didn't have to tell people about the birth experience, even though they may not have called it that. They may have many other images. It doesn't really matter; they were experiencing the joy.

Evolution into the Extraterrestial

Assuming that the 15 billion years of evolutionary process is with us and that our species can coordinate itself as a whole system, then we should be able to meet the basic needs of people on this Earth. Those "deficiency needs," as Maslow calls them in his hierarchy, are food, clothing, shelter, medical care, etc. I assume that we can and will organize ourselves and meet these needs, because if we don't, then we will probably blow ourselves up, and there won't be any future. So, if there is a future, we will first have met these needs of the people on this planet, as one body.

Going right up Maslow's hierarchy, it will become possible for most people to develop their unique growth potential. We won't have to be working day and night just to survive. There will be a total range of technologies, from "appropriate" all the way up to "space agriculture" and "controlled environment" agriculture, with new kinds of food. It won't be just everybody with a little backyard garden. Most of the survival tasks will be taken out of individual hands.

The freeing of individual capability, then, will obviously call for a whole new set of functions. Since we're not going to be producing a lot of new babies, and we're not going to be doing the old repetitive tasks for survival, I see us moving toward synergistic systems on this planet in which we will be much more deeply involved in the decisionmaking process. We will become increasingly more empathetic with the purpose of developing. The next level of our environment, I believe, is the extraterrestrial. We are going to start developing our extended environment in space. And I see a series of developments occurring which will make us into a universal species.

What is now being called the "space program" is a very infantile view of a natural capability of the universal species. We will be living and working on many worlds. The NASA Summer study of the Gerard O'Neill space-colonization proposal stated that, by the year 2004, we could have a human settlement in space that was self-regenerative, needing nothing from Earth. It could supply solar energy and industrial products for Earth, and also be self-replicative; that is, it could build other worlds in space out of solar energy and lunar materials. I am assuming that such a decision will be made, because I think it is a natural part of our evolutionary process for us to become more universal.

A new world in space is a design of a total system; therefore, it ought to help us design the most efficient way of running the "total system" that is our own planet.

Moving Onward into "Cosmic Time"

I also see us moving onward to "cosmic time." Right now, our bodies are on a mammalian life cycle. Death is scheduled into the evolutionary process, along with multicellular life and sex. We were once single-celled life, and we divided to reproduce. There was no scheduled death of the individual. I believe that the study of aging, of how the cell works, and of how DNA works will lead us to understand that clock of death. Perhaps we will be able to reset that clock, with a combination of genetic research and psychic ability to communicate with our own deeper selves. The coming generations will probably have a choice about whether or not to die, to go through the death and rebirth cycle. They may have the choice of extending their life at will, gradually moving out of the mammalian body consciously. Buckminster Fuller is talking about the "continuous human."

It's interesting to me that thanatology, the study of how to die gracefully, almost by choice, and gerontology, the study of the aging process, have come to the forefront at the same time. We need no longer feel that it is "bad" to die, because consciousness will go on beyond that death—where you have a choice of reincarnating. If you don't really need a body, you might as well die. I've read that it is a great, joyful celebration when you get out of the body; well, I've read about it, but I haven't experienced it. However, if you need a body, because you want to do work in the cosmos that is still on the physical plane, even though it is transcending the mammalian physical plane, then you will keep a body. This is a new option that evolution is opening up to us as a species.

The gerontologists, the aging scientists, space scientists, and computer scientists are bringing us to another choice: the development of new bodies which will not perish. Right now it sounds rather awkward: replacing parts, cyborgs, computerized intelligence; it doesn't sound attractive. But my feeling is, if it is a genuine evolutionary option, it will start out awkward, but will end up quite beautiful. Anything that survives in evolution is beautiful. Every stone and tree and blade of grass is beautiful.

Becoming Co-Creators and Co-Operators

Our technologies are very young. Nature's technologies are far more refined. You have to admit that the blade of grass is performing a technological feat of a very high level: it is taking water and solar energy, and transforming them into a green plant. It is making no noise, no heat, but it is a technological biochemical process. We are just at the brink of learning these processes. Our technologies are becoming more and more miniaturized, more ephemeralized. We are doing more and more with less and less, as Buckminster Fuller is fond of saying.

Lately, I've been identifying much more with the Creator than with the created. If we can make it, man and God can become closer partners. We become co-creators, cooperators with the same creative intention, operating the universe together. I think we're doing it now, but in such an infantile, inefficient, and rudimentary manner that we don't even know we are doing it. It is the nature of reality for us to do it.

So we have cosmic consciousness, cosmic action, and cosmic time, the possibility of extended life spans. Then, perhaps, we can have cosmic contact. It is now valid to assume that there are billions of planets with life on them, somewhat comparable to our own. We might also assume that the stage of contact with extraterrestrial intelligence would come when we ourselves become extraterrestrial, as is now happening.

The Coming of Cosmic Contact

I don't know if it will come through a combination of telepathy and telescope, but I have a very deep feeling that the next great quantum leap will be a contact which we can all share. I felt that the "birth experience" was a planetary contact; it wasn't personal. It might come through the mass media. Because when man first landed on the Moon, I can remember very consciously looking up at the Moon and seeing nothing, and being able to watch my television set and see it. If you look at our electronic media as an extended nervous system of a planetary body, itself being refined and interlocked and interlinked, and as we become psychically more empathetic and interlinked, combining psychic and electronic interlinkage, and develop further extraterrestrial abilities on the exoteric physical plane, my guess—and this is feminine intuition and not futurism—is that it will come through our nervous systems, which *are* our media.

As our electronic machines get more and more refined and sensitive, and as we do the same with our individual minds, it might be that our planet is getting its nervous system in order. We're now at that very awkward stage between overcomplexity and the next synthesis. We have an information overload and all these mind-blowing experiences. But as the pattern of this next synthesis emerges, I think it will click into place, and we will know it quite easily. All this technology will become quite commonplace, and we will master it and take it for granted.

The Development of a Planetary Organism

Because of a marvelous nervous system, your body is now digesting food, your eyes are seeing, your ears are hearing—without your having to pay attention to them. You only have to pay attention to them if they have a problem, and then they signal you by playing through your nervous system. I think it's going to get to be the same way on this planet. If a flood is coming or a volcano is going to erupt or if crop disease is beginning somewhere, the totality of our nervous system and our computerized information system will alert us before the "pain" occurs, so that food can be carried to the hungry spot, or if there is a potential illness somewhere it can be attended to, just as your body is doing right now.

If you put together this vision of the future, you see the outlines of a universal species naturally contacting other universal species. This vision of the future gives a meaning to the power that has been generated by knowledge, particularly in

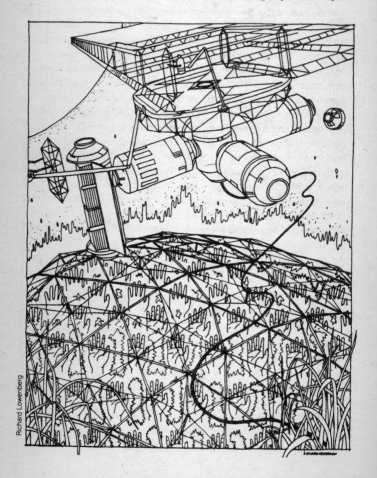

Richard Lowenberg

Western civilization. Rather than rejecting that power and saying that we have to return to a more psychic way of doing things, I see us as blending increased psychic ability with a refined use of that power.

As we now face the problems of energy, of welfare, of education, and we begin to take initiatives in a coordinated new-world-on-Earth/new-world-in-space effort, which would begin to employ more people in a nonpolluting, noninflationary manner, then the wealth that will be produced by all these efforts will, I think, be enough to make this world whole.

Now, I'm not saying that the Western world doesn't have to stop certain things it's been doing, or learn to conserve and harmonize. It does. But I think that the welfare problem in our own nation, and in those countries that are being effectively prevented from developing because their resources are being used by the developed world, will be solved by a "new worlds building" effort. Because when you consider what can be done with energy from space, and by means of industrialization in space, which doesn't affect our biosphere, you begin to see ways in which wealth can be produced for the whole planet, by the participation of the whole planet, without destroying anything or anyone. That might sound overly optimistic, but I think it is possible.

Appendix

Resource Directory

STAN KENT

Stan Kent is an Advisory Editor of the Space Age Review. *Currently, he is working on solar satellite development at Boeing, Seattle.*

If you have been intrigued, baffled, or surprised by the preceding glimpses of *Moving Into Space*, then you will probably want to explore these exciting visions further. To help your exploration, I here provide a list of resources focusing on magazine articles, advocacy groups, information organizations, and lecturers concerned with the topics covered in this book. There are many bibliographies on these topics, and I see no need to duplicate them here. Instead, I have concentrated on information which is not usually found in printed form, and about which the enthusiast traditionally learns from the grapevine of interested friends, or from television programs, or from an obscure back-page story in yesterday's newspaper. I hope this directory will eliminate the need to be in the right place at the right time.

The resource list is divided into three sections:

    (I)   General aspects of space technology, including astronomy and computers;

    (II)   Unidentified flying objects (UFOs);

    (III) Space settlement and space industrialization.

A separate section is devoted to space settlements and space industrialization because of the huge amount of material being generated in the field. Additionally, this field has encompassed numerous disciplines usually not associated with the traditional space-technology industry.

I.   General Aspects of Space Technology

NASA

The National Aeronautics and Space Administration (NASA) has all manner of materials, including magazines, books, films, lecturers, tapes, and tours of their facilities. Rather than repeat details for each item separately under articles, organizations, etc., I give here one general listing for NASA.

There are several NASA centers located all around the country. Contact the one in your area for information about specific programs, tours, films, and news releases. Address inquiries to Educational Programs Office or Public Affairs Office. Either branch will handle your inquiry.

If you live in: *Write to Educational Office at:*

If you live in:		Write to Educational Office at:
Alaska	Nevada	
Arizona	Oregon	NASA Ames Research Center
California	Utah	Moffett Field, California 94035
Hawaii	Washington	
Idaho	Wyoming	
Montana		
Alabama	Mississippi	
Arkansas	Missouri	NASA George C. Marshall Space Flight Center
Iowa	Tennessee	Marshall Space Flight Center, Alabama 35812
Louisiana		
Connecticut	New Hampshire	
Delaware	New Jersey	
District of	New York	NASA Goddard Space Flight Center
Columbia	Pennsylvania	Greenbelt, Maryland 20771
Maine	Rhode Island	
Maryland	Vermont	
Massachusetts		
Florida	Puerto Rico	NASA John F. Kennedy Space Center
Georgia	Virgin Islands	Kennedy Space Center, Florida 32899
Kentucky	Virginia	NASA Langley Research Center
North Carolina	West Virginia	Langley Station
South Carolina		Hampton, Virginia 23365
Illinois	Minnesota	NASA Lewis Research Center
Indiana	Ohio	21000 Brookpark Road
Michigan	Wisconsin	Cleveland, Ohio 44135
Colorado	North Dakota	NASA Manned Spacecraft Center
Kansas	Oklahoma	(Johnson Spacecraft Center)
Nebraska	South Dakota	Houston, Texas 77058
New Mexico	Texas	

Magazines

Astronautics and Aeronautics, 1290 Avenue of the Americas, New York, NY 10019. Editor-in-Chief, John Newbauer; monthly, $28.00/year (for nonmembers); subscription included in dues to American Institute of Aeronautics and Astronautics (see listing under Organizations).

Astronomy, 411 E. Mason Street, 6th floor, Milwaukee, WI 53202. Editor, Richard Berry; monthly, $12.00/year.

Aviation Week and Space Technology, P.O. Box 430, Hightstown, NJ 08520. Editor, David G. Jensen; weekly, $27.00/year (qualified), $37.00/year (unqualified). Qualification is based on participation in aerospace industry; address subscription requests to Fulfillment Editor.

Enterprise Student Magazine, 1176 Main Street, Apt. 39, River Edge, NJ 07661; 25 Groenedruistraat, 6466 LL Kerdrade, The Netherlands. Monthly, $11.50/year.

JBIS, Journal of the British Interplanetary Society, 12 Bessborough Gardens, London SW1V2JJ, England. Editor (Blue Cover), G.V. Groves; Editor (Red Cover), A.R. Martin; monthly, $14.00/year.

Mercury, Astronomical Society of the Pacific, 1244 Noriega Street, San Francisco, CA 94122. Editor, Richard M. Reis; bimonthly, $40.00/year; subscription included in dues to ASP.

NASA Activities. See listing for NASA center in your area.

Popular Spaceflight, P.O. Box 312, Milford, OH 45150. Editor, Michael A. Banks.

Probe, 123 32nd Street, Wyoming, MI 49508. Editor, Glen Swanson. *Probe* is a newsletter, and may be free on request. Contact editor for details.

Satellite News, 12 Barn Croft, Penwortham, Preston PRI OSX, England. Editor, Geoffrey Falworth. A monthly digest of the latest launchings on the planet.

Science Digest, P.O. Box 10076, Des Moines, IA 50340. Editor, Daniel E. Button; monthly, $7.97/year. For special student and teacher rates, write c/o James Gable.

Science News, 231 West Center Street, Marion, OH 43302. Editor, Kendrick Frazier; weekly, $12.50/year.

Scientific American, 415 Madison Avenue, New York, NY 10017. Editor, Dennis Flanagan; monthly, $18.00/year.

Sky and Telescope, 49-50-51 Bay State Road, Cambridge, MA 02138. Editor, Joseph Ashbrook; monthly, $10.00/year.

Space Age Review, 378 Cambridge Avenue, Palo Alto, CA 94306. Editor, Steve Durst; monthly, $10.00/year.

Spaceflight, published by the British Interplanetary Society, 12 Bessborough Gardens, London SW1V2JJ, England. Editor, Kenneth W. Gatland; monthly, $22.00/year.

Space World. For information, contact James Oberg, RT 2, Box 1813, Dickinson, TX 77539.

Organizations and Advocacy Groups

American Astronautical Society, 6060 Duke St., Alexandria, VA 22304. Memberships: $25.00/year; students, $15.00/year. Membership includes bimonthly newsletter and the *Journal of the Astronautical Sciences* (a technical journal). The AAS regularly sponsors meetings on space-related matters. The meetings are usually advanced in concept, and draw participants from all walks of life.

American Institute of Aeronautics and Astronautics, 1290 Avenue of the Americas, New York, NY 10019. Memberships: Associate Member (over 31 years of age), $38/year; Member (under 31 years of age), $33/year; Student Member, $7/year. Membership includes subscription to *Astronautics and Aeronautics*. Student membership includes *Astronautics and Aeronautics* and the *AIAA Student Journal*.

Astronomical Society of the Pacific, 1244 Noriega St., San Francisco, CA 94122. Memberships: $12.50/year, open to all. Membership dues include six issues of their magazine, *Mercury*. The ASP sponsors numerous seminars and meetings for members on the West coast.

British Interplanetary Society, 12 Bessborough Gardens, London SW1V2JJ, England. Memberships: Member (under 21), $20/year; Member (over 21), $22/year. The BIS was cofounded by Arthur C. Clarke, and has always represented imaginary and forward thinking for its time. The BIS magazines (included in membership dues) are excellent views of all of this planet's space activity.

Forum for the Advancement of Students in Science and Technology (FASST), 1785 Massachusetts Avenue N.W., Washington, D.C. 20036. Membership: $5.00/year. FASST sponsors some of the most rewarding symposiums and debates, with top names like Carl Sagan.

Friends of Space. Contact Dennis Kocher, 2307 Tyrolean Way, Sacramento, CA 95821.

Interface, P.O. Box 37, Altus, OK 75321. Interface is a correspondence club publishing a one- or two-page newsletter. Contact the editor for information about the club status and ways in which you could contribute.

National Association of Rocketry, 1025 Connecticut Avenue, Suite 302, Washington, D.C. 20036. If you would rather build rockets than just read about them, contact NAR. NAR will help you with the building of your model rocket and provide essential safety information.

National Space Club, 1629 K Street N.W., Washington, D.C. 20006.

National Space Institute, Suite 408, 1911 N. Fort Myer Dr., Arlington, VA 22209. Memberships: $15.00/year (adult); $9.00/year (18 or younger). Membership dues include their monthly newsletter, which always contains several interesting articles.

Space Exploration Establishment. Send self-addressed, stamped envelope to Ken Croswell, c/o SEE, 3775 Hambletonian Drive, Florissant, MO 63303.

Space Now, 1601 N. Main St., Suite 203, Walnut Creek, CA 94596. Send S.A.S.E. for membership details. Space Now is a group of concerned technicians and college students involved in promoting space.

United for Our Expanded Space Program (UFOESP), 775 Camino del Sur, Bldg. H, Unit 6, Isla Vista, CA 93017. Memberships: passive, $4.99/year; active, $15.00/year; lifetime, $100.00.

Lecturers

Many lecturers are available from the American Astronautical Society, the American Institute of Aeronautics and Astronautics, and the Astronomical Society of the Pacific. See their listings in the preceding section.

Many NASA employees are willing to lecture on their projects at no cost. Contact the NASA center in your area.

Films and Tapes

Contact the American Institute of Aeronautics and Astronautics, the Astronomical Society of the Pacific, and the NASA center in your area for films and tapes on many interesting space projects.

Activities

Want to fly the space shuttle? The last Friday night of every month is the Rockwell Corporation's open house at their Downey, California, plant. Visitors can sit in a full-scale shuttle mockup, hear lectures, and view displays on the shuttle and other space projects. There is no cost, and the plant is open to everyone. For more information, contact Pat Knapp, Space Division, Rockwell International, 12214 Lakewood Blvd., Downey, CA 90241. Phone: (213) 922-2846.

II.   Unidentified Flying Objects

Magazines and Organizations

APRO Bulletin, **Aerial Phenomena Research Organization,** 3910 E. Kleindale, Tucson, AZ 85712. Monthly, $10.00/year.

Center for UFO Studies, 1609 Sherman, Suite 207, Evanston, IL 60201. Headed by Dr. J. Allen Hynek.

GSW News Bulletin, **Ground Saucer Watch,** 13238 N. 7th Dr., Phoenix, AZ 85029. Send S.A.S.E. for current subscription information.

International UFO Reporter, 924 Chicago Ave., Evanston, IL 60202. Send S.A.S.E. for current subscription information.

MUFON UFO Journal, **Mutual UFO Network,** 103 Old Towne Rd., Seguin, TX 78155. Send S.A.S.E. for current subscription information.

NICAP Bulletin, **National Investigation Committee on Aerial Phenomena,** 3535 University Blvd., Suite 23, Kensington, MD 20795. Monthly, 4 pp., $10.00/year.

Skylook, 26 Edgewood Dr., Quincy, IL 62301. A monthly publication of the Mutual UFO Network; $8.00/year.

UFO Research Committee, 3521 S.W. 104th St., Seattle, WA 98146. Their monthly bulletin, 20 legal-size pages of worldwide clippings on UFOs and Fortean phenomena, costs $5.00/month.

UFO Research Newsletter, 3122 N. Beachwood Dr., Los Angeles, CA 90069. An excellent publication; $7.00 for 12 issues.

For information about membership in the preceding organizations, send a large (No. 10) self-addressed, stamped envelope.

Lecturers

Dr. J. Allen Hynek; Dr. Jacques Vallee: contact Jay Levey, Future Presentations, 1000 Westmount Drive, Suite 201, Los Angeles, CA 90069. Phone: (213) 652-3039.

Any of the UFO organizations listed earlier will be able to refer you to other lecturers, and some have tape libraries that they may be willing to lend. See also the list of lecturers in Section III.

III.   Space Settlement and Space Industrialization

Magazines

Claustrophobia, 5047 S.W. 26th Drive, Portland, OR 97201. Monthly, $35.00/year.

CoEvolution Quarterly, Box 428, Sausalito, CA 94965. Editor, Stewart Brand. $2.50 per issue.

L-5 News, 1060 E. Elm, Tucson, AZ 85719. Editor, Carolyn Henson; monthly, $3.00/year.

Many more articles on space colonization and industrialization can be found in the magazines listed in Section I.

Organizations and Advocacy Groups

The Earthrise Synergy Coalition, S.A. Varugnese, R.D. 2, Box 707, Sussex, NJ 07461. The Coalition is a spin-off of the L-5 Society and has many of the same goals.

The Foundation Institute, 85 East Geranium Avenue, St. Paul, MN 55117, telephone (612) 489-4466. The Foundation Institute performs contractual research for organizations or individuals interested in commerical space activities. For $20/year, or $15/year for students, you will receive a monthly copy of the Foundation Report.

High Frontiers Foundation, 38 East 52nd St., New York, NY 10022. Phone (212) 877-3800,. Ext. 401. West of the Rockies office, P.O. Box 143, San Mateo, CA 94401. Phone: (415) 881-1545. Memberships: student, $10.00/year; general, $25.00/year; family, $35.00/year; higher categories available. Contributions are tax-deductible.

The L-5 Society, Membership services, 1620 N. Park Avenue, Tucson, AZ 85719. Telephone: (602) 622-6351. Memberships: regular, $20.00/year; students, $10.00/year; includes sub to *L-5 News*. The L-5 Society is the original, and best-known, space-settlement organization.

The Network, P.O. Box 317, Berkeley, CA 94701. Memberships: regular, $7.00/year; supporting, $15.00/year; eternal, $50.00. The Network is a clearinghouse for information and for contacts among persons interested in space migration, intelligence increase, and life extension (SMI²LE).

Lecturers

Lecturers and personal speaking appearances by the following people featured in this book can be arranged through Future Presentations in Los Angeles:

Keith Henson	G. Harry Stine
Barbara Marx Hubbard	Dr. J. Peter Vajk
Dr. J. Allen Hynek	Dr. Jacques Vallee
Dr. Timothy Leary	Robert Anton Wilson

Contact: Jay Levey, Future Presentations, 1000 Westmount Drive, Suite 201, Los Angeles, CA 90069. Phone: (213) 652-3039.

For Dr. Gerard O'Neill and Dr. Brian O'Leary, contact Institute of Space Studies, Inc., Box 82, Princeton, NJ 08540.

Tapes and Films

Dawntreader, 3754 Maplewood, Los Angeles, CA 90066. Good-quality audio recording of events related to space industrialization and space settlements.

L-5 Society, 1620 N. Park, Tucson, AZ 85719. The L-5 has many excellent prepared slide shows available.

Activities

Chris Basler, a patent lawyer, has proposed the idea of a staging company to finance a space-settlement/space-industrialization project. He has asked that comments and suggestions on this idea be sent directly to him. For a copy of his paper (which details exactly what a staging company is) and for any correspondence on his ideas, write to Christian O. Basler, 250 West 94th Street, New York, NY 10025.

Space Artist

Geoffrey Chandler has exhibited his large, realistic celestial paintings in one-man shows at Stanford University, California Academy of Sciences in San Francisco, and the Oakland Museum. Other showings include many science and space conventions throughout the San Francisco Bay Area.

Mr. Chandler's "spacescapes" are distributed nationally as eight notecards by Peterprints and six posters by Pomegranate.

Mr. Chandler has been composing electronic (classical) space music for over four years. An album will be released shortly. Some of the music has been used in film scores.

Presently, he is working on a "New Age" feature film. This animated science-fiction film will emphasize inner growth, awareness, and universal harmony.

For information contact Geoffrey Chandler, 228 Westridge Dr., Portola Valley, CA 94025.

IV. New Dimensions Audio Journal

The New Dimensions Audio Journal is a quarterly 90-minute audio cassette tape publication covering the most exciting new ideas, choices, alternatives, options and solutions to appear in our time. With the New Dimensions Audio Journal you will actually listen to the sounds of transformation through the voices of many of the most respected and noted thinkers in science, health, psychology, personal growth, parapsychology, religion, social change, economics, ecology, the social sciences and the humanities. Hear them as they explore the farther reaches of the human body/mind/spirit.

Subscribe for $35 annually and receive a handsome vinyl binder to contain 4 cassette tape issues of the Audio Journal. Send your check or money order to New Dimensions Audio Journal, 267 States Street, San Francisco, California 94114.